p. 2 6yrs.
p. 2 13yrs.

The
LIFE-SMART
KID

Other Books by
Lawrence J. Greene

The LIfE-SMAℛT ᴋ*ĭd*

Teaching Your Child to Use Good Judgment in Every Situation

LAWRENCE *J.* GREENE

PRIMA PUBLISHING

Library of Congress Cataloging-in-Publication Data

Greene, Lawrence J.
   The life-smart kid : teaching your child to use good judgment in every situation / Lawrence J. Greene.
      p.   cm.
   Includes index.
   ISBN 1-55958-551-X
   1. Judgment in children.   2. Decision-making in children.   I. Title.
   BF723.J8G74   1995
   649'.1—dc20   94-39015
                                                                        CIP

95 96 97 RRD 10 9 8 7 6 5 4 3 2

Printed in the United States of America

How to Order:

Single copies may be ordered from Prima Publishing, P.O. Box 1260BK, Rocklin, CA 95677; telephone (916) 632-4400. Quantity discounts are also available. On your letterhead, include information concerning the intended use of the books and the number of books you wish to purchase.

Contents

For Addie and Alison
Two extraordinary women.
I am truly fortunate.

Acknowledgments

So many people have been supportive of my work with children over the years and have contributed in countless ways to the books I have written. These people have already been acknowledged in previous books.

This time I want to thank Dr. John Taylor for his enthusiastic support. He is the author of one of the definitive works on attention deficit disorder, a psychotherapist, and a man of great character. I also want to thank my good friend Dr. Gerald Walker Smith. He has been my confidant, sound board, and beacon for more than twenty years. Jeff Stein, another special friend whom I've known since graduate school at Stanford, encouraged me greatly during the conceptual stages of this project, and I am very appreciative of his support and friendship. Without them, this book may not have been written.

Above all, I want to thank my wife, Dr. Alison Freeman-Greene, for her incisive criticism, her insightful suggestions, her affirmation, and, especially, her love.

The
LIfE-SMAƦT
KID

Introduction

Being a child today is risky business. The world is now far more stressful and dangerous than the place most of us knew when growing up. Children in our society must cope with not only such run-of-the-mill problems and anxieties as insecurity, grades, identity crises, peer pressures, adolescence, and family conflict, but they must also handle far more palpable risks—drugs, depression, gang violence, AIDS, unwanted pregnancy, suicide, and countless other dangers that produce horrific consequences.

Children are certainly not always aware of their decision-making process, but they are nevertheless continually making choices. Some choices are relatively innocuous: Should she order the strawberry or the vanilla ice cream? Should she reveal a friend's secret? Should he study for a history test or tell his parents his homework is done so he can go to the movies with friends? Other decisions can have far more serious repercussions: Should she lie to her teacher? Take ten dollars from her mother's purse? Steal a candy bar from the supermarket? Try crack cocaine just once? Should he cheat on a final exam? Throw a party while his parents are away for the weekend? Associate with gang members? Break into his school over the weekend with friends and paint graffiti on the walls? Have unprotected sex with his girlfriend?

Your child's capacity to reason and make wise choices is clearly linked to his or her chronological age. We expect a certain caliber of logic from a teenager that we cannot reasonably expect from a six-year-old. But even a six-year-old can reasonably be expected to know the difference between fundamental issues involving right and wrong, appropriate and inappropriate, fair and unfair, safe and unsafe. We *expect* a six-year-old to have learned that it's wrong to throw pebbles at a moving car, steal another child's money, lie, or make fun of a physically or mentally disabled person.

If by age thirteen, your child cannot make age-appropriate, rational decisions, he is at risk for repeated, painful collisions throughout his life. If he cannot recognize danger, deal with setbacks, learn from mistakes, handle frustration and stress, and plan ahead, the risks are even greater. If her judgment is chronically flawed, she's likely to act impulsively at critical junctures in her life, and her actions could have disastrous implications. A pattern of poor choices, or perhaps only *one* critically flawed choice, could profoundly alter the course of your child's life.

Children who have not developed their ability to think logically play a perilous game of Russian roulette. Oblivious to the dangers, or hoping everything will magically turn out okay, these children close their eyes, put the revolver to their head, and squeeze the trigger. Their fate hinges on chance. If the chamber is empty, they tingle with an adrenaline rush, smile, and mindlessly amble onto the next encounter with destiny. They might spontaneously dive from a tree limb into a stream of unknown depth and *somehow* miraculously not hit the bottom. They might swim in surf where there are known riptides and *somehow* make it back to shore safely. They might ride a bicycle with worn-out brakes and *somehow* not have an accident. They might talk to a stranger at the mall, accept a ride home, and *somehow* not be molested. It's frightening to contemplate that the fate of these children hinges on a series of *somehows*.

The previous fortuitous outcomes notwithstanding, the laws of statistics guarantee that if a youngster plays Russian roulette long enough, eventually a chamber will be loaded. When the hammer strikes this time, catastrophe awaits. The child might run into a street without looking or ride his bicycle at night without a light and be struck by a car. She might choose not to study for an important final exam and flunk a course required for graduation. She might have unprotected sex and become pregnant or infected with AIDS. He might take a gun to school, become addicted to cocaine, walk in the wrong area of town, or wear the wrong color shirt and become another tragic police statistic.

On March 31, 1992, Senator John Glenn (D. Ohio) underscored the mindless fear, violence, and chaos to which our children are exposed every day. In a statement before the Senate Committee on Government Affairs, he cited a CBS News Broadcast that made the following sobering comparison:

Public School Problems 1940 vs. 1980

1940	*1980*
Talking Out of Turn	Drug Abuse
Chewing Gum	Alcohol Abuse
Making Noise	Pregnancy
Running in Halls	Suicide
Cutting in Line	Rape
Dress Code Infractions	Robbery
Littering	Assault

To make the 1980s list reflective of the even more sordid realities of the 1990s, we must add the following: murder, gang attacks, drive-by shootings, weapons on campus, drug dealing, teacher assaults, extortion, and violent campus incursions by nonstudents. The world in which our children live is indeed as frightening as the most terrifying Stephen King novel. Tragically, many of our children are woefully ill-prepared–intellectually, psychologically, and emotionally–for the struggle they *must* win to survive in our flawed society.

For complex economic, sociological, and psychological reasons, too many parents are failing to devote adequate time to teaching their children the reasoning skills required to prevail in a harsh, competitive, and dangerous world where one wrong choice could produce disaster. Some parents rationalize that they're so busy trying to earn a living that they don't have time to teach their children the thinking skills their own parents taught them. Others assume their children will acquire logic, critical intelligence, and reasoning either through a natural, magical osmosis process or that they'll learn them in school. Single parents face another set of monumental problems. Overwhelmed by the responsibilities of having to parent alone, they must somehow figure out a way to handle the seemingly never-ending obligations that ideally would be shared by two parents.

Typical parents today are spending 40 percent *less* time communicating with their children than their own parents spent communicating with them.* Another study, which involved a random sample of middle-class teenagers living in a Boston suburb, found that 20 percent had attempted suicide during the previous year (attempts ranged from "experimental" to "serious").† If these data are indeed accurate and representative of teenagers in our country, and if a large percentage of American children consider suicide a viable option for dealing with stress, anxiety, disappointment, and alienation, then we are in trouble. A society whose youngsters perceive gang affil-

---

*Patrick Welsh. "The New Silent Generation," *Washington Post* (November 8, 1992).
†Judith L. Rubenstein, Timothy Heeren, Donna Housman, Carol Rubin, and others. "Suicidal Behavior in 'Normal' Adolescents: Risk and Protective Factors," *American Journal of Orthopsychiatry,* Vol. 59 (January 1989), p. 59–71.

iation and violence as a means for feeling secure, gaining respect, and having a sense of family is clearly in jeopardy. The frightening stories that assault us every day in our newspapers and on TV are a clear indictment: We are failing to provide our children with the intellectual and emotional resources they need to handle life's challenges and to prevail over life's problems.

Any objective assessment of the epidemic of dysfunctional thinking and behavior enveloping juveniles in our culture leads to an inescapable conclusion: Too many children are making mindless choices that profoundly affect the future course of their lives. Like rudderless boats, they sail without bearing into a treacherous sea whose hazardous waves could destroy them. In frightening numbers, these children smash into menacing reefs because their parents have not taught them how to navigate safely through life. Their inadequately developed thinking skills are symptomatic not only of profound societal problems, but also of a tragic breakdown in the child-rearing process.

More than ever before, legions of parents are ignoring their obligation to serve as their children's primary mentors and primary moral and intellectual guides. Many of these parents then naively express shock when *their* children decide to take a weapon to school, deal in drugs, drive while intoxicated, have unprotected sex, or commit suicide. "I don't understand how this could happen!" they rail. "We worked so hard to give our children everything they wanted."

Good parenting is more than supplying a child with a nice house, a good neighborhood, roller blades, spending money, karate or gymnastics lessons, a tutor, or a psychotherapist. *Good parenting is an ongoing process of providing love, consistent values, affirmation, good teaching, and wise shepherding.*

Two fundamental truths demand to be heard:

1. Being a responsible parent requires hard work and sustained effort.

2. Parents must be prepared to devote adequate time to teaching their children how to handle life's challenges successfully.

Our society *cannot* afford to produce successive generations of cerebrally and morally anesthetized children. We *cannot* walk away from our obligation to prepare our children to meet the monumental challenges that await in the twenty-first century. We *cannot* disavow our responsibility to impart our wisdom, traditions, morals, and values to our children. Unless we are willing to examine the causal factors and develop antidotes for the malaise gripping our youth, our society could unravel. We *must* teach our children how to think and reason effectively. We *must* teach them to live according to an ethical and rational code of behavior. We *must* teach them to make wise choices. We *must* provide them with the values and the skills they need to live a just and productive life.

Although you are only as far as the introduction, you have arrived at a critical juncture in this book. Before proceeding, ask yourself the following question: *Do I have faith in my child's judgment, decision-making skills, analytical thinking skills, and critical intelligence?* If your answer is yes, there's no need for you to read further. If, however, your answer is no or I'm not sure, this book could be an important resource. It has been written by an educator who has spent twenty-five years counseling thousands of parents and teaching thousands of children to think more effectively and to achieve at a level commensurate with their true potential. The methods in this program have been taught with remarkable success to teachers and are being used in thousands of school districts throughout the United States.

Let me state three central assumptions at the onset so that you know what to expect in this book:

Assumption 1 You have concluded your child's thinking skills and decision-making ability are not as developed as you would like.

You wouldn't be reading this book unless you have some concerns about your child's ability to think clearly and reasonably, to make first-rate choices, and to assess situations, options, dangers, and opportunities effectively.

Assumption 2 You want to become actively involved in developing your child's analytical thinking and critical intelligence.

On either a conscious or unconscious level, you recognize that you are your child's most important teacher and that you have an obligation to help him or her acquire wisdom, ethics, values, and reasoning skills. This realization is the starting point in becoming your child's mentor.

Assumption 3 You want guidance, a sense of direction, and a practical strategy for improving your child's capacity to think and reason.

If you want to improve your child's thinking, reasoning, and survival skills, you must systematically teach your child how to:

Think Clearly
- differentiate appearances from reality
- assess options rationally
- act logically

Avoid Danger
- assess and reduce risks
- make astute and reasonable decisions

Plan Ahead
- establish motivational goals
- establish priorities
- develop success-oriented strategies

Think Smart
- use available resources effectively
- manage time
- learn from mistakes
- bounce back from setbacks
- neutralize obstacles

Solve Problems

- consider consequences
- analyze the underlying issues
- handle stress
- deal with anger and frustration

Prevail in a Competitive World

- handle temptations
- communicate ideas, feelings, and insights effectively
- get the job done efficiently

This book provides a practical, sequential, easy-to-implement instructional plan for teaching the skills described above to children aged 6 through 14. Interactive activities, designed to be thought-provoking and to stimulate conversation, are incorporated in each chapter to develop and enhance specific skills addressed in the chapter. They present real-life challenges, problems, and temptations your child might encounter and offer opportunity to sharpen his or her logic and critical thinking skills. Preceding each activity is its objective and the suggested age range. Some anecdotes and parables can be used with all ages with the proviso that you realistically calibrate your expectations to your child's chronological age and developmental stage. In most cases, a seven-year-old's logic and insight are less advanced than a fourteen-year-old's, although there are certainly exceptions to this generalization.

With practice, feedback, guidance, and affirmation, your child can master the skills described—assuming you begin the instructional process *before* a chronic pattern of mindlessness and counterproductive, self-sabotaging behavior has become habit. If these behaviors are entrenched, your child will require professional counseling before you can expect substantive behavioral changes.

For the program to be successful, you must be prepared to provide copious amounts of love, patience, respect, positive expectations, trust, and enthusiasm, along with a willingness to acknowledge effort and affirm improvement. This process of enhancing your child's intellectual skills should be enjoyable for everyone involved, and *you* must set the tone.

This book is not exclusively a left-brain primer (the left hemisphere is where logical thinking occurs). Training your child to think rationally when confronted with choices, problems, obstacles, temptations, doubts, setbacks, frustration, and challenges does *not* preclude encouraging your child to experience and express intense, heartfelt feelings. Youngsters who can integrate their emotions and their reasoning powers have a distinct advantage over those who think and react to stimuli impulsively. By teaching your child how to blend analytical thinking skills with emotion and passion, you provide her with a powerful fuel. Add success and pride to this mixture, and your child will be running on rocket fuel that will make her soar!

There are two additional payoffs for teaching children to think and reason effectively. As your child assumes increasing responsibility for his or her own life, your entire family will breathe a collective sigh of relief! The family dynamic will shift from anxiety about your child's judgment to faith in his or her ability to act wisely and make astute choices. This shift will produce a sense of freedom, well-being, and optimism in everyone.

The second payoff will be collected down the road. Someday you want to have to have a rich, loving relationship with your adult child. This interaction is one of the most coveted rewards of parenthood. Logic dictates that if you do not discuss substantive issues with your child during the formative years, it's unlikely you'll relate any better twenty years down the road. Unless the seeds of trust, respect, rapport, and effective communication are meticulously planted in fertile soil and carefully nurtured, there will be no fruit to harvest later!

Teaching your child to think and reason can be one of parenting's most exciting, enjoyable, and rewarding experiences. If handled adroitly, the process will enrich your relationship with your child and strengthen the threads that bond your family. Over time, this family cloth will become stronger, more durable, and more beautiful. The thinking skills you teach will become part of your legacy, a gift that will continue to produce payoffs long after you are gone. One day your child may say to her own child: "When I was your age, your grandmother taught me about planting trees to replace the ones we cut down for firewood. She told me that she learned this from her mother. Someday you'll probably teach your own child the same thing, and when you do, I bet you'll think of me, just as I'm thinking about my mother right now. Teaching children what we know is an important part of our family heritage. It's a tradition I pray will go on forever."

One final comment before you begin. Some readers may question why this book has a suggested age range of 6 to 14 years. "Why limit the upper and lower ends?" you may ask. Although the program can be used with some children younger than six, many are not yet developmentally ready to understand and apply the reasoning skills taught in this book. There are challenges at the other end of the age spectrum as well. This program can certainly be a teaching tool for older teenagers, *if* they'll allow you to assume the role of their intellectual guide and moral mentor. If, however, rapport, good communication, empathy, and trust have not been established during the formative years, it's unlikely that older teenagers will be receptive to the instructional process. Those who are resistant will probably consciously or unconsciously defeat your efforts to work with them. Methods for presenting and examining the issues with this more reticent, emotionally defensive population and strategies for handling the inherent challenges will have to be addressed in another book.

Most children are receptive to parental influence. They can be enticed away from TV, video games, and mindless Saturday morning cartoons. They can be taught to avoid unnecessary risks, analyze their options carefully, and make wise choices. Those who learn these skills have a distinct advantage over those who don't.

Children are programmed by nature to develop their minds in much the same way that animals are programmed by nature to develop their sense of smell. Although the code for acquiring analytical thinking skills is genetically implanted, for most children the path leading from mindlessness to mindfulness must be revealed. This book is about you helping *your* child find that path. You are the guide. You are the mentor. You are the teacher. This is your job.

chapter 1

Decision Making

*T*odd heard the motorcycle pull up in front of the house, and he ran to the front door before the doorbell rang. He knew it had to be Cory, his older brother's best friend. Like most eleven-year-olds, Todd was fascinated with Cory's red 1000 cc motorcycle with its sleek windscreen and sculptured white and red side panels.

Todd told Cory his brother wasn't home and asked excitedly if he could take a look at the motorcycle. Cory, proud of his new bike, was delighted to show it off. The two walked to the curb for a closer inspection. The child ran his hand lovingly over the bike's smooth curves and fantasized zooming down the freeway wearing Cory's black, white, and red leather motorcycle racing jacket, white leather pants, and reflecting sunglasses.

"You want to go for a ride?" Cory asked nonchalantly.

"Really?"

"Come on. I've got a few minutes."

Todd knew his parents probably wouldn't return from shopping for at least another hour. If he and Cory left now, they could be back in twenty minutes and his parents would never know.

When Cory first bought his motorcycle, Todd's parents had made his older brother promise he would never ride on it. They made it very clear that he would be grounded if he disobeyed them. They knew Cory had a reputation for being reckless and speeding. He also had a reputation for drinking and for refusing to wear a helmet. Todd's parents were certain it was just a matter of time before he had an accident.

Todd knew his parents would be furious if they found out he had ridden on Cory's motorcycle. But if he and Cory left right away, his parents would never know.

Crossroads

An eleven-year-old child is at a crossroad. One path leads into the sunset on a sleek motorcycle—experiencing the rush of adrenaline and the fantasy of being grown up, enhanced perhaps by knowing that he's disobeying his parents' unequivocal instructions. The deviousness and deception might even intensify the Huckleberry Finn adventure and make it all the more appealing and thrilling.

If Todd decides to disobey his parents' clearly stated wishes and risk being caught and severely punished, how should you interpret this? Is his decision an act of rashness or defiance? Does the decision simply reflect poor judgment or inadequately developed boundaries? Does he lack the critical intelligence to decide what's in his best interests? Are basic cause-and-effect principles beyond his current understanding? If he decides to ride with Cory, would this symbolize his emerging desire for more independence? Is the eleven-year-old thinking: "It's boring to have to follow the rules! I hate being told what to do all the time! How can I ever have fun if I'm always being good?" Or is he simply thinking: "If I'm lucky and we leave right now, maybe I can get away with this."

The second path—compliance with his parents' wishes—is, of course, a safer path. Say "no." Resist the temptation. Do what mom and dad want and expect. Be obedient, trustworthy, and careful. Take comfort in knowing that you make your parents proud by obeying them. Todd's parents have undoubtedly delivered the litany of family rules and responsibilities many times: "Be good, act wisely, show good judgment, and avoid danger. And be prepared for punishment if you break the rules!"

At the critical moment of decision, an adventurous child will not necessarily choose the safe path. Sometimes children select the more risky and exciting option without realizing—or unconsciously denying—that they are exposing themselves to danger.

Is it reasonable for you to *expect* your child to make the right decision if he is faced with this choice? At the critical moment, will your child obey the life-protecting rules that you lay down? You clearly have a vested interest in gauging what your child's thinking and emotional reaction would be if he were faced with a similar temptation. The anecdote offers you an opportunity to determine his reaction.

If your child is over six years of age, read the anecdote at the beginning of the chapter to him. Then ask the questions found on page 18. Don't be highly critical if his response is not the one you want. Your goals are to get a baseline of your child's current reasoning ability, open channels of communication, initiate discussion, and provide instruction and guidance. Your goals are *not* to lecture, deliver sermons, criticize, judge, or cause guilt, all of which tend to arouse defensiveness.

If your child's responses indicate poor reasoning, be careful not to communicate discouragement and disappointment. The activity has served an important function. You now know you must help your child improve his or her reasoning, critical thinking, and strategic thinking skills. Your child's less-than-ideal responses confirm your rationale for reading this book and implementing the program it offers.

Certainly, there's a down side to recognizing that your child is not thinking as logically as you would like. The bubble bursts and you're confronted with a problem you must address and resolve. At the same time, there's an up side to your new insight. You know what needs to be done, and you have an instructional resource for achieving this objective.

Below the model interactive questioning section appearing on page 18, you'll find guidelines for responding to your child in a way that should stimulate discussion and encourage the sharing of thoughts and feelings. The tone of your responses will determine whether or not you create a positive interactive context. If you're highly moralistic or critical, you'll defeat the program. Your child will dread working with you and may actively or passively resist your efforts.

Trust and Faith

Trust is vital to all intimate communication. Children develop trust when they feel appreciated and believe their feelings and ideas are respected, even when those feelings and ideas aren't congruent with those of their parents.

Criticism is *not* an effective antidote for a child's poor logic. Patience, sensitivity, respect, and empathy are far more effective. If your goal is to stimulate greater insight, you clearly want to entice your child to participate actively and eagerly in the interactive sessions. This active involvement is the most potent catalyst for intellectual growth, expanded awareness, and positive changes in behavior and attitude.

Your child will quickly gauge your expectations, attitude, and the tone of your communication. If you are impatient, self-righteous, judgmental, highly critical, or derogatory, you will elicit resentment and resistance. By clearly communicating your enthusiasm and your conviction that your child can learn what you're teaching, you dramatically improve the likelihood of insight and skill mastery. Even if children get off to a slow or uneven start, they sense when their parents have faith in their ability to sort things out and prevail over a challenge.

The Facts about Teaching Children Effectively

Negativity breeds negativity.
Disparagement breeds distrust.
Continual criticism breeds defensiveness.
Lectures breed resistance.
Sermons breed passivity.
Low expectations breed poor performance.
Lack of faith breeds insecurity.
Anger breeds fear.

* * *

Optimism breeds enthusiasm.
Positive expectations breed achievement.
Love breeds trust.
Affirmation breeds motivation.
Success breeds self-confidence.
Active involvement breeds active learning.
Faith breeds security.

Examining the Issues with Your Child

After you have read the introductory anecdote with your child, the following questions should help you and your child explore the key underlying issues. Although the anecdote can be used with children ages 6 to 14, your expectations should be realistic, geared to your child's age. Children are still in the formative stages of insight and reasoning skill. Be patient and affirming!

interactive **activity**

Age Range: 6–14
Objective: Handling the Family Rules

Questions and Issues for Discussion (anecdote found on page 13)

1. Why do you think Todd's parents made the rule about not riding on Cory's motorcycle?
2. What would they be concerned about if he or his older brother were to ride with Cory?
3. On a scale from 1 to 10, how would you rate their rule?

1	2	3	4	5	6	7	8	9	10
Not				Fairly					Very
Smart				Smart					Smart

4. What are your reasons for this rating?
5. If Todd did decide to disobey his parents and ride with Cory on his motorcycle, how would you rate this decision?

1	2	3	4	5	6	7	8	9	10
Not				Fairly					Very
Smart				Smart					Smart

6. Why would he decide to disobey his parents?
7. What would you do if you were faced with a similar decision?
8. What might happen? Tell me all the possible consequences.

For general suggestions on how to respond to your child, refer to the boxed sidebar on page 19. For specific guidelines, read on.

Guidelines for Responding to Your Child

1. If your child shows disinterest or is resistant to discussing the issues with you . . .

   Parent: I sense you don't like this anecdote (or discussion). If this is true, please tell me why. . . . (Avoid being judgmental. Listen. Your goal is to elicit feelings and thoughts and to stimulate a discussion. You might say: "That's interesting . . . tell me more.")

2. If your child seems stuck and can't come up with reasons for the rule Todd's parents made . . .

   Parent: Let's see . . . Do you think his parents might be concerned about safety? What could happen? In the story it says Cory is reckless and speeds . . .

3. If your child can't give reasons for his or her evaluation . . .

   Parent: I wonder if you considered the issue of safety when you evaluated the rule. . . . Maybe you were thinking parents' rules are sometimes unfair. (If your child says "No! that's not it," listen and encourage him to express his feelings and thoughts. Again, avoid being judgmental. His reasoning skills will improve!)

4. If your child gives responses you disagree with . . .

   Parent: That's an interesting reaction. Do you think a parent might see the issues differently? If you were Todd's parent, how would you respond if he went with Cory? How do you think I might respond? Why?

Responding to Your Child

If you're dissatisfied with the quality of your child's responses, remember that you and your child are just beginning this program! You're still in the exploratory and foundation-building stages. Don't drive issues into the ground. Resist any temptation to lecture or to insist on closure (that is, to make absolutely certain that your child has "mastered" a concept or idea). Mastery generally requires multiple exposures to a concept or procedure as well as encouragement, sensitive and constructive feedback, and repeated opportunities to practice and apply what is being taught. In some respects, the process is akin to learning a new vocabulary word that you read in a book. Most people look up the word in a dictionary several times and make a concentrated effort to use it repeatedly before they master its meaning and usage. Rest assured that this program will provide your child with many opportunities to master the thinking skills presented here.

For more comprehensive general guidelines, see pages 31–36.

Choosing the Right Path

Your child will confront many crossroads in life, and you will not always be there to provide guidance and counsel. One day he will undoubtedly be faced with a choice or temptation that could place him at risk. Like most parents, you pray that when he arrives at this juncture, he'll demonstrate good judgment, carefully weigh the risks, and consider your admonitions about safety and precaution. You pray she will not act impulsively or do something dangerous that you have expressly forbidden. You pray she'll obey your rules even if she doesn't understand the rationale for them. As a last resort, you pray the prospect of punishment will deter him from making a choice that could place his life in jeopardy. At the critical moment—the decision point—you trust that he has assimilated the self-control, wisdom, insight, and thinking skills you've taught him, and that when he arrives at the crossroad, he'll choose the right path.

Many factors will determine your child's responses at the decision points in his life. The most critical factor is the quality of the decision-making guidance you provide during his formative years. It's far more likely that he'll make good judgments and choices if you have trained him to:

> *Reason and think analytically, logically, and strategically.* ("I need to finish the instructions before I put it together.")

Respect consistent, reasonable values and behavior guide-
lines. ("I'd like this, but taking it without permission is
wrong.")

Consider carefully the consequences of his attitudes and
behaviors before he acts. ("If I get caught cheating, the
teacher will give me an F.")

Search out the underlying issues that influence events.
("My sister doesn't trust me because I told her secret.")

Examine, evaluate, and learn from positive and negative
life experiences. ("I got a poor grade on the science test
this time, but now that I know the kinds of questions
she asks, I'll do better next time.")

If you haven't begun this training process, it's time to get
started!

Figure 1.1. The Decision Process

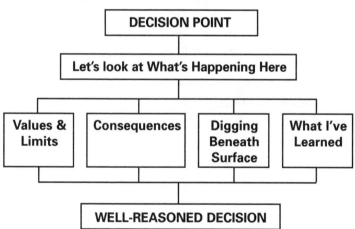

Lenses and Filters

Your child may have perfect vision, but he sees his world
through his own set of lenses and filters. These determine the

acuity and color of his perceptions. The raw materials for the lenses and filters are a composite of inherited biological and temperamental characteristics. The glass is patterned by genetic code, ground by parental training, polished by education, tinted by life experiences, and coated by culture and society.

Unfortunately, children's perceptions can become distorted. The most common causative factors include painful life experiences, inadequate education, dysfunctional family systems, and immersion in a subculture that extols counterproductive values and behaviors. Lens distortions are usually manifest as patterns of poor judgment, flawed choices, and nonstrategic thinking. In extreme cases, the distortions can result in chronic self-sabotaging or anti-social behaviors.

Even if the lenses through which your child sees the world are clear, he will still subjectively perceive and define his reality. He will interpret rules, assess risks, consider repercussions, and evaluate his options based upon his perspective, experiences, and training. When faced with important decisions, his reactions may be impulsive or restrained, balanced or unbalanced, realistic or unrealistic, reasonable or unreasonable, mature or immature. He may choose to consider some issues and disregard others. He may deny, rationalize, or convolute the facts. Or he may confront and analyze the issues and carefully examine and weigh the pros and cons. His responses to challenges, opportunities, and problems may be astute or mindless. His responses can profoundly affect the course of his life and even his statistical chances of survival.

As a responsible parent, you fervently want your child to consider carefully the pluses and minuses of important decisions *before* responding. This is especially true when the choices entail physical, emotional, academic, or vocational risks. To a large extent, child-rearing is an extended, systematic preparation for helping your child make these critical decisions.

Good judgment doesn't simply happen. Good judgment, like a good education, is the end-product of systematic instruction, guidance, feedback, affirmation, practice, and effort. Good judgment is an acquired skill, and you as a parent play the pivotal role in your child's acquisition process. Unless you are prepared to help your child understand, discriminate, and assimilate the confusing signals and data that assault him every day, he may never acquire good judgment.

Parents have always been charged with the responsibility for teaching physical and emotional survival skills to their children. When our society was essentially agrarian, the skills dealt with issues such as irrigation, fertilization, crop rotation, sewing, and canning fruits and vegetables. The realities and challenges have changed, but the basic thrust of the teaching process has not. Today you must teach your child to look both ways when crossing the street, not to talk to strangers or approach a car driven by someone she doesn't know, and to scream and run if she's accosted. On a more mundane level, you must also teach her to do her assigned or chosen chores, complete her homework, and be respectful. And you must teach her not to steal, lie, cheat, or take drugs.

At that *critical moment* when your child is confronted with a potential life or death decision ("Should I try to cross this stream even though the water is moving very fast?"), her response will hinge on the effectiveness of the training and instruction you have provided. Can she rationally assess the risks and resist the temptation to do something that is clearly dangerous? Will she refuse to ride in a car with someone who is reckless or drunk? Will she reject the drug a friend offers her? If you conclude that, despite your best efforts to teach your child how to analyze these critical situations carefully, she has not assimilated your instruction, you must be prepared to find a new and more effective methodology. The cliché expression "If it ain't broke don't fix it" should have an addendum: "If it *is* broken, and your attempts to fix it have failed, develop a new plan of action." Continuing to do the same thing over and over when it has proven ineffectual is not only a waste of time, it is illogical and nonstrategic. The monotonous repetition of a clearly flawed approach turns kids off and is guaranteed to cause their resistance and resentment. They may respond by intentionally rejecting your ideas.

Children's choices, of course, do not always involve life-threatening issues. But even their responses to seemingly benign matters can be an important barometer of their emotional maturity, judgment, and evolving sense of self. Can your child handle anxiety and stress? Can she deal with social pressures? Can she cope with occasional setbacks or rejections? Can she make and keep friends? Can she express anger or frustration without becoming sarcastic, belligerent, self-sabotaging, or antisocial?

Of far more compelling concern is how your child will react in situations that pose physical or emotional risks. If your daughter is riding her bicycle and sees a railroad gate down, will she impulsively try to beat the train to the crossing? Will she venture too close to the edge of an unstable cliff? Will she knowingly go to a party where there is risk of gang violence? Will your son steal the sweater he covets from a store? Will he take a gun to school? Will he wear gang colors that might cause him to be shot? Of course, you fervently hope your child will make the smart choice in these situations, but hoping is not enough. The critical factor that could determine the outcome is how well you have trained your child to reason and think logically, critically, and strategically.

At a decision point, your child may respect your rules, or she may consider the act of breaking or circumventing a family rule to be an adventure, a minor infraction, a cute subterfuge, a symbolic assertion of maturity and independence, or a "get off my case" slap in your face. Her conscious and unconscious evaluative process will reflect complex parent-child interactive scripts that were psychologically imprinted during the formative years of her life.

You have many options when communicating with your child. For example, let's say you are dealing with the issue of practicing the piano. You can communicate your position in the form of an order, a recommendation, an admonishment, or an implied threat. You can be clear and unequivocal or ambiguous and tentative. You can take the time to explain the rationale for your position, reason with her, and help her understand the issues, or you can be authoritarian. You can solicit her reaction and encourage her to express her feelings and defend her own position, or you can autocratically attempt to impose your wishes. At the decision point, your child will either accept or reject (actively or passively) your position. She may be forthright or manipulative and devious. She may be compliant or resentful, oppositional, and rebellious. She may carefully consider what you've said, develop a different perspective and acquire insight, or she may consciously or unconsciously disregard what she doesn't want to hear, rationalize her behavior, misinterpret facts, deny the obvious, dismiss potential consequences, or delude herself. She may perceive matters clearly, or she may see them through distorted lenses. The possible permutations are almost limitless.

Note also that your own lens could be distorted. For example, your position on practicing the piano may not necessarily be the *correct* position. You may be insisting that she study the piano despite her total lack of interest (or talent) in music. Perhaps you regret not having an opportunity to learn as a child and are intent on providing your own child with this opportunity. These may be issues *you* need to examine objectively.

You play a key role in influencing your child's perceptions and responses. You will inevitably affect the curve of the lens and the tint of the filters through which she perceives her world. By teaching her how to think analytically and rationally and training her to delve beneath the surface and examine underlying factors, you can significantly improve the likelihood that she'll think logically, act reasonably, and function effectively in critical situations. This rational thinking will, in turn, improve the chances that her responses will more accurately reflect the particular problem, challenge, or temptation she faces. There can be no guarantee that your child will always make the right decision, but the probability of her making a well-reasoned choice cannot help but improve when she's able to perceive the issues clearly.

Taking a Look at Your Child's Thinking Process

If you suspect your child is having difficulty thinking logically and analytically and making astute choices, complete the following checklist. The inventory lists many of the thinking skills requisite to effective reasoning.

In assessing your child, be sure to take his or her chronological age into consideration. Younger children (ages 4–9) can be expected to have difficulty with some of the described thinking skills. The quality of your child's analytical thinking is, of course, linked to his or her current developmental stage. You cannot reasonably expect a five-year-old to have acquired first-rate time-management or prioritization skills. However, a red flag should go up when an eight-year-old child chronically disregards obvious cause-and-effect issues (runs into the street without looking both ways or takes perilous risks on his skateboard despite your repeated admonitions). A flag should also go up if a ten-year-old cannot make age-appropriate predictions about what is likely to happen if he acts in a particular way (fails to complete his homework assignments or doesn't submit them on time). Although young children may not be developmentally ready to link certain cause-and-effect phenomena, they are ready to *begin* the process of learning how to make logical connections. Your early teaching provides them with an important head start. **Statements particularly relevant to older children are placed at the bottom of the checklist and preceded by an asterisk.** Do not expect younger children (ages 4–9) to make these logical connections consistently.

The checklist statements address several key issues related to handling challenges and opportunities effectively. These include:

Coping Skills (C)
Impulse Control* (I)

---

*Chronic impulsivity, distractibility, and inattentiveness may be symptomatic of Attention Deficit Disorder (ADD) or Attention Deficit Hyperactivity Disorder (ADHD). See *1001 Ways to Improve Your Child's Schoolwork* (Prima, fall 1995) and *Helping Your Hyperactive/Attention Deficit Child* 2nd ed. (Prima, 1994) for more information.

Planning (P)
Recognition of Danger (D)
Logic (L)
Cause and Effect (C/E)
Ethics (E)

Codes are used to classify each statement below.

✓ *Checklist:* **Does My Child Have Effective Reasoning Skills?**

0 = Never   1 = Rarely   2 = Sometimes   3 = Often   4 = Always

My child has difficulty making realistic predictions. *(Even though I won't study for the test, I'll do okay.)*

(P) (C/E) _____

My child has difficulty appreciating cause and effect and linking her actions with logical repercussions. *(Even though I haven't done my chores, Mom will let me go to the movies on Saturday.)*

(C/E) _____

My child has difficulty realizing how his behavior affects others. *(Big deal. All kids lie to their parents.)*

(C/E) _____

My child has difficulty analyzing mistakes and setbacks and learning from these experiences. *(Just because my teacher lowered my grade because my book report was late, she may not lower it next time if it's late.)*

(C/E) (L) _____

My child cannot deal with frustration. *(I didn't get the part in the play. I can't act. I'll never try out again.)*

(C) _____

My child has difficulty suspending immediate gratification. *(I can't afford it, but I'm going to buy it anyway.)*

(C) (I) (C/E) _____

My child refuses to admit when he's wrong. *(I didn't break the window because we were playing too close to the house. The ball went foul.)*

(C/E) (L) _____

My child will persist on a particular course even though
it's clear the strategy isn't working. *(I don't care if the
teacher says these problems are incorrect! This is how I'm
going to do them!)*

(L) (C/E) (P) ____

My child makes flawed judgments because he doesn't
look at key issues or denies the reality of the situation in
which he finds himself. *(I don't care if John has lied to me
many times before. He's my friend and I believe him!)*

(C/E) ____

My child has difficulty linking values and principles with
specific choices and actions. *(If I miss practice this week,
my coach won't care. I'll make the varsity team anyway.)*

(E) ____

My child often fails to consider ethics and morals when
making a decision. *(When the teacher turns her back, I'll
ask my friend for the answer to this test question.)*

(E) ____

My child disregards danger. *(Jumping off this bridge looks
like fun.)*

(D) (C/E) (I) ____

My child is having difficulty with impulse control. *(I'll put
this candy in my pocket when the clerk's back is turned.)*

(I) ____

* My child has difficulty developing a strategy that will
allow him to attain his goal. *(I don't want to take the advanced placement science course, even though I heard you
need them for pre-med.)*

(P) (C/E) (C) (L) ____

* My child has difficulty perceiving the progression and
sequence of events and ideas. *(I don't need to take the introductory course to get an A in the advanced class.)*

(C/E) (L) (P) ____

* My child has difficulty drawing reasonable conclusions
and inferences from available data. *(Everybody is taking
coats to the stadium, but I don't think I'll need one.)*

(L) (C/E) ____

* My child uses non sequiturs (conclusions that don't follow from the premise or evidence) when expressing ideas. *(The book says communication skills are linked to intelligence. Dolphins have a very complex communication system, but I don't really think they're very intelligent.)*

(L) _____

* My child has difficulty planning ahead and factoring "future time" into her decisions. *(I'll probably have enough time to read the book and do the report even if I start next week.)*

(P) (C/E) _____

Interpreting Checklist Responses

The specific issue or issues addressed by each statement is indicated with the code that follows the statement. If a pattern emerges that suggests your child is having moderate (1's and 2's) to chronic (3's and 4's) difficulty with planning, you would especially want to work on those activities in the book that address planning issues. This does not mean, however, that you want to work exclusively in your child's deficit areas. To do so would be demoralizing. You also want to provide your child with an opportunity to demonstrate her strengths!

You will note that some statements address overlapping issues (such as planning and cause and effect). These issues are often interrelated, and you would want to focus on helping your child appreciate this overlap.

If your child is younger than nine, use your discretion in interpreting your scoring. Most younger children will *occasionally* manifest impulsivity, lack of forethought, and disregard of consequences. Even if you give a younger child "4's" in several areas, this should not necessarily be a major concern. A child under eight may not be developmentally ready to understand fully the concept of future time or to apply logical thinking consistently. Intellectual development is clearly linked to chronological age and emotional maturity. Be reasonable in your expectations. Provide opportunities to practice planning and thinking logically without communicating disappointment. With practice, your child will "get it."

Although "1's" and "2's" do not necessarily indicate problems, a pattern of "3's" and "4's" does indicate possible reasoning problems, especially in the case of children older than nine. This pattern suggests your child would benefit from being systematically trained to think more logically.

The instruction, feedback, practice, and praise you will provide over the next weeks can help your child acquire all of the reasoning skills described in the inventory. It would be wise to review periodically the suggested guidelines for communicating successfully with your child and for maximizing the benefits of the instructional method. These commonsense guidelines will not only help you implement this program, they will also facilitate effective communication with your child in other contexts.

Your methodical guidance and encouragement can help your child acquire the reasoning skills described in the inventory. To gauge the effectiveness of the instructional process, fill out the checklist again after you and your child have completed the program.

Doing Something About Deficits

To address and resolve deficits identified on the Checklist, you will need to work with your child on the underlying issues. This will require strategic planning and tact on your part. Children tend to get defensive when they feel they're being "attacked" for their faults. They also tend to get defensive when they believe they're being placed under a microscope and their behavior is being unfairly scrutinized and criticized. In this respect, they are not very different from adults who feel they're being unduly criticized. The knee-jerk reaction is to protect yourself by justifying or rationalizing your behavior.

To elicit less defensiveness from your child, it can be highly effective to examine the issues, attitudes, and behavior of *another* child. This must be done without you drawing obvious parallels to your own child's behavior. Let your child *discover* the parallels. He may not do so immediately, however, as children often need time to process, distill, and assimilate insights. Changes rarely occur overnight. You must be patient. Discuss the parallels if you believe it would be appropriate and not trigger defensiveness or if your child says, "Gee, I sometimes feel the same way as that kid." If you're discussing another child's illogical response in a particular situation, and you know that your child tends to react in a similar way, don't "frontally assault" him with the insight. This will only cause him to "circle the wagons" for psychological self-protection. Resistance, passivity, or distractibility are common signals that a child feels threatened and is attempting to protect himself emotionally. You want to do everything in your power to avoid this reaction, as it will defeat your efforts to communicate successfully.

The anecdote beginning on p. 36 is intended to be a catalyst for discussion. Remember, having *fun* will not dilute the effectiveness of the activity. On the contrary, having fun will reduce resistance and *enhance* the effectiveness. Positive and pleasant associations with a learning experience invariably produce more beneficial and more lasting results than negative and painful associations.

How to Use Parent-Child Interactive Activities in This Book

The exercises in each chapter are intended to develop and enhance the specific skills examined in the chapter. The material is designed to be thought-provoking and to stimulate conversation. The anecdotes and parables, which address real-life challenges, problems, and temptations your child might encounter, are intended to sharpen his or her logic and analytical, strategic, and critical thinking. The specific objective of each activity precedes the exercise.

Right and Wrong Answers

In most instances, there is no necessarily "correct" answer or conclusion to be drawn. What matters is the process of learning how to think more effectively, critically, strategically, and logically. Your child is learning how to analyze issues, problems, and temptations, and to make astute choices. Because you have many years of life experience "under your belt," your interpretations and conclusions will frequently be quite different from those of your child. Your child is entitled to her opinions. Yours may not work for her. If, however, her interpretations, conclusions, and opinions are clearly off target, you certainly want to help her to look at the issues from a different vantage point and to reconsider her reactions. This process of encouraging your child to take a different "read" on issues must never be done in a heavy-handed way. Denigrating your child will only cause resentment and trigger resistance. Affirmation is a far more powerful tool for positively changing behavior than criticism or derision.

Moral and Ethical Issues

When dealing with activities that focus on such issues as risk-taking, morals, character, or ethics, you'll want to guide your child to key insights and to reinforce your family's values. This desire is not only legitimate, it's vital. Ideally, you will have already formulated your family's position on stealing, cheating, and lying. Your child needs to know where you stand on these issues. At appropriate points in these interactive sessions, you'll want to communicate your viewpoint on key issues involving ethics and values clearly and unequivocally (without becoming pedantic or self-righteous). Your child needs to know where you stand on these issues. Your well-reasoned position will provide a value framework for your child, and this framework will, in turn, provide a vital sense of security and continuity. It's certainly okay not have all the answers and to let your child see you thrash out the process along with him. Resist any conscious or unconscious tendency to become dictatorial, heavy-handed, and "preachy." Children often become resistant when on the receiving end of lectures, sermons, or diatribes. (See Chapter 4,

Acquiring Values, for a comprehensive examination of morals and ethics.)

Expressing Feelings

Encourage your child to ask questions and express unedited reactions. Treat these reactions with sensitivity and respect, even if they're at odds with your own perceptions or position. You want your child to become actively involved in the learning process, and you want him to feel comfortable and safe discussing his feelings with you. Lectures elicit passive involvement and mental shutdown. Guiding your child to insights about the rationale for an ethical position is a far more effective tool for influencing attitudes or behavior than attempting to browbeat your child into compliance.

Resistance

When children feel oppressed and believe their parents' rules are unfair, they may become openly resistant or defiant. They may also become manipulative, devious, or passively resistant if they're afraid to stand up to their parents. Their passive resistance, oppositional behavior, or passive aggression (such as getting a brother or sister in trouble for something they did) can be a nightmare.

When children become teenagers, most parents discover that they have less and less control over their child's behavior in situations out of their view. They will not be with their child when someone offers drugs, makes a perilous dare, or proposes breaking the law for a lark. They must trust that their child's responses to danger, problems, challenges, and temptations will be judicious. Because parental control diminishes over time, the need to teach kids to think wisely is urgent. If this teaching is to be successful, it makes sense that parents avoid eliciting knee-jerk resistance from their children. The best way to do this is to be sensitive ("I get the feeling you don't want to deal with this now."), supportive ("I saw you analyze and respond effectively to a similar situation last week."), and open-minded ("Well, that's a different assessment from the one I would make, but let's see if it can work.")

Introducing the Material

An effective introduction to the material might be "I'd like to spend a few minutes discussing something with you that I think is interesting. Let me read you a story. I'm curious about your reaction."

Make sure you find an opportune time to work with your child. It would *not* be advisable to examine a parable dealing with morality when he wants to go out and play baseball with his friends.

Teenagers can be especially resistant to examining issues they perceive as threatening, intrusive, or too personal. You might find it effective to have discussions when you and your child are alone. If you're heavy-handed or highly judgmental, be prepared for active or passive resistance to your efforts to communicate! Kids become defensive when they feel they're being continually judged and criticized.

Remember, when interacting with your child, you cannot reasonably expect instant insight and immediate changes in attitude and behavior. Few children master concepts or procedures the first time they're introduced. If you're patient, persevering, supportive, affirming, and loving, your child will begin to achieve insight. Teaching her to reason effectively is a *process*. Remind yourself that you did not learn to think logically and strategically all of a sudden. Your child won't learn these skills immediately either.

Overnight Transformations

Don't plan on immediate dramatic improvement. Children rarely make overnight transformations. They need time to process, think, interpret, associate, compare, experiment, emote, assimilate, and integrate. Significant attitudinal and behavioral changes usually occur incrementally.

Additional Suggested Guidelines for Communicating Successfully with Your Child

■ Choose activities that you feel would benefit your child. If your child doesn't have a problem with ethics, you may choose not to do exercises that address this issue.

- Select material that is relevant to your child's level of maturity and awareness. Most exercises and anecdotes are oriented to a wide age range, although some are clearly relevant to teenagers. The appropriate age range is indicated.
- You need not do all of the supplemental exercises for your child to derive benefit from the program.
- Examine selected material carefully *before* discussing it and, if you wish, modify the parables or anecdotes to make them more meaningful to your child. As the teacher and storyteller, you can be creative. Embellish with your own words, style, details, or even substitute your own anecdote that might address an issue from a different slant. For example, in the next parable, a child is saving his money to buy a bicycle. If your child is sixteen, you might substitute a car, a horse, a sports camp, or a trip. If you don't like an anecdote, metaphor, or parable, skip it. Those used in this book are designed to be models and catalysts for discussion. They are not sacred!
- Resist the temptation to lecture or preach.
- Examine the issues in a supportive, affirming context that is not emotionally charged. If the context does become emotionally charged, and you sense your child becoming resistant or defensive, STOP! Re-orient or reframe the discussion so that the interactive experience is pleasant.
- Encourage your child to express ideas and feelings freely and allow insights to "percolate." Your child does not have to "get it" right away. We all need time to assimilate new ideas, strategies, attitudes, and behaviors.
- Make the interactive sessions relatively short and gear them to your child's maturity and concentration level. If your child has a short attention span, adjust your expectations accordingly. Ten minutes may be the maximum he can focus. If his mind begins to wander, don't lose patience. Stop and resume the discussion at another time. A five- or ten-minute drive in the car to a karate class or scout meeting could be a perfect opportunity to discuss an issue with your child. Although the interactive sessions should generally occur when other siblings will not pose distractions, some exercises lend themselves to a family discussion. An anecdote or parable might be recounted at dinner, and the

entire family could participate with each child being encouraged to share his or her ideas and feelings. Use your discretion. You may sense your child needs individualized, private time with you. As a general rule, interactive sessions should not be rigidly scheduled (for example, Tuesday evenings from 8:00–8:45).

Suggested time guidelines for sessions are:

Ages 6–8: 5–10 minutes
       8–10: 10–15 minutes
       10–13: 15–20 minutes
       14–16: 20–25 minutes

These are *general* guidelines that can and should be adjusted depending upon your child's reactions to the subject or issue being examined. If your child is excited and eager, keep going. If he is resistant or begins to shut down, discontinue. You want your child to have pleasant associations with these interactive sessions.

■ Acknowledge your child for effort and clearly affirm any insight he or she achieves. Your praise will build your child's self-confidence and make the experience all the more enjoyable.

interactive **activity**

Age Range: 6–14
Objectives: Handling Goals, Tough Decisions,
             Planning Priorties, and
             Delayed Gratification

The Boy Who Wanted a Mountain Bike

Evan desperately wanted the new mountain bike. His best friend Josh had just gotten one for his birthday, and the thirteen-year-old could imagine the two of them riding their bikes through the woods near the river.

Because his father had lost his job nine months ago, Evan knew his parents wouldn't be able to buy him the bike for his birthday or for Christmas. In fact, his family was having a difficult time just paying their monthly bills.

Evan realized he would have to earn the money and buy the bike himself. The metallic blue one he wanted was very expensive. It had fourteen gears, a very light frame, and a super derailleur. Several of the rich kids at his school had the very model he wanted so badly.

Evan saved most of his allowance and the money he earned doing odd jobs at home and in the neighborhood. He also saved the money he earned baby-sitting the little boy who lived next door.

Finally, he had enough money, and he decided that the next day he would go to the store and buy the bike. But that afternoon something unexpected happened. He borrowed a friend's roller blades, helmet, and pads. He discovered he loved the thrill of speeding down the street and doing tricks. He wanted a pair right away, and he wanted a good pair like his friend had. As he wrestled with his decision about what to do, he became unhappy. Should he buy the bike and then begin saving for the roller blades? Should he buy the roller blades now and put off buying the bike? (All of his friends had roller blades, and they had started a roller blade hockey team that he wanted to join!) Should he buy a cheaper bike and use the leftover money to buy the skates? Should he buy a used bike? Should he buy used roller blades? The decision seemed overwhelming.

Note: As previously indicated, the questions that follow the anecdote are intended to be a catalyst for discussion. They are *not* intended to be a "test." The goal is to create a positive context for a rational examination of the issues and to stimulate critical and analytical thinking. (Be careful not to rattle off questions like a machine gun!) If questions other than the ones below occur to you, feel free to substitute or add these. Keep the interaction fun and interesting. Show respect for your child's thinking process even though you may not agree with his or her interpretation or responses. If you don't agree, you might say, "Does it make any sense to look at this issue in this way . . . ?" As is the case with all skills, analytical thinking is developed incrementally, and children require practice, support, and affirmation before they can achieve mastery.

Remember: You don't necessarily want your child to do what *you* would have done in the same situation. The goal is to encourage your child to look beneath the surface and examine underlying considerations. Some important issues you might want to examine include:

> Immediate versus delayed gratification. ("If Evan were to buy either the bicycle *or* the roller blades *first,* and he had to put off getting the other for several months, how upsetting do you think this would be for him? Why did you conclude this?")
>
> Options in responding to real problems, situations, and temptations. ("How could Evan handle his dilemma? How would you handle a similar situation in which you wanted two things and couldn't have them both at the same time?")
>
> The realization that some choices are more reasonable than others. ("Would it make sense for Evan to get upset because he can't afford to buy both the bike and the roller blades at the same time?")
>
> The realization that choices and decisions can have far-reaching implications, ramifications, and repercussions. ("What might have happened if Evan had decided to steal the roller blades?")
>
> The value of weighing decisions carefully and having a rationale for choices. ("Do you think it would help Evan to make his decision if he listed the pluses and minuses of each option? Let's pretend you're Evan. Make up the list of pluses and minuses.")

It's not necessary to ask all the questions in the interactive exercise for your child to derive benefit. Remember that your child's insights will reflect her chronological age, life experiences, and emotional maturity. Older children will generally be more perceptive and analytical, although they may be less communicative and more resistant if they suspect that you have a hidden agenda to get them to be more responsible. To encourage communication, you might react to resistance with statements such as, "I find that statement interesting. Tell me more about how you see (or feel about) this." Beware of overusing this response. Your child may conclude the statement is formularized and predictable and may become even more resistant to discussing the issues with you. There are many alternatives. For example, you might observe: "You seem to be saying you don't like rules. What do rules represent for you? What rules do you particularly resent?" Remember to listen to your child's responses! If appropriate, suggest a different perspective: "What would happen if people didn't stop at red lights?" "What would happen if everybody refused to pay their taxes?" "What would happen if everybody broke the law and carried a concealed weapon?"

If you sense your child becoming bored or distracted, it would be advisable to end the session before discussing everything you planned. For the interactive process to be effective and successful, it's vital that your child have positive associations with the time you spend together. There will be many more opportunities for you to practice these skills in subsequent chapters. Your goal is to help your child begin the *process* of improving thinking skills, not to "cure" him or her in one session.

Let's now look at Evan's dilemma (explain this word if necessary) and some of the issues causing his problem.

Questions and Issues for Discussion

1. Describe Evan's problem or dilemma.
2. As he struggled with the problem, what key issues do you think he needed to consider (such as how much the bike and the roller blades cost)?
3. If you were Evan, how would *you* solve the dilemma?
4. Who could you go to for advice or help?
5. What compromises might you have to make?

6. Why would you choose to solve the problem this way?
7. Let's say all your friends wanted something such as a radio-controlled car. What effect would this have on you?
8. Let's say your friends were doing something such as teasing a "weird" kid at school. What effect would this have on you?
9. Why would a kid do what his friends want him to, even though he doesn't think it's the smart thing to do?
10. What are some ways kids can resist peer pressure? (If necessary, explain what this means in concrete terms.)
11. If you decided you had made the wrong choice, what could you do then?
12. Have you ever faced a similar dilemma? Would you tell me about it?
13. Is there any moral to this story? In other words, is there something everyone could learn from this story?
14. How you would end this story?

Your child's ability to think analytically, critically, and strategically is an acquired skill. Although thinking skills are linked to intelligence, these skills can be developed and enhanced—irrespective of your child's inherited IQ—with guidance, practice, feedback, empathy, and enthusiastic support. You are your child's coach, trainer, guide, teacher, and mentor all wrapped in one package. Your child is the neophyte, rookie, explorer, apprentice, and protégé all wrapped in one package. How fortuitous it is for *you* to have this opportunity to help your child develop his or her full range of mental skills. How fortuitous it is for *your child* to have you to point out the path and lead the way.

chapter 2

Acquiring Judgment

As usual, Patrick was the first one out of the locker room. The coach nodded as the sixteen-year-old trotted past him onto the playing field to begin his warm-up stretching.

At 5'7" and 144 pounds, Patrick was the smallest player on the varsity squad. That the tenth-grader played linebacker was even more remarkable. Although not particularly fast, he was exceptionally well-disciplined. He was always in the correct position, and he had more tackles than any of the other defensive players. Aggressive, smart, and highly motivated, he was the spark plug on the team. His endurance, stamina,* work ethic, and tenacity had become legendary among his teammates. It was all but certain that he would be voted team captain the following year.

Patrick knew when he was in elementary school that he wanted to play varsity football. Realizing he was probably

---

*Define any words your child might not know or cannot figure out from the context.

going to be relatively short and light like his father and older brother, he decided he would compensate by working hard and becoming strong, tough, and wiry. For his tenth birthday present, Patrick asked his parents to buy him barbells. He had been lifting weights and working out three times a week for more than six years, and his lean muscles and physical stamina attested to his commitment to exercise.

When Patrick tried out for the junior varsity his freshman year, no one expected him to make the team. He was 5'4" and 120 pounds dripping wet! But the fourteen-year-old quickly changed the attitudes of the coach and the other players. He practiced like a person possessed, studied the defensive and offensive plays diligently, analyzed his mistakes and those of his teammates, and continually worked to improve his technique. He was the last person to leave the field after practice in the evening, and he would usually spend an extra ten minutes at the end of the day smashing the tackling dummy. Impressed with his hard work and attitude, the coach gave him the last spot on the JV roster. He never regretted the decision. In fact, most of the varsity coaches were convinced Patrick would one day play college football.

Intercepting Targets

The teenager described in the preceding anecdote defines a personal goal, develops a practical plan for attaining it, and, like a guided missile, vectors in on his target. His plan and tactics are logical, strategic, and pragmatic. He "reads" the situation, makes adjustments and compensations for his limitations, and then turns on the afterburner. Plotting his course carefully and refusing to be deflected, he attains the coveted payoff. A wiry, scrappy, scruffy, highly focused, conscientious 144-pound sophomore convinces his coaches that he has both talent and desire to be a varsity linebacker. Some might say Patrick is an overachiever. Others might say that he was the prototypical achiever who was willing to make the effort and commitment requisite to attaining his goal.

To achieve success, your child must also learn how to target personal short-term and long-term goals, plot a course, and zero in on those goals. This tactical thinking process requires that she be able to

- Think analytically
- Utilize logic and reason
- Evaluate the pluses and minuses of a course of action
- Make predictions
- Identify long-term and short-term goals
- Establish priorities
- Create a strategy
- Neutralize obstacles
- Solve problems
- Identify and manage available resources
- Handle setbacks, glitches, stress, and frustration

Your child's goals may change many times during the course of her life, but this reshuffling is inconsequential. What is consequential is that she learn how to focus her efforts and desires and how to use this focused energy to make positive things happen in her life. By establishing goals and priorities and by developing a logical, practical, and sequential plan for attaining these defined targets, she will learn how to make her way from point A to point B to point C. She will discover that these interim stops are essential if she is to reach her ultimate destination (make the varsity volleyball team, get an A in history, or be admitted to medical school). If she is a typical achiever, once she attains her objective, she will establish new goals (a 3.8 G.P.A., a college scholarship, or a residency in neurosurgery). By targeting and attaining her short-term and long-term goals, she learns how to make her life work. The resulting sense of personal efficacy and pride is vital to building her self-confidence.

Examining the Issues with Your Child

Read the anecdote that introduces this chapter with your child. Use the following questions (or make up your own) to explore the underlying issues. Although the targeted age range for the exercise is 10 to 14 years, you may be able to use the anecdote successfully with younger children and even with older teenagers. The context for the discussion should be relaxed and affirming. Your goal is not only to teach, but to *enjoy* the interaction.

interactive activity

Age Range: 10–14

Objective: Where There's a Will and a Plan, There's a Way

Questions and Issues for Discussion (anecdote found on page 41)

1. Do you find Patrick's traits admirable or not admirable?
2. Which ones are admirable?
3. Why do you find these particular traits admirable?
4. List as many of Patrick's specific decisions as you can. (For example, he was the first one out on the field.)
5. Make some predictions about the following:
   His grades. (Excellent, Good, Average, Poor)
   His popularity. (Excellent, Good, Average, Poor)
   His chances of being successful later in life. (Excellent, Good, Average, Poor)
6. Patrick obviously had a strategy. How would you rate the effectiveness of his plan?

1	2	3	4	5	6	7	8	9	10
Not Smart				Fairly Smart					Very Smart

7. Is there anything that you would be willing to work very hard to achieve?
8. What specific decisions would you have to make to achieve this goal?

Guidelines for Responding to Your Child

1. If your child doesn't find Patrick's traits admirable . . .
   Parent: In the story, it's clear that Patrick very much wanted to be the best football player he could

be. Although you might not select the same goal he chose, put yourself in his place and pretend that you, too, want to be the best player on the team. Can you understand why Patrick was willing to work so hard? (If your child is non-committal, don't drive the issue into the ground. Let it drop, and move on. There will be other opportunities to examine goal setting.)

2. If your child has difficulty identifying Patrick's specific decisions . . .

   Parent: Let's go through the story together with a pencil and underline each specific decision.

3. If your child has difficulty making realistic predictions . . .

   Parent: Let's list the kinds of behaviors and attitudes that Patrick had on the football field that might also produce good grades. The story describes how he handles challenges and how hard he works at practice. Do you think he'd work as hard at his schoolwork? (If your child responds "Not if he hates school or doesn't like to study," you might say "That's a good point. But let's assume Patrick is also motivated in school. If he worked as hard, could you predict that he'd probably get good grades?" If your child refuses to admit the logic of the point you're making with your questions, let the issue drop. You might say: "Well, just think about the link between hard work and good grades.")

4. If your child is resistant to defining a personal goal and stating what he'd be willing to do to attain this goal . . .

   Parent: I recall you once telling me that you wanted to be a professional football player (or ballerina, veterinarian, police officer). What do you think would be required to achieve this goal?

Cause and Effect

A child's capacity to use logic as a *tool* for achievement (for example, "If I study 30 minutes each night for the next five days and review my notes for an additional hour before the test, I should get a good grade.") is fundamentally linked to her understanding of the basic cause-and-effect principles. The child who reasons effectively will access her "database" of information (for example, information about taking tests) stored in her cerebral computer "hard disk." This database is comprised of observations, past experiences with similar situations and conditions, and anecdotal accountings from parents, peers, and teachers. The logical child will access and use this data to make reasonable predictions about the possible or probable consequences of her attitudes and behaviors. Her computer will help her instantaneously assess risks, react to danger, and evaluate options (for example, "If I help him cheat and get caught, I'll get an F on the exam.") Although her computer may occasionally provide the wrong answer, it will probably be accurate most of the time. As she progresses through life and confronts problems, challenges, and opportunities, she'll develop increasing trust in her reasoning skills, assuming she has a positive track record of judgment calls. She'll learn to recognize the green, yellow, or red lights that periodically flash on the "monitor." After analyzing these signals, linking what's currently happening to what's happened in the past, and projecting into the future, she'll know whether to proceed, slow down, stop, retrace her steps, or take a detour.

Your child was born with an innate, albeit rudimentary, capacity to reason. From the moment of birth, she discovered and instinctually understood a fundamental cause-and-effect principle: when she cried, you would react to her signal and address her needs. She was connected to you, and she had the power to elicit a response from her environment and the most important people in it, her parents.

Of course, many animals also discover they can cause their mothers to respond to their basic needs. To survive, they must quickly grasp that certain behaviors produce dire conse-quences. If they wander too far from the den, nest, or protec-tive parent, they will die. In most cases, this critical realization is instinctual. An antelope runs from a lion, and a kitten runs from a dog because they are programmed by genetic code to flee danger and survive.

Many animals also have the mental capacity to learn not to touch a hot stove twice. What is unique about human be-ings, however, is their capacity to make logical associations from both direct *and* indirect experiences. They can see a movie, read a book, or hear a story about someone touching a hot stove and draw logical conclusions, apply this logic, and use their insights to guide their actions.

The child who reasons and thinks logically doesn't need to experience drugs firsthand to decide she won't try them. She can infer and make predictions about the potential implications and inherent risks. By evaluating her own observations and the information she reads or hears, she will make a judgment about drugs. Ideally, this evaluative process will lead her to conclude: "Kids who take drugs act strange, get poor grades, fry their brains, get into big trouble, and ruin their lives. I don't want to be like them, so I won't take drugs."

The distinctively human abilities to analyze, identify, sort, prioritize, classify, associate, infer, deduce, predict, evaluate, apply, think logically and rationally, and use direct and indirect experiential data clearly eclipse the abilities of other life forms. These capabilities are linked to an agenda programmed by na-ture. At preordained developmental stages, your child began to crawl, walk, and talk, and, so too, at a preordained stage she began to expand her innate aptitude for thinking and reason-ing. As an eighteen-month-old, she learned the meaning of the word "no." She responded negatively to your disapproval by crying and positively to your praise by smiling. At three years of age, she began to understand the principles of punishment and delayed gratification. She also ideally began to learn how to handle frustration. Although she did not yet consciously un-derstand the insights about life that she was acquiring, and was unable to express these insights in words, she was, nevertheless, systematically etching key cause-and-effect links into both her conscious and unconscious mind. These associations comprised the foundation for her expanding reasoning capabilities.

Your child's capacity to reason is a natural extension of her evolving awareness that there are predictable consequences for specific actions and attitudes. If an angry three-year-old throws her toy at the family cat in view of her parents, she knows she will be reprimanded. This realization that a specific behavior can produce a predictable repercussion is vital to her accepting the rules that prevail at home and in the world. If your child fails to internalize age-appropriate boundaries, it's very likely she'll have difficulty with self-control and limits throughout her life. She'll always be testing to find out how far she can go before someone stops her.

Children are born with the intellectual capacity to make logical, age-appropriate, cause-and-effect associations. These associations permit children to expand their awareness of the world. As an infant, your child's developmental clock told her when to begin exploring her world. She gauged the size, shape, weight, and feel of objects in her surroundings by picking them up (a fine-motor skill) and putting them in her mouth (spatial, tactile, and kinesthetic sensory processing). At a biologically determined stage, she began to crawl (a gross-motor skill). As she propelled herself from point A to B, she registered the relationship between distance and time. She began to realize it would take a minute to crawl (the cause) from here to there (the effect). Later, she was initiated into a more formal instructional process—school—where she began to learn academic and social skills. These skills were practiced and reinforced at home through homework and parental feedback about her behavior, work ethic, performance, and attitude.

Mastering cause-and-effect principles is not only vital to a child's intellectual development; it is vital to survival. The five-year-old who wanders off at the shopping mall while her mother is paying for a purchase and who is severely admonished quickly learns that her parents will not tolerate dangerous mindlessness. She imprints that certain behaviors are perilous and that if she disregards the "house" rules, she will expose herself to unpleasant punishment.

Cause-and-effect connections also play an equally important role in a child's evolving social awareness. At a preordained developmental stage, your child became more aware of other people and began to gauge their responses to her actions. She discovered that certain behaviors were acceptable to adults and children, and other behaviors were not acceptable. She realized that tattling, temper tantrums, acting "weird," and taking other people's possessions would trigger rejection or punishment. She also discovered that other behaviors could improve her acceptance and reduce anxiety, fear, or unpleasantness. The six-year-old who is bullied by an older child at school will imprint painful cause-and-effect associations and will desperately search for ways to avoid or neutralize the effects. He may latch onto the most readily accessible solution to the problem: he may lie, telling his parents he's sick so he doesn't have to go to school, or he may give his lunch money to the bully so that he'll leave him alone. The analytical, logical child might consider other pragmatic solutions: avoid the bully, seek the protection of an older sibling, or confide in a teacher or parent.

The Danger Factor

In some cases, a child's reaction to potential danger is instinctual. In other cases, the capacity to recognize danger is a function of developed judgment.

Children are *not* genetically programmed with good judgment. Their ability to think clearly, reason, and make good choices is acquired incrementally. In a sense, the process is like building a brick wall. A child sets the bricks of her acquired knowledge, wisdom, and experience layer upon layer. With parental guidance, she learns which bricks to remove, adjust, or finesse into position. With practice, she learns how to make the layers level and how to cement the bricks together so they are solid.

Your child began to acquire the rudiments of judgment and risk assessment skills as a toddler. Although not consciously aware that she was assimilating important data from her environment, her unconscious mind continually and actively registered cause-and-effect principles that would influence her subsequent behavior. When she miscalculated and fell down or hit her head on the corner of a table, she imprinted that if she became aware of potential danger she could reduce pain. In this way, she learned from her mistakes, made key associations, and fed vital data about the harsh facts of life into her memory.

You played a key role in the inputting process. At age two, your child learned that if she reached for your coffee cup, she would be mildly reprimanded. At four, she learned that if she struck her baby sister, she would be even more severely chastised. This imprinting of basic do's and don'ts began to shape her responses to impulses and stimuli. As time passed, your reactions to her behavior had an increasingly profound impact on her appreciation and acceptance of limits, guidelines, and standards. She discovered that if she considered the repercussions of her actions *in advance,* she could avoid unpleasantness and danger. *Thinking* gave her a degree of control over her environment.

As you interacted with your child and provided feedback, she imprinted two critical cause-and-effect connections:

1. some of my behaviors are smart and others are not so smart.
2. acceptable behavior produces *pleasant* reactions from my parents, and unacceptable behavior produces reprimands, reproaches, and punishment.

Your constancy during the behavior-shaping developmental process provided a frame of reference for her evolving critical thinking and analytical decision-making skills (see Critical Thinking, page 83). Your child's realization that she could elicit specific responses reinforced (and continues to reinforce) her ever-expanding appreciation of a basic fact of life: *she is responsible for much of what happens to her.* Her actions and attitude directly affect her happiness. If she behaves, life is easier for her and everyone. This insight is the cement that binds the bricks of experience and knowledge together and creates a solid foundation for good judgment, rational thinking, and strategic planning.

Because your child's ability to evaluate situations and make appropriate decisions was initially limited, she made mistakes. She was undoubtedly sometimes perplexed by your reactions to her. Why was it unacceptable to write on the kitchen wall with a felt pen when mommy and daddy praised her for drawing on paper? Why did she *not* have to look both ways when she went into the street with daddy, but she *always* had to look both ways when she did so alone? As the data flooded into her cerebral computer, it was stored and linked with data that was previously input. Her brain connected and associated what she already knew with what she was currently learning. For example, speaking out spontaneously without editing what she said might elicit praise and approval in certain situations, while the same behavior might elicit disapproval or anger in other situations.

With each passing day, your child's database of experience and insight expanded. Your son realized he could hit the punching bag but not his younger brother. He could shoot his water gun outside the house but not inside. He could roughhouse with friends in the yard, but not in the living room.

Your child's judgment-acquiring process was linked not only to your rules, prohibitions, and reactions; it was also linked to the feedback he received from his environment. "This kid took my toy the last time we played. I don't want to play with him any more." "Aunt Alison is fun, so I'll make sure I sit next to her at the picnic." "Mrs. Winger doesn't like us to make noise when she leaves the classroom. If the kids are bad, she gets mad and punishes us." Of course, he was not always consciously aware of these connections, nor did he necessarily verbalize them in his mind as depicted above. On an unconscious level, however, he was imprinting the data. Evaluating each experience and deriving the facts of life from it, he began to acquire a storehouse of insight, wisdom, and guidelines.

When confronted with new situations, your child's brain seeks common denominators and points of reference based upon past experiences involving similar conditions and stimuli. His mind instantaneously links new data with previously-stored data. He may never have dealt with an impatient store clerk before, but he has certainly dealt with an impatient parent or teacher. The imprinted associations from these past experiences produce generalizations that will ideally influence his subsequent behavior. If he concludes that he handled a particular situation poorly, he will ideally analyze his response, reassess the situation, extract new observations and conclusions, and store this information for future reference. He is, in effect, developing a guidance system that permits him to analyze, evaluate, and respond with good judgment to danger, problems, challenges, opportunities, and temptations.

You play a pivotal role in helping your child input vital information and insights about life into his personal database. By sharing and examining your own thinking and judgment with your child and by urging him to think and reason carefully in real-life situations, you provide the critical catalyst in the equation that produces enhanced awareness and judgment. (See Interactive Activities at the end of this chapter for additional suggestions and guidance.)

interactive activity

Age Range: 9–14
Objective: Assessing Danger

To Walk or Not to Walk

As usual, Jeff and Colleen were late. And, as usual, they were upset with themselves and angry at each other. They never allowed enough time to get where they were going, and this invariably triggered arguments. For example, they would suddenly realize that English class started in five minutes, and they were two miles from school on their bikes. Jeff would blame Colleen, and she would blame him.

This time they weren't late for school. They were late for a concert. When they got off the bus, Jeff looked at his watch and clenched his teeth. It was already 7:25 P.M. The first set would start in five minutes, and the theater was seven long blocks away. He was determined not to miss the first set.

As they ran down the street, Jeff became more and more upset. The theater was in a dangerous neighborhood, and this added to his anxiety. Out of the corner of his eye, he saw a small alley that looked like a good shortcut. Jeff grabbed Colleen's arm and pointed to the alley. It was dark and scary-looking, and Colleen looked frightened when he suggested they take the shortcut. When Jeff peered down the alley, he thought he could see people lurking in the shadows. Knowing there were gangs in this part of town, he hesitated. He glanced again at his watch. The concert was supposed to start in two minutes. He didn't want to be late, but he also didn't want to get robbed or shot.

Questions and Issues for Discussion

1. If Jeff insisted they take the shortcut, how would you rate this decision?

1	2	3	4	5	6	7	8	9	10
Not				Fairly					Very
Smart				Smart					Smart

2. Why did you make this evaluation?
3. What alternatives did Jeff and Colleen have?
4. If you were late for a concert, would you go down the alley described in the story?
5. Would you be scared?
6. What would make you fearful?
7. If you would go down the alley, tell me why.
8. If you were a parent and your child was in this situation, how would you want him or her to handle it? Tell me why.

9. Would it reasonable for a parent to be concerned about how his or her child chose to handle this situation?
10. If being late is a recurring problem for Jeff and Colleen, are there any practical solutions to this problem? What are the most reasonable solutions?

Guidelines for Responding to Your Child

1. If in response to question #5 your child says she would not be scared . . .
   Parent: You say you wouldn't be frightened. But let's say your friend tells you *she* would be frightened. What do you think would frighten her?
2. If your child can't identify red flags that signal danger . . .
   Parent: Let's go back to the story and underline the things that made Jeff anxious.
3. If your child has difficulty identifying alternatives . . .
   Parent: Do you think one alternative would be to get to the concert a little late and perhaps miss part of the first set? Can you think of any other alternatives?
4. If your child has difficulty imagining himself as a parent . . .
   Parent: What safety issues do you think would concern *me*?
5. If your child thinks it's unreasonable for a parent to have concerns about the scenario described in the anecdote . . .
   Parent: Imagine how parents would feel if their child was attacked and seriously injured or even killed. What effect you think this would have on these parents?

Intuition

Intuition is one of the most supreme manifestations of human intelligence. Although we often take intuition for granted, our intuitive response to a situation or problem is actually the distillation of our life's experience and acquired wisdom. We intuitively trust one person and distrust another. We intuitively feel fearful in one situation and secure in another. We intuitively accept one choice but have grave misgivings about another, perhaps without even knowing why or without being able to verbalize our reasons.

Because intuition is often spontaneous, we may be tempted to discount its validity. In fact, an intuitive response usually represents exquisite logic and insight. Your child's reluctance to pet a strange dog whose ears are back reflects her imprinted direct or indirect experiences and associations with hostile dogs. Your daughter may not have actually been bitten by this dog, or by any dog whose ears are back, but she may have seen such a dog bite or threaten another child. Her fear, in tandem with an *instinctual* fear/avoidance reaction to danger, would cause her to recoil from the dog.

Intuition is a vital survival mechanism. Your child's "radar" about how to act and react is a precious resource, not only in life-threatening situations, but also when the conditions are less perilous. One day she may choose to work or not work for a particular company because her intuition tells her that the job is "right" or "wrong" for her. She may select someone to be her friend or roommate because she intuitively senses the person "feels right." She may decide not to go on a date with someone she meets at a party because her intuition flashes a danger signal. If you and your daughter were to analyze carefully the reasons for her decisions, you would probably discover that her intuitive response was based on an instantaneous filtering of past life experiences. In effect, she "ran" new data through her "computer" and compared this information with her stored database. The context-appropriate response then registered on the "screen." She may not be *consciously* aware of all the factors and issues she considered when she made her intuitive judgment call, but if she wanted to, she could probably identify the threads of logic and reason that ran through her decision-making process.

Right-brain functions (creativity and intuition) and left-brain functions (logic and language) are not, in fact, distinct phenomena, as some literature suggests. The novelist and the actor engaged primarily in right-brain creativity must also plan and negotiate (left-brain logic) with agents, publishers, and producers. The scientist and the engineer who use left-brain functions to calculate must also use right-brain functions to draw diagrams and find creative solutions to problems. The "bridge" connecting left-brain logic and right-brain intuition goes in both directions. (In medical terms, this bridge is called the corpus callosum.) When you provide your child with opportunities to handle situations involving right- and left-brain functions, you are, in effect, encouraging her to practice crossing this bridge. This process stimulates both brain functions. She will learn to trust her intuition (right brain) and use her reasoning powers (left brain). By stimulating your child in this way, you play a major role in helping her develop her full range of intellectual and emotional capabilities.

Sharing your own intuitive reactions to situations in life can be an excellent means for helping your child develop confidence in her own intuitive process. For example, you might describe how you based a particular decision on a "feeling" about a certain situation or individual. You could then analyze with your child what issues your mind either consciously or unconsciously factored into the decision-making process. Explain that, although you appeared to react spontaneously, your brain was actually distilling (explain this word) your past experiences and making connections and associations. Remember to gear your explanation to your child's level of developmental maturity. You might use the example of a baseball batter who expects a certain pitch in a particular situation because he's observed how the pitcher throws in previous games. Underscore that, like the batter, you made an intuitive "yes" or "no," "go" or "no-go" decision based on previous experiences and, although spontaneous, the choice was actually well-reasoned and logical.

Heightening your child's awareness that her brain is continually inputting and using experiential data will encourage her to have faith in her brain's capacity to process and distill this data effectively and to make judicious choices. Faith in oneself rests on a foundation of positive experiences. The more success your child has in trusting her intuition, the more faith she will acquire.

Of course, you want your child to consider high-risk choices carefully, analytically, and deliberately. You also want her, in appropriate contexts, to trust her spontaneous, intuitive evaluation process. She must learn *when* it's smart to make intuitive judgments and *when* it's smart to make more laborious analytical judgments.

Trust in one's intuition is directly linked to positive experiences and associations with intuitive judgment. By providing encouragement, feedback, praise, and repeated opportunities for your child to "exercise" her intuition, you increase the likelihood that she'll have positive experiences and associations with the process. The goal is for her to be able to say, "I intuitively sense this situation or choice is right!" Implicit in this statement is her confidence that in the future she'll be able to read other situations "right" as well.

---

interactive activity

Age Range: 6–14
Objectives: Recognizing Danger,
Avoiding Risks,
Resisting Peer Pressure,
Thinking Independently

Lie Down in Darkness *

(The youth's) death was easy to portray as a clear-cut case of cause and effect. On October 10, he and three carloads of friends saw the movie *The Program* at a drive-in movie not far from his home. . . . Early in the film, its hero,

---

*This edited article appeared in the November 1, 1993, edition of *Time*.

a college quarterback, tries to prove grace under pressure by lying down in the middle of busy highway flipping through a magazine as the trucks swerve to avoid him. He goes unscathed. (The teenager) did not seem especially moved by the film, his girlfriend reports. But the next weekend, he tried the same stunt himself on the double yellow line in the middle of Pennsylvania Route 62—and was hit by a pickup truck. . . . 'I've done it,' says . . . a ninth-grader at Franklin Area High School, from which the (dead youth) graduated last spring. On Halloween two years ago, she recalls, she and 20 other kids took turns arranging themselves like sardines across a road. When they saw headlights most bolted, but a few stayed pat. . . . 'All my friends were doing it, so I did it. I wasn't even thinking of getting hit.' . . . Two more youths attempted the roadway stunt on Wednesday—one a fourth-grader, the other a first-grader.

Questions and Issues for Discussion

1. Do you think the kids described in this article were aware of the dangers involved?
2. What might prompt a kid to take these kinds of risks?
3. Do you think they were showing off or trying to prove something to their friends?
4. Let's say your friends told you they were going to lie down on the highway. How would you react? Would you try to discourage them? If they refused to listen to your advice, what might you do?
5. If your friends did this stunt, how would you rate their behavior?

1	2	3	4	5	6	7	8	9	10
Not Dangerous				Fairly Dangerous					Very Dangerous

6. Have you ever been tempted to do something dangerous that you saw in a movie or on TV?
7. When a movie star survives a dangerous stunt, does this mean kids could do it successfully as well? Why did you conclude this?

8. What would the parents of the kids described in the anecdote say if they knew what their children were doing? How would they feel?
9. Why do kids sometimes not think about danger and take risks?
10. If you were tempted to do something very risky, what might cause you to stop and reconsider?
11. Might you be tempted to do something very dangerous because your friends decided to do it?
12. Let's assume you did do something very dangerous because your friends dared you. How would you rate your decision?

1	2	3	4	5	6	7	8	9	10
Not				Fairly					Very
Smart				Smart					Smart

Guidelines for Responding to Your Child

1. If your child tells you the kids in the story weren't aware of the risks . . .

    Parent: Let's look at some of the red danger flags these kids may not have considered. Would the driver of an oncoming car or truck necessarily be able to see someone lying in the road? Would they be able to stop in time? Would they expect the kids doing the stunt to get up and move away in time? Might they unintentionally swerve into a child who is getting up to run away?

2. If your child cannot come up with reasons why kids might pull this stunt . . .

    Parent: I'm wondering about what prompts kids to act or dress in a certain way. Do movies, rock groups, and TV influence kids? Why do you think this happens? What makes some things "cool" and other things "not cool?"

3. If your child has difficulty examining the issue of showing off . . .

> *Parent:* Do you have any friends who show off? How do they show off? Why do they do this? Give me some examples of what your friends might do to show off. When you want to show off, what do you do? Do adults also show off? Can you think of an example?

4. If your child has difficulty coming up with ideas for discouraging his friend from doing this stunt . . .

> *Parent:* Do you think it might be possible to find someone your friend really respects, for example, an older kid or your brother and have him tell your friend that the idea is dumb? What about telling an adult? This would be tattling, I know. But imagine how you would feel if your friend were killed and you didn't do everything in your power to discourage him. Can you think of any other ideas? Could you live with the fact that your friend might be mad at you if you told an adult about the plan?

5. If your child doesn't give the stunt a very negative rating . . .

> *Parent:* Do you think the kid lying in the road is in control of what happens to him? What might happen if the driver of a truck coming down the road is sleepy? What other possibilities could significantly increase the risk to the child trying this stunt?

6. If your child has difficulty recognizing or discussing the extent to which she is influenced by TV or the movies . . .

> *Parent:* Tell me who your favorite singer, musician, TV personality, or movie star is. What is it about this person that appeals to you? If you wanted to be like this person, how would you act or how would you try to dress?

7. If your child has difficulty realizing that movies can depict something inherently dangerous as being fun or harmless . . .

Parent: Do you recall that scene in the movie we just rented in which the actor jumped from one train to another? Do you think the stuntman practiced that scene repeatedly until he was able to do it successfully? Could someone who was not a trained stuntperson do that without getting hurt? Could I do it? Could you do it? Are some of the stunts fake? Do stuntmen sometimes have wires attached to them to protect them from falling? Would that stunt happen in the real world? If a kid tried a dangerous stunt from a movie, what would happen? Do people who die in movies really die? In the real world, when you have an accident, do you simply get up afterward and walk away? When someone really dies, does he simply get up, get into his car, and drive home for dinner like an actor or stuntman does?

8. If your child has difficulty empathizing with your likely emotional reaction if you learned that he had done the stunt described in the article . . .

Parent: If someone told you that your dog was chasing cars on the expressway, would you be concerned? What if someone told you your little brother and his friends were roller blading on a freeway? Is it natural to be concerned when someone you love is taking risks and might be hurt or die as a result? Imagine you are the parent of the first-grader described in the last sentence of the article who attempted the roadway stunt. Would you be concerned? What would you be feeling?

9. If your child has difficulty figuring out why children might disregard danger and take risks . . .

Parent: Let's say a friend suggests you swim to a small island in the middle of a river. You're a good swimmer, but the water is moving fast and the island is several hundred yards away. You want to go with your friend because you think it might be fun. He dares you to swim with him. What would go on in your mind? What issues would you weigh? If you decided not to do it, how would you tell your friend? What might his reaction be? What would you do if he accused you of being scared and being a baby? What would you do if you wanted his approval, but your judgment told you that you might not make it to the island? Let's assume you go into the water and realize you were making a mistake. Would you turn back or would you continue? If you thought it was too dangerous, would you discourage your friend from trying it, too? What would you say to your friend to convince him not to take the chance?

Assessing Risks

Danger is a fact of life. Children face risks whenever they ride their bicycles, go swimming, skate, ski, and, in some cases, simply walk down the street.

If you want to teach your child to assess risks carefully and avoid obvious perils, you must develop an effective teaching strategy. Continual nagging about danger is *not* the answer. Although a young child doesn't yet have a great deal of overt power, he does have covert power. He can always find ways to circumvent your wishes and admonishments. You may tell him not to play in a particular area, but you cannot monitor him constantly. If he's intent on disregarding (or "forgetting") your instructions, you'll be forced to become a police officer, an unpleasant prospect for everyone in the family.

The child who receives repetitive lectures about safety and danger may become excessively frightened, fearful, and tentative, or he may simply block out what he's being told. Some children manifest resistance to their parents' admonitions by rejecting the advice and by being openly resentful and rebellious. The red flags that signal an oppositional family dynamic are continual arguments, blaming, hurt feelings, and anger. Other children may manifest opposition to their parents' advice by becoming passively resistant and covertly resentful and rebellious. They may agree to do what their parents say simply to "get them off their backs," and then do what they wanted to do all along. Other children may manipulate and lie to get their own way. (If disrespect, resentment, rebelliousness, passive resistance, or manipulation are chronic, such behaviors are symptomatic of a family dysfunction. Professional counseling is essential.)

The alternative to sermons, lectures, showdowns, shoot-outs, and bruised feelings is to teach your child non-pedantically *how* to make wise decisions, solve problems, and exercise good judgment, critical intelligence, and strategic thinking. Children who have been trained to use logic and to trust their intuition are far more likely to assess risks carefully and respond judiciously.

Investing the time to assess and enhance the quality of your communication with your child is certain to pay off. Although learning how to establish an effective dialogue with your child can be challenging and frustrating, the rewards will more than compensate for the hard work and occasional frustration. Good parent-child communication during the formative years establishes the foundation for good parent-adult child communication twenty years down the road.

Tragic Conditions, Tragic Choices, and Tragic Outcomes

We live in a world where those who lack the requisite intellectual and psychological resources and judgment to survive, compete, and prevail are often crushed and callously discarded like so much refuse. The homeless wander aimlessly and hopelessly through our city streets, and tens of thousands of children in the U.S., the richest country in the world, go to bed hungry. In third world countries, thousands of emaciated, disease-ridden children starve to death each day. In the morning newspapers, we occasionally see their silent suffering and their sad, clouded eyes framed by gaunt, defeated faces captured in the lens of a curious photo journalist. The mentally ill stand on street corners talking to people they alone can hear, and addicted drug users live and die in sordid crack houses. The emotionally crushing list of human tragedies seems endless.

The world has always been perilous for those who are ill-prepared to deal with life's realities because of bad luck, unfortunate circumstances, or poor judgment. Danger has plagued human beings throughout history. In the past, the village offered protection from the forbidding forest, the jungle, marauding animals, and criminals. The bow, the knife, the spear, the gun, the wisdom of the elders, the strength and courage of the warriors and hunters, the astuteness of the leaders and rulers, and the constant vigilance of the village inhabitants were essential to individual and collective survival.

In the jungle of the modern industrialized western world, we no longer have to fear the crocodile, the lion, or the cobra. But dangers still surround us. In fact, these dangers have multiplied exponentially. Your child must learn to protect himself from the mugger who lurks in a dark alley and the drug dealer who entices him with powders and crystals that produce initial euphoria and then addiction and degradation. He must protect himself from the pedophile and the rapist who would destroy his innocence and scar him emotionally for life. He must protect himself from the gangs who would shoot him from a speeding car, the scam artists who would deceive with false promises, and the exploiters who would profit from his naiveté.

Your child has *already* begun the perilous process of leaving the protection of the family nest. He must walk to the bus stop, ride public transportation, walk down the hall at school, and enter the men's room in a movie theater. All these situations represent potential danger. Tragically, the age of innocence ends all too soon! If you haven't adequately trained him to assess, avoid, or reduce the risks, and if he ventures into the jungle without being "intellectually armed," he will be unable to protect himself. He may become the prey of the modern counterparts to the tiger, the cobra, or the bandit. A continual pattern of brainless choices and impulsive behavior could imperil his life.

Although it can be argued that excessive fearfulness and paranoia are pathological, it can also be argued that some paranoia is vital to survival. Caution, healthy skepticism, vigilance, risk assessment, and strategic planning are your child's most potent protective resources in today's jungle. These are the modern equivalents of the bow, the knife, and the spear. Children must learn how to reduce the risks and avoid calamities. They must be taught to use their heads!

If there was an actuarial chart that compared children who reason and think logically and strategically with those who act and think impulsively and senselessly, it would undoubtedly reveal that children in the first category live longer, have fewer accidents, and achieve at a higher level than their more impulsive counterparts. Logic and reason are not "optional equipment." They are necessities.

Note about the following activity: As you read the following news article with your child, don't "tip your hand" by shaking your head disapprovingly. You want to use the story as a catalyst for discussion and to guide your child, without moralizing or sermonizing, to his or her own insights about risks, mindless behavior, and intoxication. Of course, you can and should discuss your feelings and reactions, but resist the temptation to lecture your child about the evils of drinking. If you do, he or she may simply tune you out. Your goal is to help your child draw logical conclusions from the data so that these conclusions and the analytical process will have a positive impact on his or her future actions and decisions. This objective can be best accomplished by helping your child learn how to examine the underlying issues and the inherent dangers logically and rationally.

interactive **activity**

Age Range: 8–14
Objective: Acquiring Judgment

Beer-Drinking Youth Killed by Oil Tank Explosion

Sherman, Texas—
Several teenagers partying at an oil tank accidentally caused an explosion early yesterday that killed one of them and injured four others, officials said.

Grayson County Sheriff's Department chief investigator Skip Walley reported that the blast occurred at 2:30 A.M. at the Chevron oil tank about 60 miles north of Dallas.

According to Walley, seven teenagers were holding a late-night beer party, Walley said. "Four of the young men climbed up on top of the oil well. One of them . . . got the top open, couldn't see down inside of it, so he leaned over and either lit a match or a cigarette lighter." One of the other teens underwent surgery, and another was admitted to the intensive care unit. A third was hospitalized for burns and the fourth injured teen was treated and released.

Questions and Issues for Discussion

1. What do you think the specific factors were that caused the accident described in the news story?
2. Do you think the decision to have the party at the oil storage tank was made before the teenagers got drunk?
3. If the teenager hadn't been drinking, do you think he would have lit a match to look inside the tank? If you believe he might have done it anyway, what factors would he be disregarding?

4. Do you believe alcohol can hurt a person's judgment?

5. Do you think that the teenager who lit the match had good judgment before he became drunk? Why do you think this?

6. How would you respond if some friends proposed that you do something you knew was foolish or very dangerous?

7. If you wouldn't participate, how would you handle the problem of backing out? What if they teased you or said you were a coward?

8. Why might a kid be reluctant to reject a dangerous idea or scheme that a friend proposes? What might be the social consequences of refusing to participate in the scheme?

9. How important would it be to you if a friend accused you of being a coward because you refused to go along with a dangerous scheme?

1	2	3	4	5	6	7	8	9	10
Not Important				Fairly Important					Very Important

10. Let's assume that one of the teenagers described above had misgivings (define this term if necessary) about having a beer party at an oil storage tank. Even though he has doubts, what factors might cause him to agree to join them? (such as drinking, peer pressure, etc.)

11. Let's assume the person with misgivings gives in and joins his buddies. How would you rate this decision?

1	2	3	4	5	6	7	8	9	10
Not Smart				Fairly Smart					Very Smart

12. What would you do if you were with friends, and one friend began acting irrationally or dangerously?

Guidelines for Responding to Your Child

1. If your child has difficulty identifying the specific factors responsible for the accident . . .

> ***Parent:*** Let's number each factor described in the article that might have contributed to the accident.

2. If your child cannot project how he (she) might respond if someone proposed doing something very dangerous or foolish . . .

> ***Parent:*** Well, what do you think you would do if someone proposed that you steal and copy an exam from your teacher?

3. If your child cannot figure out how to back out of something his friends propose . . .

> ***Parent:*** Let's look at some options. I suppose you could make up a lie. . . . You could, of course, be honest and tell them you won't do something you think is silly or dangerous. . . .

4. If your child has difficulty identifying specific coercive pressures. . . .

> ***Parent:*** Think about a time when your friends suggested doing something that everyone thought was a great idea. Perhaps it was playing basketball after school, or crashing a party. If you didn't want to be part of what was happening, and your friends very much wanted you to participate, what might they say to convince, coerce (define term), intimidate, or shame you into being part of what everyone else was doing?

5. If your child has difficulty deciding how he would react if a friend started acting strangely or dangerously. . . .

> ***Parent:*** Imagine you're with a friend who has been drinking. He suggests you go for a ride in his father's car. You know his father is away and has expressly forbidden your friend to use his car . . .

Your child was not born knowing how to think "straight." If he is to acquire this vital capacity, you must be his teacher. His good judgment and wise choices will be directly attributable to your careful, systematic instruction. By training him to be aware of the consequences of his actions and decisions and by teaching him to assess risks and think rationally and strategically, you can significantly improve the odds that he will actualize his full potential.

You can be certain that during the course of his life, your child will arrive at many crossroads. At these decision points, he will be forced to select a direction. Your guidance during the formative years at the decision point can be pivotal. You *can* influence the quality of your child's thinking skills, and you *can* help him acquire the judgment and wisdom he needs to triumph in a competitive world.

chapter 3

Brain Power

Tyrone, Kevin, and Brian raced up the driveway on their bicycles. It was a perfect summer day to go fishing. Their last stop before heading for the lake was to pick up their buddy, Martin. The boys had packed an ample supply of sandwiches, soft drinks, potato chips, and candy in their backpacks. They had strapped their disassembled fishing poles and their bait and tackle boxes to their bikes. It would take them 45 minutes to pedal to their favorite fishing spot. If they left right away, they could be there by 9:30, when they were certain the fish would be hungry.

As the twelve-year-olds dismounted their bikes, each pushed down the kickstand. Tyrone's and Kevin's bikes rested upright. Brian's wobbled and fell over. Brian set it upright, but once again it wobbled and fell. He glanced at his friends and shrugged. He and Tyrone went into the garage to find out if Martin was ready.

Kevin had a puzzled look on his face. While Tyrone and Brian went to look for Martin, he went over to examine

Brian's bike. At first, he suspected that the weight of the pole and gear strapped to one side had caused the bike to fall. But on closer inspection, he discovered that the bolt attaching the kickstand to the frame was loose. Finding a wrench on the workshop bench in the garage, he quickly tightened the bolt, pushed the kickstand down, and nodded with satisfaction when he saw that the bike remained upright. The entire procedure had taken two minutes. When Brian saw that Kevin had fixed his kickstand, he showed his appreciation by remarking, "Hey, that's cool." Within two minutes, the boys were speeding down the driveway.

This Doesn't Make Sense

Put four twelve-year-olds together, throw in a nice summer day and the prospect of going fishing at the lake. Why would one kid be thinking about fixing the kickstand on his friend's bicycle when it was clearly "no big deal"?

Kevin saw it differently. When the bike fell over, a buzzer went off in his mind. Something was wrong. When the kickstand is down, a bike *should* remain upright.

On the surface, Kevin's reaction to the falling bicycle might not appear especially significant. His reaction, however, signals that he likes things to work the way they're supposed to work. His curiosity and appreciation for the principles of cause and effect compelled him to figure out why the bike kept falling over. Once he investigated and identified the source of the problem, he quickly resolved it.

From his reaction, it would be reasonable to make several inferences about Kevin's thinking process.

> He's intrigued when something defies logic ("Bikes should remain upright when the kickstand is down.")
> He thinks deductively. ("The bike has fallen twice. Obviously, something must be wrong somewhere.")
> He's observant, analytical, questioning, and thorough. ("I must figure this out. Let's take a closer look at what's happening. I see what the problem is.")

He's confident he can remove obstacles standing in his
way. ("It's no big deal. I can easily fix it. Where can I
find a wrench or pliers?")

He doesn't like to be thwarted. ("I like making things
work right.")

He enjoys figuring things out. ("There must be a reason
why the bike is falling.")

He applies what he knows when confronted with a problem or challenge. ("I've fixed problems like this before.")

Contrasting Kevin's reaction to the falling bike with that
of his friends might lead to the conclusion that Kevin is the
more intelligent child. Perhaps this is true, but it's conceivable
that Brian and Tyrone are equally intelligent. Kevin's analytical
thinking process, however, clearly differentiates him. Like most
kids, he likes to fish and have fun with his friends, but he also
shares the distinctive mind-set of those who want the principles of physics, mechanics, and cause and effect to function in
an orderly and predictable way. Such people ascribe to a basic
tenet: "When it's broken, and you want it to work, figure out
what's wrong and fix it."

Given Kevin's reaction to the falling bike, it would be reasonable to predict that in high school he would be the type of
student who would carefully check the accuracy of his footnotes
on a term paper, verify the results of a lab experiment, and go
over a geometry proof before submitting it. You would also expect him to make sure he has all the necessary equipment before
embarking on a ten-day backpacking trip. You would expect
that, as an adult, he would make certain the brakes and tires on
his car are in working order before he begins a vacation with his
family, and you would expect him to make sure the project his
boss assigned is complete, accurate, and submitted on time.

Attention to detail, thoroughness, logical thinking, and a
need to make things work right are the benchmarks of *applied
intelligence*. With your help and guidance, your child can acquire these traits. He can learn how to use his mind more effectively, think more analytically, and become more observant,
questioning, and thorough. He can learn how to confront a

puzzling problem, examine and evaluate the data, figure out what needs to be done, apply what he knows, and fix what needs to be fixed. The payoffs for his curiosity, effort, and follow-through will be pride, satisfaction in a job well done, and confidence in his problem-solving skills.

Once your child experiences the thrill of using his mind to prevail over challenges, he'll become addicted. He'll discover that his desire, focused intellect, and perseverance can move *seemingly* unmovable obstacles and solve *seemingly* insoluble problems. He may have to struggle to make something work the way he wants it to work, but he'll learn in the process that his brain can serve as the *instrument of his will*. This realization will cause his sense of his own power and efficacy to soar.

Examining the Issues with Your Child

Read the introductory anecdote with your child. Use the following questions (or make up your own) to explore the underlying issues. The context for the discussion should be relaxed and affirming. Your goal is not only to teach, but also to *enjoy* this interaction with your child.

---

interactive **activity**

Age Range: 6–14
Objectives: Learning to analyze problems and
          Identifying causal factors

Questions and Issues for Discussion (anecdote found on page 71)

1. Why do you think Kevin was willing to take the time to examine the kickstand?
2. Why do you think Brian and Tyrone weren't willing to take the time?
3. If you were with Brian and Tyrone and your bike fell over after you put down the kickstand, what would you do?

4. How would you rate Kevin's decision to figure out what was causing the bike to fall?

1	2	3	4	5	6	7	8	9	10
Not				Fairly					Very
Smart				Smart					Smart

5. What adjectives would you use to describe Kevin?
6. What predictions would you make about him? His grades in school? His ability to solve problems? His intelligence? His work ethic? His self-confidence? His popularity with other kids?
7. If you were backpacking, would Kevin be the type of person you would want to take along? Why? How do you think he would handle a crisis or emergency?
8. Do you think Kevin was born with the ability to analyze and solve problems, or do you think he learned how to do so? Can kids make themselves smarter? How could they do this?

Please note: Since the preceding questions are straightforward, you will probably not require guidance on how to respond to your child. If you run into problems and need help, follow the parent response Guidelines found in previous interactive activities. These guidelines are summarized in the following boxed sidebars.

Eight Key Principles for Communicating Effectively with Your Child

Be patient
Be empathetic and supportive
Orchestrate successful experiences
Create positive associations
Express positive expectations
Resist being highly judgmental and critical
Affirm your child for progress
Enthusiastically acknowledge your child's achievements

Handling Off-Target Responses

After listening empathetically to your child's response, you may be able to stimulate greater insigyt by saying:

- ■ "That's interesting. . . . Tell me more."
- ■ "Can you think of any alternative ways to handle this?"
- ■ "Have you considered looking at this issue in this way?
- ■ What's your reaction to this suggestion? . . ."

Remember, your goal is to encourage active involvement in these interactive exercises. If your child acquires negative associations with the activity, he will become resistant and will actively or passively defeat your efforts to work interactively with him.

Intelligence

That *you* play a key role in the development of your child's thinking skills has been repeatedly underscored in this book. There are, however, other important factors in the thinking skills equation. Your child's capacity to reason is also clearly linked to his maturation level. You can reasonably expect a certain level of insight, understanding, and logic from a twelve-year-old (such as, "If I don't have a good G.P.A., I won't get into a good college.") that you cannot reasonably expect from a five-year-old.

Another key factor must be added to the thinking skills equation: intelligence. The greater your child's intelligence, the greater her ability to analyze, comprehend, evaluate, perceive connections, unravel puzzling issues, apply logic, and solve complex problems. There are, of course, exceptions. When there are discrepancies between intelligence and applied thinking skills, these may be attributable to trauma, abuse, emotional problems, a dysfunctional family system, attention deficit disorder, or to sensory, emotional, or intellectual deprivation during the formative years.

A Working Definition of Intelligence

Intelligence is the capacity to think creatively and logically, recognize similarities and differences, analyze and critically evaluate information, perceive underlying issues, solve problems, link past experiences with current experiences, learn from mistakes, find common denominators, handle multiple complex variables, understand abstractions, distill information, recall data, and utilize insights and learned information when confronted with challenges, problems, and opportunities.

Example: "I see this problem is similar to the one I just read. I simply need to do one additional step. If I use the same technique I used to solve the previous problem and do the extra step, I can solve this problem easily."

Educators generally agree that 70–80 percent of intelligence is inherited and genetically based. The remainder can be affected by environmental factors and can be enhanced with education, training, nurturing, and exposure to intellectually stimulating and enriching experiences during the critically important formative years.

Bright children have a wider range of resources for handling challenging situations. These resources provide distinct academic advantages. Children with high IQ's generally have less difficulty understanding abstract ideas in textbooks and lectures, thinking analytically, reasoning deductively, drawing inferences, making logical predictions, finding alternative solutions, handling advanced academic subject matter, and communicating their insights and ideas.

You may not be able to dramatically alter your child's level of intelligence, but you can most definitely have a significant impact on how she *uses* her intelligence. You can teach her to think more effectively, efficiently, and pragmatically. You can teach her how to get the most "mileage" out of her inherited intellectual capacity. You can teach her to think smarter and develop judgment. You can teach her how to acquire and use insight and wisdom. It is on this level of practical, applied intelligence that you as a parent can have the most positive and profound impact.

Smartness

A high level of inherited intelligence does not guarantee that your child will use his intellectual powers to full advantage. Many bright children suffer repeated setbacks they might have avoided. They make chronic errors in judgment and disregard the predictable implications of their actions and attitudes because they haven't learned how to think logically and strategically. The net effect is a glaring discrepancy between their *potential ability* and their *developed ability.* Although intelligent, they underachieve because they don't know how to focus their intellect. They are like gifted, natural athletes who have the potential to become consummate professionals but who never fully develop their talents because they weren't properly coached or because they chose not to practice.

Being intelligent and being smart are *not* synonymous. The child with an IQ of 140 may amble through life in a fog. He may park his new bicycle in front of a store without locking it to something or allow himself to be goaded by his friends into jumping from a tree into a fast-moving stream, carrying a weapon to school, stealing a car, or taking drugs. Unfortunately, bright kids who don't think smart often end up doing very "dumb" things.

> ### *A Working Definition of Smartness*
>
> Smartness is the capacity to apply intelligence pragmatically, get from point A to point B efficiently, calculate odds, plan strategically, prioritize what needs to be done, understand cause-and-effect phenomena, anticipate and avoid problems, bounce back from setbacks, focus efforts, overcome obstacles, and survive and prevail in a harsh and competitive world.
>
> *Example:* "I got a bad grade on the last history test because I studied the wrong material. This time when I study, I'll look over the previous test and use it to help me predict what the teacher is likely to ask on the next test. I'll also ask my friends who received good grades on the last test what specific material they plan to study for the next test."

The smart child is a survivor. She uses her head to get what she wants or needs in life. She is goal-oriented and performance conscious. When she confronts a problem, challenge, or opportunity, she asks herself—on either a conscious or unconscious level—a series of key questions:

What do I want to achieve?
What are the potential difficulties I will face?
How can I get the job done efficiently and painlessly?
How can I avoid pitfalls and mistakes?
How can I increase my chances of success?
Who (or what) can help me attain my objective?
What's my timetable?

Intelligence and smartness overlap. To think smart, a child must possess intelligence. She need not, however, be brilliant to be successful in school or in her chosen vocation. The smart child may not be the best student in her class, but she typically gets better-than-average grades, passes her courses, graduates, and goes to college. By calculating the odds, plotting a course, and getting the job done, she gets the most out of the hand she's been dealt.

Although the brilliant student (as measured on an IQ test)* may do magnificently in school, she may be unable to handle everyday problems or to make her life work. There are members of Mensa, an elitist organization for the mentally gifted, whose achievements are certainly *not* commensurate with their measured intelligence.

It's fortuitous when a child possesses both intelligence *and* smartness. In tandem, these two resources can generate awesome power. The smart and intelligent child has more academic and vocational options. She can become a neurosurgeon, an astrophysicist, a college professor, an architect, an engineer, or a novelist, assuming she's strategic enough to establish her goals, chart a course, focus her resources, and get the job done.

Whatever your child's genetically based intelligence level, the quality of her applied intelligence can be enhanced with training. Logic is the turbocharger in her intellectual propulsion system. Under your tutelage, she can learn how to generate maximum mental RPM's and torque. Each time you encourage her to analyze and evaluate an issue, problem, challenge, opportunity, or decision, and each time you help her produce a logical response, you are revving her engine and enhancing her reasoning skills. These skills will serve her throughout her life.

interactive activity

Age Range: 8–14
Objective: Making Astute Judgments about
　　　　　People and Situations

Joining the Gang

Jenni and Alexis had been friends since kindergarten. They did everything together. They enrolled in the same

*See my book *1001 Ways to Improve Your Child's Schoolwork* (Prima, fall 1995) for a comprehensive discussion of IQ.

gymnastics program, they were on the same soccer and softball teams, and they were in the same Sunday school class. Now that they both were thirteen, they would go together to the mall on Saturday afternoons and visit with their friends.

Jenni was surprised and disturbed when Alexis started hanging out with some girls who were in a street gang. The girls smoked, cut school, and took drugs. At first Alexis was on the fringe of the group. But then she started wearing similar clothing and using the hand signs that the gang members used to communicate.

Jenni couldn't understand why her friend was attracted to these girls. They were all "losers" in Jenni's eyes. They did poorly in school, acted and dressed weird, and were unfriendly and discourteous to everyone. "Why would Alexis want to associate with them?" she wondered. She knew her friend had talked about going to college and becoming a doctor.

When Alexis told her she was planning on actually joining the gang, Jenni thought her friend had lost her mind. That Alexis actually believed she could talk Jenni into joining the gang too seemed even more incredible. The last thing in the world Jenni wanted to do was to associate with those girls. Jenni wanted to do well in school, go to college on a basketball scholarship, and become a lawyer someday. All the girls in the gang seemed like they were on a track that led straight to juvenile hall, and that was the last place in the world Jenni wanted to go.

Jenni told her friend that she wanted nothing to do with Alexis's new friends. She tried to help Alexis see that she was making a big mistake, but her friend refused to listen. Instead, Alexis got mad and said she would no longer be Jenni's friend. Jenni felt very sad about losing her friend and very sad about Alexis's decision to join the gang. Alexis had changed so much over the last two months. She seemed so angry at everyone, and Jenni couldn't figure out why. She finally decided the problem wasn't hers. She had done all she could to help Alexis, and she had to accept the fact that they had chosen very different paths.

Questions and Issues for Discussion

1. Why might Alexis be attracted to a gang? What might appeal to her?
2. What might be happening in Alexis's life, or might have happened in the past, that could cause her to consider joining a gang?
3. What are the pluses of being in a gang?
4. What are the minuses?
5. How would you rate Alexis's decision to join the gang?

1	2	3	4	5	6	7	8	9	10
Not				Fairly					Very
Smart				Smart					Smart

6. Why did Jenni think that Alexis was making a mistake?
7. What were Jenni's reasons for not accepting the invitation to join?
8. Based upon what you know about gangs, do you agree with Jenni's description of the gang members?
9. How would you rate Jenni's decision not to join the gang?

1	2	3	4	5	6	7	8	9	10
Not				Fairly					Very
Smart				Smart					Smart

10. Do you agree with Jenni that joining a gang would hurt her chances to go to college and achieve her other goals? In what ways might joining the gang cause her problems?
11. How would you rate Jenni's decision to reject Alexis's suggestion that Jenni also join the gang?

1	2	3	4	5	6	7	8	9	10
Not				Fairly					Very
Smart				Smart					Smart

12. What would you do if you were in a similar situation and your best friend tried to convince you to join a gang?
13. What are the risks of being in a gang?
14. If a group you belong to does something you don't approve of (for example, beat up someone) and you

refuse to join in, might you nevertheless be held responsible because you belong to the group?

15. Let's say you join a group but don't approve of something the group decides to do (you're in the minority), is it easy to refuse to go along with the others?

16. Was there anything more Jenni might have done to change her friend's mind?

Note: Since this interactive activity is fairly straightforward, specific guidelines for responding have been omitted. for general guidelines for communicating and responding to your child, see pages 31–36.

Critical Thinking

Things are *not* always as they appear, and what you see is *not* necessarily what you get. Although these statements are clichés, they still ring true. The seemingly million-dollar opportunity may be a sham. The seemingly honest salesman may deceive you. The seemingly insoluble problem may be solved if examined from a different perspective. The seemingly plausible argument may be fatuous when the underlying contradictions are exposed.

The capacity to peel away the surface layers and get to the *heart* of an issue before drawing conclusions, making decisions, and reacting is the essence of critical thinking. This careful, rational procedure distinguishes those who think actively from those who think passively. It differentiates the wise from the naive, the veteran from the rookie, and the competent from the incompetent. Children who have been trained to think critically don't simply accept everything they hear or read *at face value*. They ask penetrating questions as they read and listen. They don't accept illogical explanations or justifications. They are dubious of the "hard sell." They look beneath the surface and ask questions. They don't accept slick, facile, non-plausible, or "politically correct" explanations. They make an intellectual effort to reach for the truth. They reject the implausible. They are not easily led, and they are not easily manipulated by those who take liberties with the truth.

To think critically, your child must have the skills of a surgeon and a lawyer. Whereas the competent surgeon uses her scalpel and her knowledge of anatomy and medicine to incise, penetrate, investigate, expose, and correct the underlying problem, the competent attorney uses her knowledge of the law and her adversarial skills to question, confront, debate, and expose that which is untruthful, distorted, misleading, and deceptive. The surgeon's probing mind and the lawyer's adversarial mind are vital to success in advanced academic courses, especially at the college and graduate school levels where professors take great pride in challenging their students intellectually. Those who convince their instructors that they can dig beneath the surface, ferret out the facts and the truth, differentiate the substantive from the non-substantive, understand the issues, draw rational conclusions, use what they've learned, and defend their position with logic and reason are rewarded with good grades, coveted letters of recommendation, and prestigious job offers.

The ability to think critically is an equally valuable and essential resource in the workplace. Those who can identify and solve problems and get the job done efficiently will find themselves on an accelerated career track. They will be prized by their employers, and they will be rewarded with promotions and raises.

The gradual shift in educational emphasis and focus from the mastery of basic skills in elementary school to higher level analytical and critical thinking in high school and college can be disconcerting for students who have not been adequately trained to use their brains. In advanced courses, simply being able to memorize and regurgitate information is no longer sufficient. Instructors and professors expect their students to be able to analyze, evaluate, critique, synthesize, generalize, compare, contrast, expand, and comprehend the information they assimilate in books and from lectures. Students must be able to challenge erroneous statements and conclusions, and they must be able to withstand challenges to their own statements and conclusions. They must be able to think incisively and apply what they learn when they are given problems to solve. They must be able to demonstrate their mastery of the subject content, concepts, process, and application.

A Working Definition of Critical Thinking

Critical thinking is the capacity to: probe beneath the surface; analyze information and data; ask penetrating questions; challenge the validity of assumptions; identify contradictions, inconsistencies, and deceptions; respond skeptically to facile, simplisitic statements and deceptions; recognize key ideas; apply reason and logic; consider the pluses and minuses of options objectively; see matters from different perspectives; assess and perceive flaws in arguments, recommendations, advice, and conclusions; and predict potential consequences.

Example: "He claims the holocaust never happened. How can he explain the awful pictures taken of the thousands of dead bodies in the concentration camps? And how can he explain the firsthand eyewitness accounts of war correspondents, army officers, and enlisted men who liberated the camps and attested to the horror? This man is clearly an idiot, and his argument is bogus!"

The overlapping characteristics of intelligence, smartness, and critical thinking (see pages 77 and 79) clearly suggest that the different manifestations of intellect are interrelated. Although an intelligent child would be expected to have a greater capacity to think critically, there are notable exceptions to the assumption that *Superior IQ = Superior Thinking.* Just as an intelligent child may not acquire practical thinking skills (smartness), he may also not learn to think critically. Despite his intelligence, he may be conned by a dishonest salesperson and respond impulsively or emotionally instead of analyzing his "facts," evaluating the pros and cons, and questioning the salesperson's motives. Unless he disciplines himself to assess decision-making situations carefullywith context-appropriate skepticism, he'll fail to identify blatant (and not-so-blatant) fallacies, inconsistencies, contradictions, and deceptions.

Whereas some children certainly have a greater natural facility for playing basketball, others have a greater natural facility for thinking critically. This notwithstanding, *critical thinking is a skill* that can be taught and refined with effective training, guidance, feedback, and practice. Just as a basketball player's skills will improve with good coaching, so, too, will a child's critical thinking skills improve with good coaching.

Critical thinking skills can often compensate for a less than stellar IQ. The child who knows how to ask the right questions and assess the answers will often achieve at a higher level than the brilliant child who meanders through life in an intellectual stupor.

During the last five decades, many fads have been periodically introduced in the field of education. Most are implemented for a year or two and then quietly disappear, to be replaced by a new fad. (These programs are usually created by professors in graduate schools of education. A grant is written, a pilot program set up, and, after statistically-based research, the new program is then sold to schools or to a major publishing company whose sales force aggressively touts it.) One of the more recent examples of this phenomenon is the heralded inclusion of "innovative" critical thinking components in elementary and secondary curricula. This new emphasis represents a response to a disquieting realization by parents and educators: too many schools have developed a production-line mentality and are churning out millions of ostensibly educated graduates who act like they are brain dead.

Good teachers, of course, have been training students to think critically for generations. Until the late 1980s, however, critical thinking was largely ignored by many American elementary and secondary schools because the system emphasized quantitative rather than qualitative learning.

Ideally, the recent and long overdue renaissance in teaching thinking skills will not simply be another educational fad. Critical thinking programs are desperately needed by our children, and we must insist that they be made a permanent and integral component in the instructional methodology. These programs are currently under attack in many parts of the country because they actually encourage children to *think, feel,* and *question,* thus threatening parents who are psychologically and emotionally invested in controlling all aspects of their children's lives.

Educators and publishers who consider the incorporation of critical thinking components in textbooks and curriculum to be revolutionary suffer from exaggerated self-importance. They fail to acknowledge that Aristotle, Socrates, and Plato were systematically training their students to reason more than three thousand years ago. The deplorable thinking skills of millions of American children today attest to the fact that we have strayed far from their teaching methods.

It would be unrealistic to expect a classroom teacher to assume the entire responsibility for teaching your child how to think. You clearly must play an active role in the instructional process. You must model how to ask penetrating questions and how to search for the underlying truth. Asking your child questions about current event issues and real-life concerns can be the springboard. For example, you might ask: "What are the advantages and disadvantages of raising taxes?" "Does capital punishment deter people from committing murder?" "What issues would cause the workers at this plant to vote to go on strike?" "Why would a town council vote to forbid smoking in restaurants?" "What factors should you consider as you wrestle with your decision to take Spanish or French in high school?" "What are the advantages and disadvantages of taking AP (advanced placement) courses?" "Why do you think car insurance is expensive for teenagers?"

Ideally, your child will continue to develop and refine her critical thinking skills throughout her life. She will use these skills in whatever career she chooses. If she becomes a scientist, she must be able to evaluate professional literature and assess her research options. If she becomes a college professor, she must be able to evaluate her students' work. If she becomes a business executive, she must be able to analyze new marketing plans and investment opportunities. If she becomes an attorney, she must be able to assess the evidence and the veracity of those testifying in court. Each of these procedures demands a trained and disciplined mind that can think critically.

Your child must accommodate herself to a basic fact of life: she lives in a performance-driven, results-oriented society. If she's incapable of evaluating issues critically, she'll struggle to compete in a world that rewards those who can "use their heads," handle the challenges, solve the problems, and come up with the right answers.

The child who possesses the ability to ask penetrating questions, demands incisive answers, and makes astute judgments has a distinct advantage over the child whose thinking is flaccid. The immobilized mind quickly atrophies; the mind develops only when stimulated.

The Pros and Cons of Having a Thinking Child

A child who has been trained to think critically would not accept statements she reads at face value *simply because they're written in a book.* If she knows something about the subject, she would use her knowledge and insights to evaluate the information and the author's point of view. She would respond skeptically to exaggerations, generalizations, and sensationalism. She would need proof before she would believe statements that seemed implausible or biased, especially if these statements contradicted what she herself knew or if they did not adequately address important issues.

Although critical intelligence is usually perceived as a precious resource, it can be a double-edged sword. Some parents might equate critical thinking with a Stradivarius violin upon which their child can learn to play beautiful music. Others would perceive critical intelligence as a destabilizing force that will challenge cherished family beliefs, undermine family values, and tear apart the family fabric. Rather than seeing critical intelligence as a precious violin, those who are threatened by independent analytical thinking would probably equate it with a Pandora's box which, once opened, will unleash demons who can never again be restrained.

It's true that a child trained to think critically would question and challenge that which doesn't make sense. He would struggle to reconcile contradictions. He would assert his right to think independently, and over time he would create his own truths. This does not mean, however, that he would reject his family's religious, ethical, and moral values (see Chapter 4 for a discussion of values and ethics). Critical thinking does not translate into rebellion, nihilism, antisocial attitudes, or immoral behavior. Rather, critical thinking translates into developing a probing, analytical, rational, evaluative mind that seeks truth and insight.

The benchmark of someone who does not think critically is unquestioning acceptance of what he's told and mindless, emotional, irrational reactions to stimuli. The child with an untrained mind is the proverbial clean slate upon which others will write their truths. He will follow their lead willingly. He will obey because he has been taught that obedience is the most laudable of all traits. He will find a semblance of security in associating with kindred obedient spirits who also mindlessly accept what they are told. This identification provides strength (if strength is defined as certainty and conviction) and tenuous peace of mind. This peace of mind can quickly deteriorate when the basic precepts and beliefs are questioned or challenged. This often occurs when brainwashed individuals are deprogrammed and realize that, upon closer, objective inspection, all that they believed so fervently was a tissue of lies, manipulation, and deceit.

Although there are psychological pluses when a child is trained to accept unquestioningly what he's told, there are also risks in his failing to develop critical intelligence. This is especially true when the values and beliefs he accepts without question are evil. Throughout history, tyrants and fascists have exploited the naiveté of those who blindly followed them.

As a parent, you must decide for yourself where you stand on the issues of critical intelligence. You must decide if critical thinking is a treasured violin or a treacherous Pandora's box. You must decide if you want your child to look for flaws and fallacies so that she can acquire accurate information, form her own conclusions, and think for herself. You must decide if you want her to develop the ability to make her own judgments and acquire her own wisdom and insight to complement and supplement the wisdom, insights, values, and beliefs she has assimilated from you.

Many institutions in our society are built upon the willingness of their members to accept on faith what they are taught. There is, of course, a place for *faith*. Some would argue there is even a place for *unquestioning faith*. Certainly, encouraging a child to acquire critical intelligence could pose a dilemma for some parents. They may be reluctant to encourage a process that could threaten beliefs and values they themselves have been trained to accept unquestioningly. For other parents, there is no dilemma. They believe in training their child's mind to question, and they're prepared to deal reasonably with any fallout that might result.

If you want your child to develop independent critical thinking skills, you must provide the violin, the lessons, and the practice time. The notes your child produces will reflect both her aptitude *and* her training. Although few people have the natural talent of an Isaac Stern or Itzak Pearlman, there are many less brilliant musicians who still produce beautiful music.

Examining the Issues with Your Child

Read the following anecdote with your child, and pose the following questions (or make up your own). Your goal is to help your child discover the thrill of thinking incisively and appreciate the value of having a questioning mind. The child who acquires critical thinking skills is far less likely to be led or misled. He will have the mind-set: "prove it to me before I'll believe it."

Naiveté and innocence are appropriate for the very young. Unfortunately, the realities of the world all too soon impinge on this state of innocence. Every child must ultimately realize that "all that glitters is not gold." Those who don't will order "magic" diet pills and send away for "incredible" free offers throughout their lives. These children are destined to be repeatedly deceived and disillusioned.

interactive activity

Age Range: 10–14
Objectives: Acquiring Critical Thinking Skills

What's Not in the Book

Rebecca's father loved to read history books. The period that interested him the most involved the epoch of the trappers, pioneers, farmers, and ranchers who began migrating to the west in the early nineteenth century. He shared his enthusiasm with Rebecca. When she was a little girl, he would read to her about the different Indian tribes. He read countless stories to her about Sitting Bull, Custer, and Buffalo Bill. Rebecca quickly realized and appreciated her father's sympathy for the Indians, whom he believed had been treated terribly by the settlers and the U.S. Government.

When Rebecca was thirteen years old, she decided to write a term paper on the Indian tribes who lived in the western states. She searched through three encyclopedias, and with the help of the librarian, she located several books and articles on the subject. In one of these books, she read the following passage:

The Cherokee, Apache, and Shawnee tribes hated the settlers who crossed their territory, appropriated their lands, and carved out homesteads for themselves. Ferocious attacks on wagon trains were common, and many settlers were killed. Farms and ranches were burned to the ground by marauding war parties. In retaliation, federal troops frequently attacked and burned Indian villages. To resolve this difficult problem, the United States Government set aside reservations for the Indians, signed treaties that promised the Indians land and food, and then resettled entire tribes in these designated areas. . . .

As she read the passage, Rebecca found herself becoming angry. Because of the many hours she spent reading about American Indians and discussing the issues with her father, she knew a great deal about this period. In her mind, she began to ask questions: "Why shouldn't the Indians resist the settlers who were crossing and taking *their* land? My dad and I read that many Indian villages were destroyed by U.S. army troops. Many of the trappers cheated the Indians, and the hunters on the plains killed millions of buffalo. These animals provided food and clothes for the Indians. What right did the United States Government have to resettle entire tribes on reservations? And what about the treaties? I read in another book that the U.S. Government continually lied to the Indians and repeatedly broke their treaties. Some of the reservations were like prison camps. I wonder how many settlers were killed compared to the number of native Americans who were killed."

In her term paper, Rebecca tried to present a balanced account of what happened on the western plains. She quoted from several articles and books and commented on fallacies she found in the authors' statements and points of view. Determined to "set the record right" and present the truth, she cited other books and articles to support her interpretations and conclusions. She spent more than fifteen hours researching and writing her term paper. The pride she felt when she finished more than justified her effort.

Her dad said the paper was first-rate. Her teacher agreed. She gave Rebecca an A+.

Questions and Issues for Discussion

1. What made Rebecca so angry when she read the passage?
2. Do you think the author of the passage would have expected a thirteen-year-old student to question the information?
3. Do you think Rebecca is a typical eighth grader? What qualities might set her apart from many of her classmates?
4. Do you think she would question the validity (if necessary, define this word) of other information she reads in books or hears from other people?
5. Rebecca clearly knows a great deal about this period in history. Can a person question information even if he doesn't know a great deal about something?
6. Can you think of any general questions someone who reads and thinks critically (looks for and challenges flaws, inaccuracies, and distortions) might ask? For example, "On what does this person base his or her statement, and do I agree with this?" Can you think of any other questions (such as, What are his motives? What has he not included? Why is she making this statement? How does this agree or disagree with what I know about this subject? What are the credentials of the person making the statement? Who besides this person can verify what is said or written? Your expectations and explanations of what words like "credentials" and "verify" mean should, of course, be geared to your child's developmental level.)
7. Has there ever been a time when you questioned the truthfulness or the accuracy of something you heard or read? Tell me about it.

8. How would you rate the critical questions that Rebecca raised as she read the passage?

1	2	3	4	5	6	7	8	9	10
Not Smart				Fairly Smart					Very Smart

9. Based upon the description of her behavior, how would you rate her intelligence?

1	2	3	4	5	6	7	8	9	10
Not High				Fairly High					Very High

10. In the anecdote, it said that Rebecca tried to present a *balanced* account of what really happened. What does this mean to you?

11. Describe an incident when you challenged the truthfulness of something you read or were told.

12. Rebecca received an A+ on her term paper. Based upon what you've learned about how she thinks and how she works, estimate the grades you think she would receive in her subjects at school.

1	2	3	4	5	6	7	8	9	10
Poor				Average					Excellent

13. What caused you to make this estimate?

14. How would your rate your own critical thinking skills?

1	2	3	4	5	6	7	8	9	10
Poor				Average					Excellent

15. How do you think critical thinking skills can be developed and improved? Would desire and practice help? How could you practice?

16. In what areas do you think you have good critical intelligence? For example, are you able to figure out why a quarterback is having a bad game?

17. Why would someone be willing to work as hard as Rebecca did when she wrote her term paper? What would motivate that person?

18. Is there any subject or issue about which you feel a great deal of interest or passion? For example, does homelessness, gang violence, or the mistreatment of

animals cause you to get upset? Does the idea of becoming a professional athlete or journalist trigger excitement and passion?
19. What is it that makes you interested or passionate in these subjects?

Suggestions for Improving Your Child's Critical Thinking Skills

1. Select current newspaper or magazine articles and ask your child to identify the author's assumptions and editorial position. You might choose an article dealing with ecology (such as actions that might endanger a species), health care (such as universal coverage), working conditions, international trade, etc. Your critical evaluation of the material may lead you and your child to agree or disagree with the author's interpretations, conclusions, or position. Remember: you want your child to generate his own questions and to reach his own conclusions. If you do all the work, then the critical thinking experience will be passive rather than active. You may need to model at first, but your ultimate goal is for your child to be able to initiate questions and ferret out the underlying issues, contradictions, and inconsistencies.
2. Listen to the nightly news with your child. Select a topic and follow the questioning procedure outlined above.
3. Select a passage from your child's history textbook and analyze it critically with him.
4. Examine real-life situations. Question and challenge the validity of common assumptions and simplistic thinking. For example, you might describe a situation in which a salesman is trying to convince you that a particular lawn irrigation system conserves water. What questions would you need to ask to verify that the salesman's statements are accurate? This skepticism is a cornerstone of critical thinking.

Strategic Thinking

Your child's ultimate success in life may hinge on some very fundamental, but very important, procedures. These procedures include planning ahead, organizing time, identifying the possible problems that might impede him, applying the lessons he has learned, handling obstacles and barriers, and getting the job done expeditiously. This strategic, tactical thinking is clearly an application of smartness.

Unlike IQ, your child's STQ (strategic thinking quotient)* can be significantly developed and enhanced with guidance, practice, and feedback. Just as IQ should theoretically predict and correlate with academic achievement (the higher your child's IQ, the more likely he will do well in school), your child's STQ should predict and correlate with his success in life. Imagine that your daughter tells you she wants to join a very desirable after-school club. There's a waiting list to join this club, and the members vote on who is admitted. A very popular child does not want your daughter in the club. Perhaps she's jealous or threatened by your daughter and fears that she would become more popular and her own standing in the club might suffer. Distraught about the likelihood of being excluded, your child asks for advice. You wisely decide not to tell her what she should do. Instead, you help her identify her options:

- Should she accept not being admitted into the club?
- Should she consider joining another club?
- Should she complain to the faculty or parent advisor?
- Should she talk with the other child who is blocking her and try to come to an understanding with her?
- Should she appeal directly to the other club members?
- Should she challenge the other child in some way, "neutralize" her, and use this to impress other children?

Your child must decide when it's more strategic to knock over, go around, or avoid a barrier. Her ability to analyze a sit-

---

*STQ is a term I have coined. There is, to date, no standardized test that measures STQ.

uation objectively (as opposed to emotionally), weigh her options, anticipate potential outcomes, use her intelligence pragmatically, and develop a practical, effective plan is the benchmark of sound strategic thinking.

Working Definition of Strategic Thinking

Strategic thinking is the capacity to: define personal long-term and short-term goals, establish priorities, avoid pitfalls, calculate the odds, plan tactically, manage time, organize resources, understand cause and effect, anticipate and prepare for potential problems, apply acquired insight and wisdom to new situations, learn from mistakes, handle setbacks, defeats, and frustration, and neutralize impediments.

Example: "Working at a pet hospital during the summer vacation will give me great hands-on experience with animals. If I do a good job and impress everyone, I can ask the doctor for a recommendation to veterinary school when I apply during my last year of college."

The diagram below represents how the different types of intelligence are interconnected and overlap. Although IQ (genetically-based intelligence) and applied intelligence (smartness, critical intelligence, and strategic intelligence) are linked, they can be differentiated. In a specific arena, one type of intelligence may be more vital than another. For example, getting a good grade in an advanced physics or calculus course requires a high IQ. Although strategic intelligence (planning skills) and critical intelligence (evaluating different experimental methods) may also be valuable, these forms of intelligence do not play as vital a role as IQ.

A very bright child (*high intelligence*) may be able to read at four years of age, solve calculus problems at nine, and remember virtually everything she studies. She may, however, be easily influenced by other children and experiment with drugs because her friends are doing so (*inadequate critical intelligence, smartness, and strategic intelligence*). Another child may

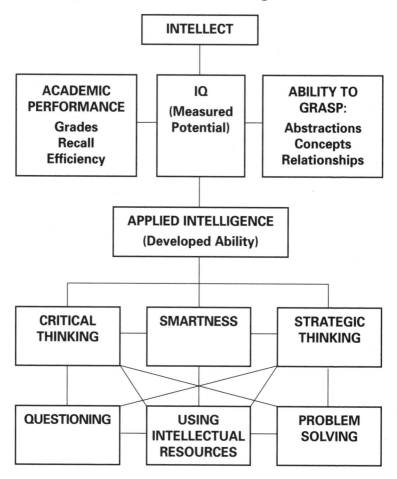

Figure 3.1. How the Forms of Intelligence are Linked

understand concepts and abstractions and may perceive fallacies and logical inconsistencies (*high level of intelligence and
critical intelligence*), but she may continually lose coats, keys,
and sweaters (*inadequate smartness*) and may get poor grades
on homework assignments because she forgets to complete
the work or doesn't submit her assignments on time (*inadequate smartness and strategic intelligence*).

The child who thinks strategically knows where she's headed and has a fairly good idea how to get to there. She draws the most efficient route on her map and checks off each interim stop along the way. If possible, she'll proceed directly to her defined destination. She can also determine when she must take a detour to get where she wants to go.

You play the pivotal role in developing your child's strategic intelligence. By showing her how to plan her own birthday party, organize her room, budget her time, and figure out what went wrong, you provide invaluable opportunities for her to practice thinking tactically. By asking your child "How do you propose to get the job done?" you stimulate strategic thinking. By asking your child "What could you do to impress your volleyball coach?" you demonstrate the value of tactical planning. These solution-oriented skills comprise the cornerstones of strategic intelligence.

---

interactive activity

Age Range: 6–14
Objectives: Acquiring Time-Management Skills and
Appreciating Cause-and-Effect Principles

I Didn't Get Around to It

Margo didn't study for the science test. She ran out of time. When she got home from school, she went over to Julie's house and stayed there until dinnertime. They tried on some of the new clothes Julie had gotten for her birthday, and they called Jessica to talk about their plans for the weekend. After dinner, Margo watched two of her favorite sitcoms. This took an hour, and it was now eight o'clock. She worked on her math homework for twenty minutes and spent another twenty minutes finishing her book report. Then she went to the kitchen for a snack. This took fifteen minutes. Once back in her room, she played with her cat for fifteen minutes. After this, she called two of her friends and talked to each for twenty minutes. It was 9:50, and Margo felt really tired. She was usually in bed by 10:00 P.M. and she knew that trying to study after 10:00 was impossible. She couldn't concentrate when she was sleepy. Margo decided she would get ready for bed and study for the science test on the school bus the next morning. But once she got on the bus, she began to talk with some friends, which left her about ten minutes to study for the test. When she got off the bus, Margo knew she hadn't reviewed everything. She hoped she could somehow pass the test anyway. If she didn't, she realized she might get a D on her report card. Her grades in science had been terrible for the entire semester.

Questions and Issues for Discussion

1. It's clear that Margo made several decisions about how she was going to spend her time after school. Let's go back into the story and underline each thing she decided to do.
2. What specific behaviors indicate that Margo was choosing not to study for the science test?
3. What could she have eliminated to make time for studying?
4. Let's say the science test counts for 20 percent of her semester grade. How much time would be reasonable to set aside for studying for an important test?
5. One specific fact was mentioned that should have motivated her to study extra hard. What was it?
6. How would you rate the way in which Margo used her time?

1	2	3	4	5	6	7	8	9	10
Poor				Fair					Excellent

7. How much time would you spend studying for an exam in a course in which you were not doing well?
8. How smart would you say Margo is? (Emphasize that smartness is how well you use your head, and not how intelligent you are.)

1	2	3	4	5	6	7	8	9	10
Not Smart				Fairly Smart					Very Smart

9. Although the story doesn't say, predict the grades Margo is probably getting in her other courses.

1	2	3	4	5	6	7	8	9	10
Poor				Fair					Excellent

10. Let's say Margo is planning a major project such as a party, a vacation, or a term paper. On the basis of what you read about her above, predict how well she would organize herself, plan, and manage her time.

1	2	3	4	5	6	7	8	9	10
Poor				Fair					Excellent

11. If Margo's parents were concerned about her schoolwork, her study habits, her planning, and her organization, how could they bring up the subject in a way that would not make Margo defensive or angry?

Thinking Critically and Strategically

The way your child responds to life's challenges and to her obligations and responsibilities is a litmus test of her critical and strategic thinking skills. The thinking child will either consciously or unconsciously ask herself seven key questions when she confronts a challenge:

- What do I want to achieve?
- What are my assumptions, and are they valid?
- What are the possible problems I might face?
- How can I get the job done efficiently and effectively?
- How can I avoid mistakes?
- What are my contingency plans?
- How can I increase the odds of success?

Although the thinking child realizes the shortest distance between two points is a straight line, she also realizes that occasionally she may need to make interim stops before reaching her goal. She recognizes that getting an A on her next English test (a short-term goal) is a stepping-stone to attaining a high enough G.P.A. to be accepted at the college of her choice (her long-term goal). If her goal is to make the tennis team, she's willing to spend hours practicing. She voluntarily commits the requisite time and effort because she believes her plan will allow her to attain her objective.

Thinking children carefully consider the potential effects of their decisions and behavior *before* acting or reacting. This allows them to avoid many problems. A student may not like her biology teacher, but if she's thinking strategically, she'll realize that his recommendation for college could be important, and she would be careful not to alienate him. This capacity to think tactically differentiates her from her counterparts who have never learned to think critically and strategically. If she miscalculates and experiences a setback, she'll assess the situation objectively and make the necessary adjustments. In contrast, the nonthinking child rarely learns from negative experiences and, as a consequence, is destined to repeat mistakes.

A heightened awareness of what is happening in one's environment is another benchmark of the alert, thinking child. Such a child uses her awareness to guide her actions. If she finds herself at a rowdy party, she might decide to leave before there is a melee and the police are called. Because she can assess situations objectively, question assumptions, and anticipate possible problems, she will make fewer judgment errors. If her science teacher emphasizes facts and data in class and on tests, she will modify her study strategy and devote extra time to memorizing these facts. She will also review her previous tests and quizzes and will try to anticipate what questions her teacher is likely to ask on the next test. If she concludes that she doesn't understand the material, she'll pore over the assigned unit carefully, ask herself questions about the content, review her notes, and perhaps study with a friend or make an appointment with her teacher to ask for help. Before she finishes studying, she'll make certain she comprehends the content and can answer the questions she has asked herself. Her thoroughness, motivation, problem-solving skills, and pragmatic thinking will significantly improve the likelihood of her doing well on the test.

The nonthinking child responds quite differently. She might not bother to look at her previous tests when she studies. She might not take the time to analyze what her teacher has emphasized in class. She might opt to memorize facts without bothering to understand what she is studying. She might "forget" to proofread her book report, check her math problems, or learn the assigned irregular Spanish verb conjugations and new vocabulary words. She might not ask herself questions as she studies or become actively engaged in the process of preparing for tests. She may talk for two hours on the telephone with her boyfriend on the night before an important final exam. Her *lack* of thoroughness, motivation, problem-solving skills, and pragmatic thinking will significantly reduce the likelihood of her doing well on the test.

The nonthinking child also signals her mindlessness in other ways. She may talk back to an English teacher she doesn't particularly like and alienate him. She may hitchhike. She may flirt with her best friend's boyfriend. She may date someone taking drugs. The strategic child who possesses developed critical thinking skills would be appalled by this behavior and consider it "dumb."

IQ tests are designed to measure a child's *potential* to succeed in school. These tests, however, do not measure the child's ability to apply her intelligence pragmatically, nor do they assess how well she can use her intelligence to attain her goals. Over time, the child who floats through life in a cerebral daze will become increasingly habituated to passive, ineffectual thinking. The long-term academic and vocational implications of this behavior can obviously be disastrous.

The time to begin the process of teaching your child to think is *now.* In a supportive, non-threatening way, ask questions about her plan for handling a particular problem, challenge, or issue (for example, "What's your strategy for getting the coach to dismiss you early from practice so you can meet with your tutor?") In a non-confrontational and non-hostile manner, challenge her assumptions (but don't do so continually, or she may become resentful). Listen attentively and empathetically to her response, position, or interpretation before expressing disapproval, especially if she proposes to handle the situation differently than you would. If her plan is patently flawed or ineffectual, you might say: "What about the idea of . . . ?"

With younger children, you might make statements that are obviously absurd, such as: "I don't think any foreigners should be allowed to emigrate to the United States." Urge your child to challenge your assertion and give her reasons for doing so. Examine some of the absurd policy statements politicians make and discuss why their ideas couldn't work. Analyze newspaper articles and critique proposed strategies for handling a problem or situation such as urban crime or teenage pregnancy.

Virtually every child of normal intelligence can be taught to think more critically and strategically. If this is your goal, you must *intentionally* create a home environment that encourages and affirms pragmatic, tactical thinking. By training your child to probe, analyze, question, and plan, you can significantly raise her STQ (Strategic Thinking Quotient) and CTQ (Critical Thinking Quotient).* These resources will provide your child with a competitive advantage in a world that rewards the most diligent, focused, and tactical thinkers with the most coveted prizes.

interactive activity

Age Range: 6–14
Objective: Applying Intelligence

The Girl Who Knew What She Wanted

Caitlin had known that she wanted to be a reporter ever since she was nine years old. Her mother's best friend Kim worked for a newspaper, and she was Caitlin's hero. When she came over for dinner, she would talk about

---

*Both STQ and CTQ are terms I have coined.

stories she was working on and discuss how she would interview people to find out what was really happening. Sometimes she would go to the library and do research. Sometimes she would go to the scene of a crime and poke around. She got to meet and interview famous people who came to town, and she would occasionally get a scoop and find out something before any other reporters discovered the information.

Even though she was only eight at the time, Caitlin began to read the articles written by her mom's friend. (Caitlin was one of the best readers in her class.) Her mom would help her when she occasionally had difficulty with a word. She always felt a thrill when she saw her "friend's" byline, and she began to fantasize about someday seeing her own name under an article. By her ninth birthday, she had made up her mind. She would go to school and become a reporter, too.

Once she made her decision, Caitlin decided to find out what was involved in preparing for her chosen career. When she asked her mom, she suggested that Caitlin go to the library and ask the librarian for books that might tell her how to become a journalist. She also suggested that Caitlin speak with her reporter friend because Kim would be a great source of information.

After reading two books about famous newspaper reporters and talking with Kim, Caitlin knew exactly what she had to do to prepare for her career. Kim had suggested that she read at least one newspaper every day and figure out what she liked about certain articles. She told her to be aware of the reporter's style, the way in which the information was presented, and the types of subjects that were covered. She recommended that in high school, Caitlin join the staff of the school paper. Kim also suggested that she begin writing letters to the editor about issues that interested her. She could discuss subjects that made her angry, such as the mistreatment of animals, gangs in school, drugs, and curfews for kids. Because publishing a well-written and well-thought-out letter from a kid is very appealing to an editor, she advised Caitlin always to indicate her age when she wrote a letter. This might encourage the editor to select her letter to print.

Caitlin learned that it would be smart to major in either journalism or communication when she went to college. Kim advised her to try to join the staff of her college newspaper. She would need to get good grades and good recommendations from her high school teachers and college instructors. Getting a summer internship at a newspaper would also be a big boost, especially if she could impress her supervisors with her hard work and writing skills. Kim told her she had to read her own material very critically. She needed to be very self-critical, identify her weak skills, and focus on making herself a better writer. This meant carefully analyzing her work and looking for mistakes, unclear sentences, and poor grammar.

Once Caitlin knew what she needed to do, she put together a plan of action. She defined her long-term and short-term goals. She was determined to be a reporter someday at a major newspaper. She knew it would be hard work, but she was certain she would make it.

Questions and Issues for Discussion

1. Do you think having a goal, as Caitlin did, is helpful to a child? What are the advantages?
2. Caitlin was fascinated by the work her mother's friend did. Have you ever know someone who has inspired you or whose career you find fascinating? Has it motivated you to consider this career for yourself?
3. Given what you've read about Caitlin, what do you think her chances are of achieving her goal?

1	2	3	4	5	6	7	8	9	10
Poor				Fair					Excellent

4. If you were describing Caitlin to a friend, what adjectives would you use?
5. To get information, Caitlin went to the library and spoke with her mother's friend. Are there any other sources of information Caitlin might have used to find out more about becoming a journalist? For example, is there anyone she might have written to for information (the editor of the local newspaper, reporters, a university department of journalism, etc.)?

6. Let's go through the story together. We'll underline and number each action or tactic that would help Caitlin achieve her goal. We'll include the suggestions from her mother's friend and the ideas Caitlin discovered as a result of doing her library research and reading. Let's see how many we can find.

7. If Caitlin's goal is to become a reporter at a good newspaper, how difficult do you think it would be for her to attain her goal?

1	2	3	4	5	6	7	8	9	10
Not				Fairly					Very
Difficult				Difficult					Difficult

8. How would you rate Caitlin's strategy?

1	2	3	4	5	6	7	8	9	10
Poor				Fair					Excellent

9. What sort of problems and obstacles might she run into?

10. Do you think there are any minuses to becoming a reporter. What might they be?

11. What would improve her chances of being admitted into the journalism department at a good university?

12. What would improve her chances of being accepted on the staff of her school newspaper?

13. Tell me about a long-term goal you have. Let's write down your plan or strategy for attaining this goal. What would your short-term goals be (for example, getting a good grade in Spanish)?

14. How could you get more information that might help you achieve this objective?

By teaching your child to think strategically and critically, to establish long-term and short-term goals, and to plan for contingencies, you are preparing her to win in life. Her judgments will be more astute; her efforts will be more focused, and her achievements will be more rewarding. As the classic Wheaties commercial said: "Champions are not born, they're made!"

chapter 4

Acquiring Values

*M*egan couldn't believe her eyes. Connor was cheating on the make-up test.

Megan had missed three days of school because she had a bad sore throat. When she returned on Friday, her teacher told her she could make up the weekly history test she had missed on Monday. The twelve-year-old was relieved to hear this. It was an important test that could make the difference between her getting an A or a B on her next report card. By studying over the weekend, she would have two days to prepare.

Megan was a serious student who worked very hard to get good grades. She planned to use the weekend to review the assigned chapter and study her notes. The sixth-grader had already made up her mind she wanted to go a good college. That weekend Megan spent more than three hours studying. By Sunday evening, she felt confident she had learned what would be covered on the test.

When she entered the history classroom after school on Monday, Megan discovered that Connor was making up the same test. After instructing the two students to sit down, the teacher handed an exam to each child. Glancing quickly through it, Megan saw that it consisted of twenty multiple-choice questions, twenty true-false questions, and one essay question. They had forty minutes to finish.

The teacher sat down at her desk and began grading papers. Five minutes later she announced she was going to the teachers' lounge. She instructed Megan and Connor to continue working and to put their completed tests on her desk if they finished before she returned at 3:40.

After the teacher left, Megan glanced over at Connor. She noticed he had taken a small piece of paper from his pocket, and she watched as he used the information written on the paper to answer the test questions.

Connor finished before the teacher returned. Placing his test on her desk, he glanced at Megan nervously and left the room. Although she was tempted to look at Connor's test, Megan decided to resist the temptation. When she finished her final essay, she placed her test on top of Connor's. Just as she was leaving, the teacher returned. She asked Megan if she had found the test difficult. Without thinking, Megan blurted out that she had seen Connor cheat. The teacher looked upset then thanked Megan for telling her what had happened. Megan quickly left the classroom.

When she got into bed that evening, Megan's conscience was troubling her, and she slept fitfully. She felt guilty about telling the teacher about Connor. But she also felt angry. She had studied hard, and Connor might get a better grade because he cheated. It seemed very unfair! Although she believed she had done the right thing by telling, she still felt horrible and ashamed about being an informer.

Morals, Values, and Ethics

A twelve-year-old is confronted with a moral and ethical dilemma. She sees a classmate cheat on a test, and his dishonesty challenges her values and ethics. Reacting to the injustice, she spontaneously informs her teacher. Although she could certainly justify "telling," Megan's conscience nevertheless troubles her. She had studied hard and had played by the rules. When you work hard and are honest, you're supposed to be rewarded for your effort and honesty. Megan expected others to play by the same rules. That Connor might get a better grade because he cheated was both unfair and infuriating. He wasn't playing according to the rules.

In a child's world, informing on another child is considered a betrayal. Megan snitched, and many children would consider her behavior more reprehensible than Connor's cheating. Perhaps this attitude explains, in part, the cheating scandals that periodically erupt at military service academies. Asking students not to cheat is one thing. Asking them to inform when others cheat, knowing this will lead to the cheater's expulsion, is another. Given the childhood conditioning not to inform, this honor code requirement is an ultimate test of moral fiber, ethics, and values.

The stricture about not informing is prevalent not only in a child's world; it's also prevalent in the adult world where otherwise honest people often look the other way when someone cheats or steals. Rationalizing that another person's dishonesty is none of their business, they tell themselves not to get involved. The unspoken code is "see no evil, speak no evil." It's ironic that convicted felons are the most obsessed with the issue of snitching. The very people who blatantly reject society's laws, in turn, create their own alternative system of inflexible rules. To inform is the ultimate act of dishonor and the ultimate transgression, often punishable by death.

Megan was clearly torn between two codes. Should she inform, or simply close her eyes to Connor's dishonesty and accept his receiving a grade he didn't deserve? Impulsively, she chose the first option, and her conscience paid the price.

A twelve-year-old's ethical dilemma and subsequent guilt are a paradigm for the conflict we, too, may experience when we realize that by asserting our moral values, we may be perceived as mean-spirited. Do we tell the checkout clerk we saw someone steal? Do we intervene if we see a teenager beating up another teenager? Do we inform the cashier that he has given us too much change? Do we tell the bank they made a $100.00 mistake in our favor? Some people would find these decisions difficult. Others would respond "yes" to certain questions and "no" to others. And some would immediately and emphatically answer "absolutely" to all the questions.

The foundation for your child's understanding of right and wrong and of acceptable and unacceptable behavior was poured early in life. You provided the cement and the blueprint for this labor-intensive process. During the formative years, you reprimanded your son if he ran into the street without looking and scolded him if he repeatedly spilled his milk. You admonished him if he teased his sister or played catch too close to the living room window and lectured him when he took something that didn't belong to him. You rebuked him if he told a lie and chastised him if he hit another child. When he behaved and conformed to the family's rules, you affirmed him; when he didn't, you punished him.

The ongoing process of communicating and reinforcing the "do's and don'ts" form the underpinnings of your child's evolving value system. For this strata to hold firm, several critical ingredients must be provided. These include:

- mutual trust and respect
- a clearly defined family value system
- support and affirmation
- empathy
- love

When children are deprived of these critical ingredients during their formative years, they are more likely to reject their parents' values and, in extreme cases, to express their confusion, anger, and disillusionment by either actively violating or passively resisting the family rules. The absence of values, trust, respect, and affirmation explain, in part, the proliferation of gangs in our society. Gang members often state:

"The gang is my family. They give me respect. They protect me, and I protect them." These youngsters crave the respect, trust, protection, sense of identity, and values that families traditionally provided. They want to belong, to feel appreciated, and to feel secure. These are the basic emotional needs of all human beings.

Examining the Issues with Your Child

Read the anecdote at the beginning of this chapter (page 109) with your child. The following questions are designed to help you and your child explore the underlying issues.

interactive **activity**

Age Range: 6–14
Objectives: Examining Values and Ethics

Questions and Issues for Discussion

1. Do you think Megan should have told the teacher that Connor cheated?
2. Why do you feel this way?
3. Did she have any alternatives for handling the situation? If so, what were her alternatives?
4. Why do you think Megan's conscience bothered her?
5. Megan had mixed feelings. She felt guilty, but she also felt angry. Do you think she was justified in feeling guilty? Do you think she was justified in feeling angry? How would you have felt?
6. How would you have handled the same situation?
7. Have you ever been in a similar situation?
8. What do you think about cheating in school? Is it okay to cheat in some situations? For example, if you forgot to study for a test, would you be justified in cheating?

Guidelines for Responding to Your Child

Although guidelines were not provided for the interactive exercises in the preceding chapter, they are included here because the issues you are exploring are "tricky." To achieve the results you want—a greater awareness of ethics, values, and morality—you'll need to respond with special care. If you do not respond with empathy, or you wittingly or unwittingly moralize or pontificate, you risk "turning your child off" and triggering active or passive resistance.

1. If your child appears unwilling to discuss the anecdote . . .

   Parent: I have the impression that this is an unpleasant topic for you to discuss. Could you tell me why? If your child doesn't want to tell you why or can't express the reasons, you might let the matter drop and proceed to question #3. An alternative would be for you to share a personal experience from your own life that describes how you once wrestled with the temptation to cheat and either gave in, or didn't give in to the temptation. Describe your moral dilemma without coming across as being "holier than thou."

2. If your child has difficulty expressing feelings . . .

   Parent: It can be difficult to talk about feelings such as guilt or anger. I want to tell you about a time when I did something that made me feel angry (or guilty). *Have a personal anecdote ready.* By sharing your own feelings, you're modeling emotional openness. Ideally, this will be a catalyst for your child to share her feelings. You're saying: I trust you enough to tell you something that's not so perfect about me without fearing you're going to judge me harshly, and I hope you can share feelings and experiences with me without feeling that I'm going to criticize you. I'm human, and I'm certainly not perfect. You're human, and I don't expect you to be perfect. Examining how we feel and how we respond to situations and problems helps us learn more about ourselves. It also helps us grow and become better human beings."

3. If your child has difficulty thinking of alternatives to Megan's decision to inform the teacher . . .

   Parent: Do you think Megan might have said something to Connor when she saw him cheat?

4. If your child is having difficulty projecting himself (herself) into the situation described in the anecdote . . .

   Parent: Close your eyes, and imagine yourself sitting in a classroom taking a test. . . . Describe how you're feeling. Now imagine another child is cheating. . . . What are you feeling?

Being Clear About Where You Stand

During the early years, children lack the experience, wisdom, and insight to assess situations and determine the appropriateness or inappropriateness of their behavior. Their data base of acceptable versus unacceptable responses is still in the formative stage, and their capacity to compute and understand is limited by their chronological age and lack of life experiences. These children need a "value hook" to grasp for emotional stability and security. They need to know where their parents stand on key ethical issues, and they need to know what's expected of them. Those who are uncertain about the rules, codes, and boundaries will continue to probe and test the limits in their attempt to determine where parental tolerance ends and accountability begins.

Inconsistent, ambiguous family rules, ethics, and behavior guidelines cause children to become confused and insecure. Children exposed to this ambiguity are invariably unhappy.

Your child's effort to determine how far he can go before he finally gets his hand "slapped" ("slapped" is used *metaphorically* and does not suggest that children should be hit!) is a critical component in your child's learning curve. Setting limits is akin to putting tabs on a word-processing program. The cursor is programmed to know where the preset stops (behavior boundaries) are and to return to the margin (the family's moral and ethical value base.)

The figurative "slap" that defines the limits of parental tolerance may assume the form of a reprimand, a loss of privileges, or a punishment. Later, the slap could be more disastrous: an F in a required course, a stay in juvenile hall, or a car wrapped around a tree. Ideally, the first round of limit setting will suffice and prevent the child from needing to continue testing.

Children who are unsure of the limits may never complete the testing phase characteristic of two- and three-year-olds. If they're still struggling to define the boundaries for acceptable and unacceptable behavior when they reach adulthood, they are high-risk candidates for becoming entangled in the criminal justice system.

Children who do not respect the external boundaries imposed by their parents and their society and those who have not internalized these boundaries often become troubled, alienated teenagers. They later evolve into unhappy, marginally-performing adults. As their nonadaptive attitudes and behavior become increasingly entrenched, they will have difficulty adjusting to the demands and competitive realities they encounter in school, at work, and in society. Confused about (or rebelling against) the rules and codes, they are at risk for becoming the outsiders, the underachievers, and, in extreme cases, the drug takers, prostitutes, and outlaws.

Youngsters who lack a clear reference point for their values, actions, and attitudes are often drawn into a surrogate social system that provides alternative structure, identity, and rules. They may join gangs or align themselves with one or two other equally adrift and disenfranchised children. Lacking the maturity, experience, insight, and wisdom to evaluate which behaviors are viable and which are not, they ensconce themselves in the substitute value system. The nightmarish repercussions of this phenomenon are vividly described in Golding's novel *The Lord of the Flies,* where children left to their own devices create a violent, psychopathic society. Every day a similar nightmare is enacted on the streets of our cities and towns. Packs of teenagers kill and maim each other and rationalize their actions with a "code of honor" that sanctions their ghoulish behavior and symbolic "rights of passage."

A child's value confusion can usually be traced to his parents' and his society's value confusion. Parents who haven't formulated their *own* ethical and moral position on honesty, effort, and responsibility cannot reasonably expect their children to assimilate clearly defined values. In the same way, a society that tacitly encourages rule-bending and rewards "marginal" dishonesty (such as income tax laws that tacitly encourage cheating, government pork barrel projects, government junkets, and political patronage) cannot reasonably expect citizens to respect its laws. Double messages ("You can't really do this, but it's okay sometimes within certain limits.") invariably produce disrespect for rules and laws.

Children have powerful intuitive radar. They can "read" the rebounding impulses from their parents' values (or lack of values) with great accuracy. Parental indifference, ambivalence, rule enforcement inconsistencies, and hypocrisy invariably lead to moral confusion.

Children can sense when their parents are clear about and committed to their beliefs. Parents who say, "don't cheat, steal, or lie," and who are themselves overtly or covertly dishonest cannot expect to have their ethical admonitions taken seriously. These parents "go through the motions" of being responsible, and their children go through the motions of assimilating their token values. When parents *repeatedly* break promises, lie, or make phony excuses for their lack of consistency and commitment ("I know I promised to go to your soccer game, but something important has come up."), this hypocrisy sends a baffling double message to a child. She hears that it's okay to cut corners, rationalize, and deny responsibility for her actions. Parents who become role models for this "do as I say, not as I do" sham should not be surprised when their children have difficulty conforming to society's laws and strictures.

Children who have not assimilated an ethical code of behavior from their parents have, at best, an ambiguous reference point for their own attitudes and behavior. They are at risk for making chronically flawed ethical decisions throughout their lives and for repeatedly suffering the negative consequences of these choices.

The alternative to talking about ethics and morality is to *communicate* your family's values and *demonstrate* them every day. In expressing clearly and unequivocally your position on the issue of honesty, you might say: "In this family, we don't steal, cheat, or intentionally hurt another person by hitting them or making fun of them. When we do these things, we don't feel good about ourselves. This family believes in acting righteously and morally and in behaving in a way that makes us proud." After saying this, you must *act* on your words and *model* your ethics.

Your unambiguously defined boundaries and unambiguously communicated rationale for these boundaries provide your child with a solid foundation for making her own value judgments. Your daughter will know she cannot justify stealing from a store simply because she covets something, nor can she justify lying simply because it's the easier, more convenient option.

One of the litmus tests of effective parenting is to develop an effective method for handling firmly your child's violations of the rules without having to resort to threats, lectures, and continual punishment. Although admonitions and punishment may be appropriate responses in certain situations, they are generally less-than-ideal ways to deal with rule breaking and misbehavior. Children tend to tune out lectures and threats, even when they are reinforced with consistent punishment. Over time, continual criticism and negative reinforcement lose their potency. By the time the repeatedly punished child becomes a teenager, he may be inured to being grounded or denied access to the family car, especially if he's resentful and angry about having been repeatedly and "unfairly" punished. He may express his resentment and hostility by becoming withdrawn or by acting out. He may overtly break the family rules, despite the consequences, or he may covertly break the rules. (This subterfuge is a form of passive-aggressive behavior.) The child's self-sabotaging actions, which may be consciously or unconsciously driven, are directly linked to value confusion, low self-esteem, anger, and poor family communication.

Discussing misbehavior calmly, explaining the rationale for your reactions, avoiding recriminations, and creating a positive "let's work together and look at this issue" attitude are generally far more effective in modifying counterproductive behavior than threats and heavy-handed punishment. Punishment, however, can certainly be a legitimate response to certain transgressions. You will need to make a judgment call. Whatever response you select, it should be rational, reasonable, and congruent with the outcome you want to achieve. If, for example, you discover your six-year-old is stealing, you must decide whether "talking it out" or punishing him is the more effective way to stop the behavior. You may decide to deal with the problem by discussing it and then discover that strategy does not work. At this point you, you may decide to combine explanations with graduated consequences (that is, punishment). Resorting exclusively to heavy-handed punishment could boomerang and cause your child to become more devious about stealing.

It's ironic that many death row inmates were raised in physically and psychologically abusive, repressive, but ostensibly "moral" families where their parents consistently adhered to the oft-cited simplistic principle of "spare the rod and spoil the child".* Autocratic parenting with swift, mindless "justice" does not guarantee a moral, law-abiding child. In fact, it's likely

*Helen Prejean, *Dead Man Walking*. New York: Random House, 1993.

to produce the opposite effect. Of course, highly permissive parenting methods can produce equally disastrous results.

Figure 4.1 represents the multiple factors that affect your child's evolving value system. The synergy of these interacting factors will have a profound impact on your child's ethics and his or her ability to adjust successfully to society's rules and demands.

A Shelter from the Storm

Parents face a monumental challenge: how do they impart values, standards, and guidelines when society is experiencing a breakdown in morals and ethics? Americans are murdering, stealing, kidnapping, raping, and abusing their children in record numbers. Drug abuse is epidemic. Crimes against people and property have proliferated to the point where we're

Figure 4.1. Creating an Ethical Child

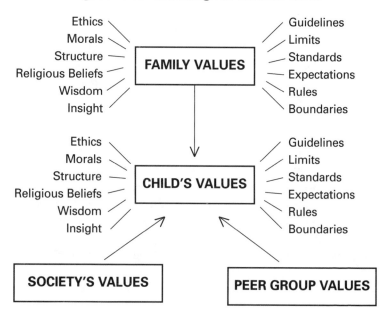

becoming hardened to the grim data that assaults us every day through the media. Our prisons are overflowing. Traditional family institutions are fracturing. Children, especially inner city children, feel an overwhelming sense of hopelessness and despair. Politicians connive, lie, and prostitute themselves to special interest lobbyists, and then posture piously about honesty, integrity, and American ideals. Large corporations deceive, exploit, and pollute while their executives refuse to acknowledge responsibility until the situation becomes so scandalous that they no longer can brazenly deny the truth or deflect public outrage. Pleading "no contest" in court, they pay their symbolic fines without admitting responsibility or culpability.

The list of examples of dishonesty and hypocrisy by putative business and political leaders seems endless. We have become a disillusioned and distrusting society. Tobacco companies argue deceitfully that their products do not pose health risks and that nicotine is not addictive. Homeless people sleep in doorways, and the hungry are not fed. Criminal and civil courts are hopelessly logjammed, and the justice system punishes some (usually the poor) and exonerates others who may be equally guilty (usually the rich who can afford the best attorneys).

In the latter part of the twentieth century, intact two-parent families are becoming an anachronism. Economic necessity forces millions of parents to drop their children off at child care at 7:00 A.M. and to pick them up at 6:00 P.M. Schools are underfunded, teachers are inadequately trained, and classes are too large. Many schools lack the money to purchase textbooks or pay school counselors. Administrators must cram thirty or more children with widely divergent skills, cultural backgrounds, and languages into one classroom. They then expect one underpaid and, in many cases, demoralized teacher to develop a strategy for teaching this hodgepodge. Children walk down the hallways of their schools in fear of being attacked, and even teachers must fear being assaulted.* Overwhelmed parents find

*The National Educational Association estimates that every day 100,000 students bring weapons to school, 6250 teachers are threatened, and 260 are assaulted. Source: Jon D. Hull. "The Knife in the Book Bag," *Time* (Feb. 8, 1993), p. 37.

they must work long hours to pay the bills and, in some cases, to keep one step ahead of the collection agency.

Parents attempting to impart morals, values, and ethics to their children must plot a course through a treacherous sea of moral incertitude, physical danger, and psychological risks. Helping your child understand, assimilate, and practice what you value can be a formidable challenge. Given the magnitude of this challenge, the temptation to become authoritarian and dictatorial can be very strong. Although wise parents realize they must establish a framework of "do's and don'ts," they also realize that an "I give the orders around here" approach will often elicit active or passive resistance, resentment, and, perhaps, rebellion down the road.

Whereas laxity and ambivalence triggers confusion and insecurity, dictatorship triggers alienation and rebellion. Somewhere between these extremes is the right course—reasonable rules and boundaries. The challenge is to find a balance that works for you and your family, one that avoids conflict, resistance, and oppositional behavior.

When you clearly communicate and model your family's values and beliefs, you provide a guiding beacon. Without this light, your child can get lost in the storm or smash against the rocks. Without a safe and secure haven, he can suffer anxiety, fear, and insecurity. Without love, support, nurturing, empathy, and affirmation, he may never develop self-esteem or self-confidence. The world can appear terribly frightening and foreboding to a young child who finds himself alone in the dark, buffeted by towering, ominous waves.

Helping Your Child Acquire Values, Morals, and Ethics

Define your personal values and family code of ethics. ("Intentionally hurting another person causes pain and suffering. If we can avoid hurting another person, we'll do so because we care about that person's feelings.")

Establish reasonable, clearly defined behavioral boundaries. ("Cheating is wrong because it gives a dishonest picture of your accomplishments. We would rather you be honest and get a poor grade on a test than discover you've received a good grade because you cheated. We value your honesty far more than we value a grade on a test.")

Clearly communicate your position on integrity, responsibility, effort, commitment, education, etc. ("My job is to work hard and support this family. It's my responsibility. Your job is to get an education so that you can get what you want from life. This is your responsibility.")

Model ethics. ("I can't give you as much help as you would like in writing your term paper because then the term paper would be mine and not yours.")

Explain the reasons for your values in terms your child can understand. ("We don't steal because we hurt another person when we take things that belong to him. We also hurt ourselves when we steal because we lose our self-respect.")

Examine hypothetical situations to prepare your child to handle situations requiring value judgments. ("Imagine you're in a store and see a shirt you like, but you don't have the money to buy it. The clerk goes into the storeroom. What would you do? What would you be thinking about as you make your decision?")

Communicate that honesty is a cherished family tradition. ("When I was in school, a friend suggested that we steal some money from our mothers and go to an amusement park. For a moment, I was tempted, but I realized I couldn't go through with it. I loved my mother too much to steal from her, and I knew that if she ever found out, she would be hurt and disillusioned with me.")

Consistently model your values. ("Unfortunately, I can't take you to the baseball game because I've already promised your sister that I would take her to the movies. I keep my promises to her, just as I will keep them to you.")

Have and express positive expectations. ("I know you'll handle this situation honorably.")

Let your child know you are available to serve as a sounding board. ("This is a tough choice, and if you need help sorting out this problem, please ask me.")

Affirm your child for good judgment and moral behavior. ("I think you handled that situation wonderfully. You've carefully weighed the pluses and minuses, and you've come up with a good solution.")

Acknowledge improvement and progress. ("It's frustrating to have to deal with this problem, but you certainly seem to be making good progress.")

Respond with sensitivity to your child's moral dilemmas. ("Having to tell your friends that you can't do what they're suggesting can be difficult. Going along with what they want can be very appealing, even though you realize that doing so would be wrong or dangerous. We all want to be liked and accepted by our friends.")

Offer guidance without being autocratic and dictatorial. ("What do you think about suggesting an alternative plan to your friends that wouldn't pose as many risks?")

Provide copious amounts of love and affirmation, not only for their accomplishments, but simply for being a precious part of your life. ("You make me very proud to be your parent!")

These communication suggestions increase the likelihood that your child will develop:

- A sense of security
- Age-appropriate independence
- Responsibility
- Ability to handle society's realities and demands
- Self-esteem
- Self-confidence
- Social awareness and adeptness
- Values and ethics
- Empathy for others

Children who haven't internalized their family's values, boundaries, expectations, and guidelines almost invariably become dysfunctional in one way or another. Because they lack judgment, self-control, self-esteem, and a stable frame of reference, they are predisposed to making chronically flawed decisions. This counterproductive behavior could persist throughout their lives and could cause them to sabotage their careers, interpersonal relationships, and marriages.

Unfortunately, dysfunctional adults often bequeath their nonadaptive behaviors to their own children. Those who are emotionally and ethically adrift cannot possibly model positive values and behaviors. They do not establish reasonable limits. They do not act responsibly. They do not communicate respect for society's laws. These failures perpetuate the cycle of individual and family malfunction.

"Producing" an Honorable Child

The challenge of helping your child become genuine, honorable, and aware of her moral obligations and responsibilities is indeed awesome. For example, let's say you suspect that your child has done something wrong. You ask her, and she admits that she broke a family rule. You might respond by getting upset or angry. You might chastise her. Or you might say: "I appreciate that you told me the truth even though I know it was difficult. I hope you never lie to me because some day you may need me to believe you and trust you. If I know you always tell the truth, I will be there for you, and I will support you 100 percent." These words unequivocally underscore your position on honesty and truthfulness. By communicating in this way, you achieve three critical objectives:

1. You give your child credit for being able to understand the rationale for your position.
2. You affirm your faith in her.
3. You build a foundation of trust and mutual respect.

Your goal is for your child to imprint a key cause-and-effect link. Her choices and behaviors will produce predictable consequences that can be either pleasant or unpleasant. She'll realize that by telling the truth, she earns your respect, support, and admiration. By lying, she'll elicit your disappointment and disapproval. This clearly expressed value framework provides a sense of security vital to the development of character. Your child will engrave psychologically that certain actions and attitudes are *constants* in her world, irrespective of the inconsistencies, injustices, and moral aberrations that may surround her in the world at large.

No matter what your parenting strategy, there are no guarantees that your child will assimilate and practice your values. Despite good child-rearing practices and clearly defined family values, some youngsters may still become dishonest, manipulative, and, in extreme cases, sociopathic or psychopathic. The explanation for these perplexing anomalies can usually be traced to a complex mix of inherited personality traits interacting with subtle (or not-so-subtle) environmental factors. Although there are no guarantees that consistent ethical and moral instruction combined with love, affirmation, and respect will produce a moral child, these ingredients definitely enhance the odds.

When a child blatantly rejects her parents' values and manifests a chronic pattern of flawed decisions and self-sabotaging behavior, her parents *must* identify the underlying causal factors and seek appropriate treatment. If they can't identify these factors or need help in dealing with them, they must seek a qualified mental health professional to assist them.

Emotional trauma can cause significant distortions in a child's perception. These distortions, in turn, often trigger anger, depression, resentment, confusion, and insecurity. In some cases, the distortions may produce rebellion and anti-social or self-destructive behavior. Individual or family counseling is vital when parents observe these behaviors.* The longer the underlying problems go untreated, the greater the risk of serious, lasting emotional damage.

Even seemingly "benign" problems such as learning disabilities, concentration deficits (Attention Deficit Disorder), or study-skill deficits can cause children to become frustrated, demoralized, angry, and resistant. Continual negative experiences at school can have a cumulative psychologically corrosive effect. Struggling students who do not receive effective learning assistance often become phobic about school and self-deprecating about their intelligence and abilities. Their feelings of inadequacy usually generate a complex web of counterproductive defense mechanisms called *psychological overlay*. The commonly associated behaviors include poor motivation, irresponsibility, procrastination, and academic shutdown. Unless the underlying learning deficits that cause these behaviors are properly identified and treated, and the child's sense of academic hopelessness is reoriented, a debilitating psychological problem may develop.†

Assimilating and Applying Values

At decisive moments in life, your child will need to respond quickly. A friend might say to your nine-year-old: "Let's steal some gum when the clerk turns her back." Your twelve-year-old may see a wallet fall out of an old woman's purse and be

---

*Family counseling is appropriate when a child's acting-out behavior is primarily attributable to family discord, poor communication, or mixed messages about rules and values. Individual counseling (psychotherapy) is appropriate when a child is unhappy, depressed, chronically rebellious, and self-sabotaging.

†For more information about these issues, see my books *Learning Disabilities and Your Child, Kids Who Underachieve,* and *1001 Ways to Improve Your Child's Schoolwork.*

tempted to pick it up and run away. Your teenage son may be tempted to speed away from a gas station without paying because he wants to use his money to take his girlfriend to a movie. Each of these hypothetical scenarios have obvious, logical, and predictable cause-and-effect implications that your child may or may not consider when he finds himself at a crossroad. You pray, of course, that he'll respond (albeit quickly) with reason and good judgment, weigh the pluses and minuses, resist the temptation to act impetuously, and make the judicious choice. You also pray he'll respond morally and ethically.

Some people will argue that values are relative and not absolute. This argument may be at the core of our society's moral malaise. *Stealing is wrong.* If the behavior isn't categorically identified as wrong, our civilization will sink into lawlessness and crumble. Parents must teach their child that stealing is unequivocally unacceptable. If they don't, their child is on a collision course with society. He may conclude that if he covets something that belongs to someone else, he can simply take it. If he conveniently rationalizes, "Well, everybody steals," he could end up in prison some day. Society will punish him because his parents have not fulfilled their obligation to teach him the difference between right and wrong.*

The distinction between right and wrong is often obvious, but this is not always the case, as the next anecdote will illustrate. The distinction can by clouded by such issues as loyalty, betrayal, and conflicting codes of honor.

Crossing the Dishonesty Line

We live in a society that gives lip service to honesty, despite our vaunted Judeo-Christian traditions and our ostensible com-

---

*Perhaps our society should require parents to accompany their adult children to prison when it can be proven that they've failed to provide them with moral values. This would certainly motivate parents to document their parenting practices in much the same way as they document their expenses for the IRS.

mitment to morality. Every day the media assaults us with a seemingly endless barrage of dishonesty and corruption. This epidemic of immorality is attributable, in part, to an unspoken code that accepts, and even encourages, certain types of dishonesty. Many would sarcastically call this the "American way." The dishonesty permeates many of our institutions. Perhaps the most blatant example is found in our taxation system.* In principle, the system is predicated on citizens being honest, but in practice, the system tacitly encourages prevarication, "cutting corners," and "fudging." When citizens become too greedy in claiming fictitious deductions or evading taxes, the government enforcers become vindictive. The judiciary then punishes those who have intentionally and egregiously crossed the line that demarcates "acceptable" from "unacceptable" dishonesty.

Other examples of hypocritical morality abound. Professional athletes are tacitly encouraged to play "dirty," but not too dirty. If they cross the line, they're penalized by the referee or fined by the commissioner. Physicians, chiropractors, and podiatrists can overcharge Medicare to a certain extent, but if they're excessively dishonest, they can be prosecuted. Corporations can pollute within limits, but if they pollute blatantly, they will be fined. Stock market speculators can have access to some insider information, but if they get too greedy and make too much money, they risk being prosecuted. Elected representatives can accept gifts and junkets from lobbyists, but if they take an overt bribe, they can be sent to prison. The list seems endless.

The prevalent attitude seems to be: "Get away with as much as you can, but be careful not to go too far, or you'll get your knuckles rapped." This "play it cool" attitude is passed on to our children and places them in a classic double bind: you're dumb if you're too honest, and you're dumb if you're too dishonest and get caught.

Some would respond to this societal indictment: "Don't be naive! It's been like this in American society from day one."

---

*In fairness, it should be noted that Congress and tradition are responsible for our taxation laws. The IRS simply enforces the laws as written.

They would argue that instantaneous media coverage (from the nightly news to *60 Minutes* to daily newspaper exposés) brings the transgressions to public attention as never before and creates the distorted impression that our society's dishonesty has reached epidemic proportions. It's certainly true that our society has always been plagued by graft, and it may also be true that the media makes corruption appear more prevalent today. The challenge concerned parents face is: "What can I do to raise a moral and ethical child? How can I prepare my fifteen-year-old to reject a friend's scheme to break into a teacher's office and look at the final exam? How do I train my six-year-old not to make fun of a handicapped child? How can I train my eighteen-year-old to reject the suggestion that he sell drugs to make some 'easy money?' How can I counteract the influence of a society that seems to be increasingly dishonest and immoral?"

Millions of responsible parents want to swim above the tide of hypocrisy, corruption, deceit, and dishonesty. They want their children to live in accordance with wholesome values, morals, and ethics. They want their children to have a conscience and practice a righteous code of behavior. These parents also want their children to pass this code of righteousness on to their own children some day.

Our sensibilities have clearly been bludgeoned by the pervasive moral crisis in our society. We have fitfully adjusted to being fearful for our children's physical safety. We have reluctantly become inured to the mind-boggling statistics that attest to rampant crime and violence and an epidemic of seemingly insoluble social problems. A wave of dissatisfaction and alarm, however, appears to be sweeping our country. Despite the evidence of a society running morally amok, legions of parents desperately want to teach their children to be honorable and honest.

Examining the Issues with Your Child

Read the following anecdote with your child and use the questions to help your child explore the underlying issues. The targeted age range is 8 to 14, but you may want to experiment using the anecdote with younger or older children. Remember: the context should be relaxed and affirming. Your goal is not only to teach, but also to enjoy the interaction.

---

interactive activity

Age Range: 8–14
Objectives: Wrestling with Right
and Wrong, Making
a Difficult Decision,
and Dealing with
Temptation

A Tough Call

Brendon couldn't believe what his friend Josh was saying. Josh had discovered how to open the locked door to their history teacher's room. He was suggesting they hide in a closet after school, slip into the room late in the afternoon, and look at the semester final exam. Josh wanted Brendon to hide behind some locker in the hall and be the lookout in case the janitor showed up.

Brendon's history grade was currently a B–. If he could get an B on the final, he would get a B on his report card. This would raise his G.P.A. to 3.1 and improve his chances of getting into a good university.

Still, Brendon was puzzled by Josh's plan. He couldn't understand why his friend would even propose stealing the exam. Josh was carrying a B+ in history, and it didn't make sense that he would consider breaking into Mrs. Arena's room. Although Josh was very bright, he was also very lazy. With only a couple of hours of studying, he could get a B+ or even an A on the final without any difficulty. But Josh didn't want to spend his time studying. He preferred hanging out with his friends, shooting baskets, and flirting with girls.

For a moment, Brendon was tempted by the plan. Knowing the questions in advance would certainly make studying for the final easier. Josh was also very persuasive. He argued that it would be a "piece of cake" to get into the office, look at the exam, and get out before anyone found out. He assured Brendon they wouldn't get caught. After a few minutes of indecision, Brendon made up he mind. He told Josh he wouldn't help him. The risks were too great. It also felt wrong. He decided he would study for the test and take his chances.

When Brendon told Josh his decision, his friend was upset and accused Brendon of being scared. Brendon wouldn't budge, and Josh wouldn't budge either. He told Brendon he would follow through with the plan with or without him. He would simply find someone else to be the lookout.

Brendon tried unsuccessfully to convince Josh to reconsider, but his friend wouldn't listen. In his desperation to prevent his friend from making a serious mistake, Brendon was tempted to leave an anonymous note for the teacher telling her not to leave the exam in her desk. The situation made him very depressed. He didn't want to betray his own values, and he didn't want to betray Mrs. Arena, a teacher he respected. But he also didn't want to betray Josh. His friend was about to make a really bad decision, and Brendon felt powerless to stop him. What a mess!

Questions and Issues for Discussion

1. After a few moments of indecision, Brendon arrived at a decision point and decided not to go along with Josh's scheme. On a scale from 1 to 10, rate this decision.

1	2	3	4	5	6	7	8	9	10
Not Smart				Fairly Smart					Very Smart

2. Why did you evaluate the decision in this way?
3. What do you think might have happened if Brendon had agreed to go along with the plan?
4. Josh also arrived at a decision point. What was his decision? How would you rate it on a scale from 1 to 10?

1	2	3	4	5	6	7	8	9	10
Not				Fairly					Very
Smart				Smart					Smart

5. What were your reasons for evaluating his decision this way?
6. If Josh carried through with his plan, what do you think the potential consequences would be?
7. Were there any other decision points for either of the boys in this story? What were they?
8. Let's say you're doing badly in a course and a friend suggests you cheat or steal a copy of a test. What concerns would you have? Would the decision be easy or hard to make?
9. What would you do if you refused to go along with the plan and your friend accused you of being a coward?
10. How much do dares influence kids? ("If you don't jump, you're a chicken!") How much do dares or being called a coward influence you?
11. In the story, Brendon tried to discourage his friend from going through with his plan. He kicked around the idea of anonymously telling the teacher to protect the test, but he rejected this idea. Did he have any other alternatives in trying to discourage Josh from going through with his plan?
12. Have you ever had to deal with a similar situation? What did you do?

Guidelines for Responding to Your Child

Guidelines are provided because the issues of honesty, ethics, and morality may be challenging and emotionally charged. The temptation to resort to lectures and sermons should be resisted.

1. If your child appears unwilling to discuss the anecdote . . .

    Parent: I had an experience when I was in school that was similar to the one described in the story. . . . (Have a personal anecdote ready to use as a catalyst for discussion.)

2. If your child has difficulty giving reasons for the rating . . .

   Parent: Did you rate the decision this way because you considered what might happen if they got caught? Or perhaps you also considered the issue of doing something dishonest?

3. If your child has difficulty understanding what a decision point is . . .

   Parent: Yesterday I had to decide whether to spend a lot of money to repair our car or sell it and buy a new one. The decision point was when the mechanic told me how much the repairs would be. I had to consider the investment in light of the fact that the car has over 100,000 miles on it. Can you think of a decision point in your own life during the last week? Tell me about it.

4. If your child has difficulty examining and discussing the hypothetical "What would you do if a friend suggested . . ."

   Parent: Let's look at another situation. Let's say we're in a restaurant, and the waiter forgets to charge for dessert. Your brother suggests we not tell him about the mistake. What would your reaction be?

5. If your child has difficulty discussing how he would handle a friend's dare . . .

   Parent: I remember I was swimming with some friends in the river near my house. A friend dared me to dive from the limb of a tree . . . (Have a story ready that describes how you successfully or unsuccessfully dealt with a friend's dare. It's okay to describe a situation in which you made an error in judgment.)

6. If your child has difficulty defining alternatives Brendon might have used to discourage Josh from making a mistake . . .

   Parent: I can think of a possible alternative. Perhaps Brendon could have asked his parents for advice.

7. If your child has difficulty describing a situation in which he wanted to discourage a friend from making a mistake . . .

   Parent: I remember when I felt my brother was going to do something very dumb. . . . (Have an anecdote ready.)

---

interactive **activity**

Age Range: 6–14
Objective: Dealing with Honesty,
Loyalty, and Betrayal

The Girl Who Didn't Want to Tell on Her Sister

Whitney was surprised when her teenage sister said she had a favor to ask. Jessica hardly ever bothered to talk to her, much less ask for a favor. Jessica asked Whitney if she would hide a paper bag of "stuff" in her room for a few days. She said her boyfriend wanted her to hold onto the bag until the weekend. When Whitney asked what was in the bag, Jessica replied nervously, "I don't know." Then Whitney wanted to know why Jessica couldn't hide the bag in her own room. Jessica replied, "I think Mom sometimes comes in my room and looks around. I don't want her to find it." Whitney again asked "Why?" Jessica replied, "If you won't do it, just tell me. I don't want to be asked a lot of questions!"

To please her sister, Whitney agreed to hide the bag. It was carefully wrapped and taped and weighed less than a pound. She found a place to put it in her closet under some summer clothes. The next day Jessica was actually nice to her. Whitney promised not to tell anyone about the bag, not even her best friend Roberta.

The following day, Whitney's curiosity got the best of her. She went to her closet and retrieved the bag. She sniffed it, and it smelled funny. It had a sweet odor, like tea. Whitney carefully removed the tape without tearing the bag. Inside she discovered green leaves and stems. After sniffing the leaves, she knew from her drug education class that the bag contained marijuana. Quickly rewrapping the bag with the tape, she stuck it under the clothes and shut the door to her closet.

Whitney began to tremble. "What should I do?" she muttered to herself. She didn't want to have drugs in her room. She didn't want to tell on her sister and get her in trouble with her parents. And she didn't want Jessica to be angry with her for causing her to lose her boyfriend or maybe even go to jail. She couldn't even talk it over with Roberta because she had promised Jessica not to tell anyone. And if Roberta told her parents, it would be a real mess.

Questions and Issues for Discussion

1. Why do you think Whitney was so upset and concerned?
2. List all of Whitney's possible choices in dealing with the dilemma that Jessica forced upon her.
3. What are the pluses and minuses of each possible choice?
4. If you were faced with a similar dilemma, what would you do?
5. Why would you choose to solve the problem in this way?
6. What risks might you face if you decided to do nothing?
7. Is there anyone you could go to for advice or help?
8. Let's say you did tell your best friend and she or he said "No big deal. I do this for my brother all the time."

Would you do something because your best friend was doing it?

9. What if you were in a similar situation and concluded that you made the wrong choice in trying to help your sister, brother, or best friend. What could you do then?

10. Have you ever faced a similar dilemma in which you wanted to do the right thing but didn't want to have to betray a confidence? Would you be willing to tell me about it?

11. Let's say Whitney hides the bag even though she thinks there's marijuana inside. How would you rate this decision?

1	2	3	4	5	6	7	8	9	10
Not Smart				Fairly Smart					Very Smart

12. Is there a moral (lesson) to this story?

Guidelines for Responding to Your Child

1. If your child has difficulty understanding or empathizing with Whitney's concern . . .
   Parent: Do you think she might be concerned about her parents' reaction if they found out?

2. If your child has difficulty listing Whitney's options . . .
   Parent: Well, would one option be to tell her sister "no"? What else might she do?

3. If your child has difficulty evaluating the pluses and minuses . . .
   Parent: What are the possible consequences if she says "no" to her sister?

4. If your child cannot project how she might deal with a similar situation . . .
   Parent: What sort of thoughts would go on in your mind if you were faced with the choices Whitney faced?

5. If your child cannot identify anyone who might help her with a major dilemma . . .

> **Parent:** Would you feel comfortable discussing the dilemma with your teacher, with another brother or sister, a friend? What do you think would happen if you discussed the problem with me? How do you think I would handle it?

6. If your child indicates she might do something because her best friend would do it . . .

> **Parent:** What might happen if your best friend suggests stealing something?

7. If your child has difficulty understanding that, if she concludes she made a bad choice, it may not be too late to change her course . . .

> **Parent:** Let me tell you about a time when I made a bad choice but was able to fix things before it was too late. . . . (Have a personal anecdote ready!)

8. If your child has difficulty drawing a moral from the anecdote . . .

> **Parent:** Could we come up with something about being true to yourself or about being able to say "no"?

Remember that your goal is to use a hypothetical situation to help your child develop and refine her reasoning skills, not to pass judgment or castigate her for poor reasoning. You want to acquire insight into your child's analytical thinking process so that you can identify and address deficits. You want to help your child develop good analytical thinking skills so that she can make astute judgments when she finds herself at one of life's critical junctures. During these interactive sessions, you must discipline yourself to be *process oriented* ("*How* can you make a good decision in this situation?") rather than judgment-oriented ("That seems like a dumb thing to do.") You must treat your child with respect, even if her answers are not what you expect or want. If you lecture, admonish, or deride her for poor thinking, she's likely to shut down and become angry, resentful, and resistant. You want her to feel comfortable discussing important personal issues with you that could have a profound impact on her life. At the same time, you want to assure her that you're sensitive to the dilemma of "telling" on a sibling or friend. Other issues in this anecdote that you would want to examine with your child include:

- The challenge of attempting to help a friend or sibling who is making a seriously flawed choice.
- The ethical conflict of revealing a secret in a way that might be perceived as a betrayal.
- The issues of sibling loyalty versus self-protection and self-preservation (Whitney might be considered an accomplice if the police were to become involved).
- The identification of resources and support systems (parents, teachers, etc.) that could help with dilemmas.
- The rationale for your family's position on drugs and the risks associated with using or selling them.

Although communicating your beliefs about drugs is clearly a primary goal in this interactive exercise, the anecdote touches upon other ethical considerations involving friendship and loyalty. Your child is undoubtedly deeply enmeshed in her sense of loyalty. "Betraying" her sister would undoubtedly be a traumatic experience for her. (*You* realize, of course, that *not* making this difficult choice could hurt the other person far more.) Urging your child to consider *in advance* how she would handle similar dilemmas and how she could navigate a reasonable course when faced with choices that might involve displeasing someone is of monumental importance. For example: What would she do if she discovered her best friend was taking drugs? What would she do if her best friend was dating a boy who was stealing cars or dealing drugs?

You want your child to realize that in certain situations she must be guided by both her heart *and* her head. You also want her to realize that there could be a time when she might be forced to make a "hard" choice that could temporarily, or, even permanently, alienate someone she likes. She may need to make this choice to protect the person she likes or to protect herself. In this situation, her head must absolutely prevail!

Making a decision that may appear to be a betrayal can be heart-wrenching. If you're to have credibility and if your child is to trust you and communicate openly, you must acknowledge how traumatic this choice can be. You must be sensitive to the dilemma, and have empathy for the stress and pain the dilemma would trigger.

chapter 5

Building the Foundation

*R*yan felt his stomach churning as he walked home from school. He knew he should be at basketball practice. He had gotten as far as the locker room, but he couldn't go through the door. After asking one of his teammates to tell the coach he was sick, he began the half-mile trek home.

Ever since he was four years old, Ryan had been told that he had extraordinary natural athletic ability and that someday he'd be a professional athlete. Although only a high school sophomore, the 6'2" teenager was already a three-letter man playing varsity baseball, basketball, and football. His coaches liked him because he worked hard, and they respected him for being a team leader.

The plan for becoming a professional athlete, however, had gone astray. Ryan no longer wanted to play varsity sports. He wanted to become an actor. Playing competitive sports wouldn't allow time for him to try out for parts in school plays. Ryan realized that if he were serious about acting, he'd have to use every free moment memorizing lines and rehearsing. Forced to make a decision, he had chosen acting after a great deal of soul-searching.

Despite his decision, the sixteen-year-old felt anxious and depressed. He dreaded having to tell his coach he was going to quit the basketball team. He also dreaded having to explain to his teammates why he was quitting. He knew they wouldn't understand and would feel betrayed. With him on the team, they had a chance of winning the league title. How could he let them down? Knowing how upset his coach and teammates would be triggered waves of guilt. Ryan had had bad dreams the previous night, but he woke up in the morning convinced he had made the right decision. He would talk to the coach tomorrow. Tonight he would tell his dad.

The prospect of talking to his dad was even more painful than talking to his coach. Ryan's father was extremely proud of him and would brag to everyone about his son's touchdowns, home runs, and jump shots. Although Ryan liked making his dad proud, the bragging made him uncomfortable. He felt like he was under a microscope, and everything he did was being scrutinized and analyzed. Having a bad game was his worst nightmare.

Ryan's father had also played high school basketball. He had wanted to play in college, but because his family was very poor, he had been forced to go to work to help support his mother and sisters. Now he dreamed about his son playing college ball. Ryan didn't know how to break the news that he would no longer be playing varsity sports.

Ryan could hear one voice inside his head: "Don't be a quitter! Your dad deserves to be proud of you." But then he'd hear another voice: "You don't enjoy basketball anymore. You could be using your free time to improve your acting skills." The two voices caused him to feel confused and uncertain, but then he would remind himself that he wasn't quitting because he was afraid of the challenge or unwilling to work hard. He was quitting because he wanted to be a professional actor, and he realized he would have to make some tough choices if he was going to achieve his goal.

To Please or Not to Please

A teenager finds himself at a crossroad. After weighing the pluses and minuses of his options and struggling to identify what he wants in life, he decides to change course. It's a radical change. He recognizes his own natural athletic talents, but he decides that what he desires more than anything is to become an actor.

One might reasonably infer that Ryan has no assurances that his acting ability is as exceptional as his athletic ability. He knows that he enjoys acting more than playing intramural sports, and he has faith in himself. His decision to quit the basketball team and abandon varsity sports, however, has an expensive price tag attached. He will have to disappoint people he cares about: his coach, his teammates, and, most important, his father. Despite his guilt feelings and anxiety, he's determined to follow the path he has chosen and accept the consequences.

Courage manifests itself in many ways. There are two common denominators: the willingness to take a risk and the commitment to a particular belief or cause. Sometimes courage is impulsive. A soldier charges up a hill under enemy fire to rescue a buddy, or a woman jumps into a river to save a child. Sometimes courage is more calculated. A rescue team parachutes into a forest fire to save the lives of firefighters who are in danger.

Courage may also involve exposing oneself to emotional rather than physical risks. It may mean your saying "no" to a friend's request that you do something unethical when it would be more convenient to rationalize and say "yes." It may involve helping someone because it "feels right" despite the risks or inconvenience this might entail. It may involve going against popular opinion or standing up for something in which you strongly believe, despite the disapproval of those you admire, love, or fear. It may involve asserting your own legitimate needs at the expense of another person's needs, or subordinating your own needs because you perceive another person's needs should rightfully come first (such as insisting, despite your own injuries, that an injured child be taken first by the rescue helicopter).

You can be certain that your child will confront situations in her life that demand courageous decisions. To a large extent, her choices will directly reflect her self-concept. If she has good self-esteem, she'll make choices that affirm her positive sense of self. Her judgments and priorities will be congruent with her values, goals, and self-confidence. She'll choose to study for a final exam rather than go with friends to the park on Saturday afternoon because she feels she *deserves* to get good grades and win a scholarship to a first-rate university. She'll keep a secret because she feels she *deserves* to be trusted. She'll ditch an abusive boyfriend because she feels she *deserves* to be treated well. She'll reject the drugs offered to her at a party because she feels she *deserves* a healthy body and healthy mind. She'll not cheat on a test because she knows she doesn't need to resort to cheating to get a good grade and be- cause she feels she *deserves* to respect herself. She'll turn down an offer for a well-paying job that doesn't provide the desired experience or opportunities because she feels she *deserves* to be happy and fulfilled in her work.

Your child will not always be consciously aware of the reasons for her judgment calls, but her unconscious mind will operate at full throttle when she makes important deci- sions. Her choices will reflect her conviction that she's a "good" person who merits getting what she needs and wants in life, or a "bad" person who merits pain, failure, and un- happiness. Self-esteem is the fulcrum for this decision-making seesaw.

A child's courage to act on her convictions and to trust herself and her intuition is a precious resource. *The child who likes herself will take care of herself.* She wants life's coveted payoffs: love, achievement, security, pride, and respect. As she rides on life's carousel, she's convinced she has every right to reach for and capture the brass ring. The teenager described in the introductory anecdote clearly possessed both courage and self-esteem. He was determined to assert his needs and desires despite the disapproval his decision was bound to elicit.

During the formative years, a child's self-esteem and self-confidence are like newly planted seedlings. To thrive, they must be planted in rich soil, nurtured, protected, and exposed to the right amount of sunlight. If they are improperly nourished or denied sunlight, they will shrivel and die. A child's self-esteem and self-confidence can also shrivel and die if he's denied essential nutrients. Parents wittingly or unwittingly deny their child these nutrients when they attempt to impose their own conscious or unconscious psychological needs, career agendas, thwarted desires, and cherished fantasies onto their child. When this happens, they are placing their own needs first and are sending a powerful message to their child: *Your uniqueness, individuality, and emotional needs are not important.*

The line differentiating reasonable career guidance from unreasonable coercion stretches across a dangerous minefield. If the mines are tripped, the shrapnel can psychologically maim a child and rip through the family fabric like razor blades.

The parent who tries to live vicariously through a child's accomplishments imposes a heavy emotional burden on the child. He's asking her to assume responsibility for *his* contentment. The child may conclude that this is her role and destiny in life. Another example of parent-imposed behavior is the child who never marries because she has consciously or unconsciously concluded that her responsibility is to be the caretaker for her aging parents. The child who agrees to conform to this script cannot help but feel unfulfilled, frustrated, resentful, and angry. If she refuses to conform, she will probably feel guilty. She's clearly in a double bind—damned if she does and damned if she doesn't. She'll respond to this emotionally wrenching dilemma by becoming withdrawn and depressed or by acting out her rage in some counterproductive way.

Interviews with adults who as children were expected to fulfill their parents' thwarted desires often reveal profound and lasting resentment. Hidden or not-so-hidden parental agendas can break a child's spirit. The child may want to please his parents so desperately that he may never get on with his own life. The scenario breeds emotional dependency and impedes the development of self-esteem and self-confidence. Although the child may ultimately be successful in the career his parents have chosen, his ostensible achievement may produce little satisfaction.

I Want to Make You Proud

Most children want to please their parents and covet their parents' pride in their accomplishments. Achievement is one way a child can say, "I love you and want you to be proud of me. My successes will show you that I appreciate what you've done for me. I want to give you pleasure."

The natural desire of children to please their parents can become distorted when they receive double messages from parents ("Honey, of course I want you to do what's best for you, but I was really hoping you would take over my law practice someday"). Guilt trips are insidious tools of behavior modification. They exploit and distort a child's natural desire to please. Parents who fail to identify their child's legitimate emotional needs, are insensitive to these needs, and don't individuate psychologically from their child risk triggering emotional turmoil in their children. These parents shouldn't be surprised when this turmoil generates confusion, depression, and counterproductive behavior. Children caught in the grip of negative emotions often sabotage themselves, unaware that they have become their own worst enemies.

Resentful, angry, and alienated children often get revenge by doing everything in their power to upset, disillusion, and thwart their parents. Their self-sabotaging behavior sends a clear signal that both child and family are in trouble. If the behavior is chronic, it's imperative that parents find a well-trained family therapist, social worker, or psychotherapist who can help them identify and reconcile the misunderstandings, distorted perceptions, bruised feelings, and communication breakdowns. Parents who are smart enough to realize they need professional assistance and who seek such help have their priorities straight. They want their child to have the best shot at making her life "work," and they're committed to doing whatever is necessary to improve the likelihood of this happening.

Fundamentals of Providing Wise Counsel and Guidance When Your Child Is at a Crossroad in Life

- **Express faith in your child's ability to make good judgments, even though you may not always agree with all of her decisions.** ("I know you'll make a wise choice.")
- **Guide your child through an examination of the issues.** ("Let's look at the pluses and minuses of being a doctor.")
- **Communicate your support and empathy.** ("If you decide that you want to discuss the problem with me, I'll be here.")
- **Acknowledge how difficult it can be to make a tough decision.** ("It is tough having to disappoint someone you care about.")
- **Communicate respect and trust.** ("You've handled this difficult situation very honorably. I'm proud of you!")
- **Affirm your child for progress.** ("Each time you analyze a problem, I can see that you are doing better and better at identifying the underlying issues.")
- **Praise your child for achievements.** ("You've done a great job identifying the pros and cons in this situation.")
- **Resist the temptation to impose your perspective and attitudes on your child, even if you believe her logic is off-target and her choices are flawed.** ("You've made a decision about how to handle this problem. I suggest you think overnight about the alternatives we discussed before acting on your decision. If you're still convinced your solution is the best, then go for it.")

My Life Is My Life

The introductory anecdote is a paradigm for the conflict that may develop between parents' expectations and children's expectations. Certainly, parents can and should have expectations. They expect their child to be honest and ethical (and they have a concomitant responsibility to create a family context that teaches and models honesty and ethics). They have the right to expect their child to be responsible, conscientious, and sensitive to the feelings of others (and they have a concomitant responsibility to create a family context that teaches and models these qualities). These expectations are quite distinct from expecting a child to go to West Point.

Wise parents realize that their child must plot, with appropriate guidance, his own course in life. Historically, of course, this was not the case. The male children of farmers usually became farmers, and female children usually married farmers. The sons of blue-collar workers usually became blue-collar workers, and the children of physicians often became doctors. The world is different today. A father can no longer guarantee his son a job at the plant or an apprenticeship in his union. Many physicians are no longer sure they want their children to follow in their footsteps, given the pressure, problems, and frustrations they now face.

Although some might debate the wisdom of Ryan's decision to abandon sports, the choice rightfully belonged to him. The sixteen-year-old was not responsible for making his father's life rewarding through his achievements. His father might fantasize his son playing college basketball, but this fantasy also had to work for Ryan. It had to be congruent with his personality, interests, talents, needs, and desires. To avoid a potentially serious family conflict, Ryan's father would have to remind himself that his primary objectives are, namely, to help his son:

- Develop a clear sense of his own identity and talents.
- Identify his own interests and define what *he* wants in life.
- Establish his own goals, priorities, and agendas.

- Become his "own person" and take charge of his own life.

Once Ryan's father clarifies these objectives, subordinating any fantasies and expectations about a child's career becomes natural and appropriate. Certainly, any parent would be justified in wanting to examine calmly and rationally the pros and cons of a major decision with his child. Ryan's father would be justified in expressing his concerns and misgivings, especially if he's convinced his son has not carefully considered important issues or the implications of his decision. This does not, however, justify insisting that his son conform to a career agenda he's created. Ryan had no obligation to play basketball because it would make his dad, coach, and teammates happy. His obligation was to create his own life plan. If his judgment ultimately proved wrong and he became disillusioned with acting, he could always pick up the pieces and move on. No doors would have permanently clanged shut. He could always play sports the following year, or he could embark on another completely different career track.

Ryan wasn't running away from hard work or a challenge. He was thinking rationally and strategically, and he was guided by his intuition. This intuition rested on a solid foundation of self-esteem and self-confidence. What more could any reasonable parent desire or expect from his or her teenager?

Parents who delude themselves that they are justified in guiding their child along the career path they've selected are acting egocentrically and, perhaps, even narcissistically. The classic example is the intense, driven parent who stalks the sidelines of the tennis court, baseball field, football field, soccer field, or hockey rink, exhorting his or her child to practice harder and perform better. (This is distinct from the genuine enthusiasm of parents who support their child's efforts and share in the joy and excitement of the event.) Obsessed with living vicariously though their child's achievements, these sideline "parent-coaches" have failed to individuate from their child. The performance pressure they exert often causes children to conclude that they're deserving of love only for their achievements. Such highly conditional parental love and acceptance can be psychologically damaging and can produce debilitating guilt and alienation.

The needs of parents and their children can certainly be congruent. The child of a physician may decide to become a physician because she enjoys helping people and believes a career in medicine will be fulfilling. So, too, might the child of a gold medal ice skater aspire to compete in the Olympics without being coerced to carry on the family tradition. Parents who encourage a child's ambition to attain her personal goals are acting responsibly. If the child subsequently changes her mind, these parents would help her carefully weigh the pluses and minuses of her options. If her reasons for changing course make sense (for example, the goal no longer is important because the child's interests have changed), they would support the decision. For a parent to coerce or manipulate a child into maintaining her original goal to satisfy the parent's own ego needs is self-centered and irresponsible.

The foregoing should not be construed as advocating a "hands-off" policy when your child is wrestling with important educational or career decisions. Parents have a responsibility to help their children identify talents and interests and establish personal goals. They have a responsibility to encourage them to persevere when they encounter temporary glitches or minor setbacks, or when they're tempted to quit because it's the easy way out. Parents have a responsibility to encourage their children not to cut their bridges before they're certain of their decisions. They have a responsibility to urge their children to keep open as many options as possible. And finally, they have a responsibility to help their children figure out how to identify, develop, and focus their talents and energies so they can attain their goals.

Examining the Issues with Your Child

Read the introductory anecdote with your child. The activity targets children ages 10 to 14, but you may want to try it with a younger or older child. If your child is resistant or unable to relate to the issues, move on. An alternative would be to share and examine a personal "tough choice" anecdote from your own life experiences if you believe this will be more productive.

---

interactive activity

Age Range: 10–14
Objectives: Goal Setting and
Decision Making

Questions and Issues for Discussion (anecdote found on page 141)

1. Do you think Ryan's anxiety about telling his dad his decision and fear of disappointing him was justified?
2. If you were in a similar situation, would you be afraid to disappoint me? How would you deal with the situation?
3. How do you think I would respond?
4. How would you evaluate Ryan's decision?

1	2	3	4	5	6	7	8	9	10
Not Smart				Fairly Smart					Very Smart

5. What reasons might Ryan's dad give to encourage his son to continuing playing basketball?
6. Do you think that by giving up basketball, Ryan might be establishing a pattern of running away from challenges?
7. Why did you conclude this?
8. Do you think it would be fair if Ryan's dad becomes angry at him because he has decided to quit sports? Would it be unfair if his dad remained angry? Should parents insist their child pursue goals they believe are important, even though their child may not be interested in these goals? What are your reasons?

9. Let's assume that, to please his dad, Ryan decides to continue playing basketball and doesn't try out for the school play. How would you rate this decision?

1	2	3	4	5	6	7	8	9	10
Not Smart				Fairly Smart					Very Smart

10. Why did you rate the decision this way?
11. Let's assume Ryan decides *not* to continue playing basketball and tries out for the play. How would you rate this decision?

1	2	3	4	5	6	7	8	9	10
Not Smart				Fairly Smart					Very Smart

12. Why did you rate the decision this way?
13. Have you ever been in a similar situation? (Parents: Be prepared to describe an analogous double-bind situation you've encountered in your own life.)

Disagreements and Conflicts

When children are young, parents have a great deal of power, and, in a showdown, they can assert their authority and prerogatives. As children mature, however, the power fulcrum shifts, and it becomes increasingly difficult for parents to be autocratic and dictatorial. Unhappy teenagers can always figure out ways to resist their parents' desires and sabotage rules they feel are unfair. They may acquiesce under duress, but they'll feel angry, resentful, and alienated. These feelings can produce disastrous repercussions and seriously damage the parent-child relationship.

Most adolescents struggle with the process of asserting their need for greater freedom and independence. The progression that leads from a parent-regulated child to a self-regulated young adult follows a biologically and culturally imprinted timetable. Children typically earn greater freedom and independence by virtue of their increasing physical and emotional maturity and demonstrated good judgment.

The initial forays of teenagers into the world beyond the family nest can be disquieting for parents. Teenagers who were once innocent and highly dependent begin to make more and more key choices on their own. They decide what they want to do with their bodies and their lives, and their decisions may not always be the ones parents would prefer. The potential for family conflict, resentment, active or passive resistance, and anger increases significantly when an adolescent feels his parents do not trust him or his judgment and are intent on imposing their own rigid agenda on his life.

Disagreements are common when parents and children engaged in an emotionally charged discussion have divergent perspectives, levels of maturity, experience, analytical thinking skills, and personal agendas. If they have radically different "reads" on a situation and draw radically different conclusions, the chances of a disagreement becoming an unpleasant showdown increase significantly. These showdowns invariably generate counterproductive behavior and recriminations, especially if both parent and child are intent on asserting their own position and are unwilling to listen or empathize with what the other is saying. At this juncture, parents have two options: they can attempt to reason with their child, or they can attempt to impose their will with threats and punishments.

A dispute between a parent and a child has three possible outcomes:

1. Both win (a **win-win** situation)
2. One wins and one loses (a **win-lose** situation)
3. Neither wins (a **lose-lose** situation)

The ideal outcome in any disagreement, whether between a parent and a child, two adults, or two nations, is for both to feel they've won *something*. Losing, especially losing continually, triggers frustration, demoralization, resentment, hostility, defiance, resistance, and counterproductive vindictive behavior. These behaviors may be overt (the child openly does something expressly forbidden) or covert (the child surreptitiously or manipulatively breaks the rule.)

Eliciting voluntary cooperation is clearly preferable to demanding obedience and compliance or resorting to threats and punishments. Reasoning with a child and helping him realize that certain behaviors are in his best interest are also clearly preferable to coercing him into conforming to an imposed agenda. The child who emerges from a disagreement without feeling he has been beaten down by his parents' superior power will be more inclined to consider his parents' position, act rationally, and make wise choices. The parents win, and the child also wins.

The following figure represents parental options in response to disagreements and conflict:

In a dispute with a child, the parent is responsible for orchestrating a win-win outcome whenever this is appropriate

Figure 5.1. Parent-Child Conflict

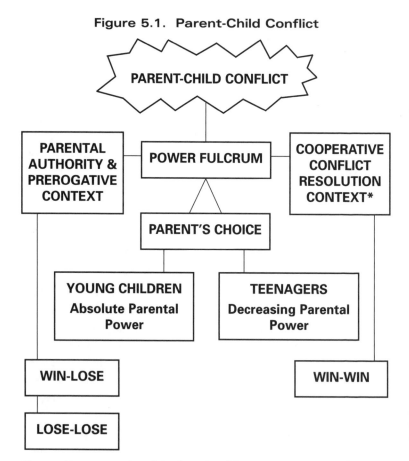

*See graphic representation of the dynamics of these options on page 156–157.

and reasonable. *This does not mean all issues are negotiable!* In some situations, the parent's wish must prevail (see "When Overt Parental Pressure Is Justified," page 159). Still, the likelihood of a win-win resolution improves significantly when both parties are willing to:

> Define and objectively analyze their issues, priorities, and respective concerns
> Communicate without anger and recriminations
> Demonstrate empathy, trust, and respect

When either the parent or the child has a conscious or unconscious agenda to be the exclusive winner in a disagreement, the potential for an emotionally charged conflict increases dramatically. Conversely, when both parties are willing to seek a reasonable and mutually acceptable compromise (a win-win, since both sides get something), the potential for resolving a conflict increases dramatically. The ball for creating this win-win context is clearly in the parents' court. They must take the initiative and assume the responsibility for creating this dispute-resolution context. (Please note: In some situations, compromising with your child is *inappropriate*. Parents must win some disputes, especially when a child's position is entrenched and clearly untenable or irrational. Driving with a suspended license would be an example of an issue that is nonnegotiable. The teenager *must* abide by the law, even if he is unwilling to concur with the underlying logic for the law.)

Parents who consciously or unconsciously orchestrate *power struggles* to force their child to see the issues from their perspective and conform to their wishes risk igniting hard-to-extinguish conflagrations. Many statements are predictable flash points. A parent might say: "This is a dumb decision! Why would you want to be a second-rate actor when you could be a first-rate athlete? The men in our family play ball. I played ball, and I'd like you to play ball (join the Marines, become an engineer, etc.). Competitive sports builds character and discipline." This sledgehammer diatribe is going to press hot buttons. The parent is attacking his child's judgment, family loyalty, masculinity, and character, and he shouldn't be surprised if this causes his child to become resentful, hostile, rebellious, and emotionally distant. Short of physical or sexual abuse, nothing is more corrosive to a parent/child relationship than demeaning verbal assaults. These shoot-outs undermine the child's respect and trust and erect virtually insurmountable barriers to effective, intimate family communication. Although the parent may appear to win the argument, and his child may submit to his wishes, his vitriolic words will produce a lose-lose outcome in the long run. What child would want to share his feelings, thoughts, and self-doubts with a parent who cares only about his own egocentric needs?

Some parents use manipulative pressure to get their child to conform to their blueprint. They might say: "You realize, of course, that you're really disappointing us. We were hoping you'd win an athletic scholarship and carry on the family tradition. I guess we'll have to accept your decision and deal with our disappointment." This tactic might "work" and the child may acquiesce, but it could also backfire and produce resentment and anger. In the final analysis, manipulation usually produces a lose-lose situation. The child may submit (thus lose), but he'll undoubtedly feel resentful. Or the child may resist, contravene his parent's wishes, feel guilty, and be punished

Figure 5.2. Win-Win Conflict Resolution

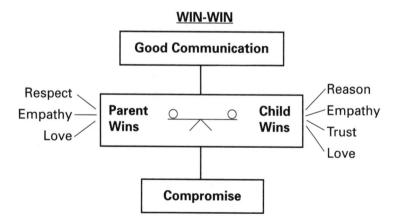

Figure 5.3. Win-Lose Conflict Resolution

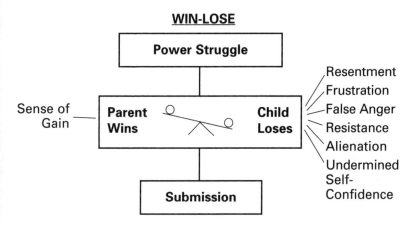

Figure 5.4. Lose-Lose Conflict Resolution

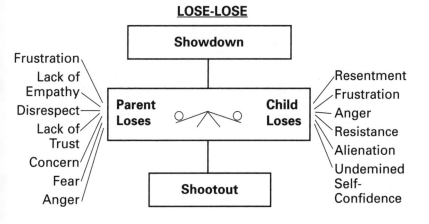

(thus lose). The parent may not realize that he, too, is losing because the cumulative effect of the resentment and guilt will cause the child to become distrustful and alienated.

Other parents may use fear to influence their child's attitudes or modify his behavior. They might say: "You realize, of course, that you'll never be able to support yourself as an actor. In New York and Los Angeles, thousands of young people who want to be actors live in poverty and become dishwashers, busboys, and parking lot attendants. At forty, you'll discover you've wasted your life and achieved nothing. Is that what you want?" This tactic may produce the desired outcome—apprehension, anxiety, and compliance—but it will probably also produce resentment and alienation. The parent thus unwittingly creates a lose-lose situation. He loses and the child loses.

When parents are convinced their child is making a serious error in judgment, they, of course, have the right, in fact the obligation, to express their concerns. The way in which they communicate their concerns, however, is critically important. The parent might say: "Let's look at your decision. Let's list the pluses in one column and the minuses in another." The parent might also *diplomatically* suggest minuses the child hasn't considered. For example:

> **Parent:** You probably already know that very few high school athletes ever make it to the pros. Perhaps 10 percent go on to play college ball, and perhaps 2 percent of the best college athletes are drafted into the pros. I imagine that an equally small percentage of kids who act in high school ever become professional actors. Only the very best make it. And even if they have talent, luck plays a key role in their success. A young actor may be doing summer stock, and a famous director may happen to see the play and offer a tryout for a movie. Another young actor may be parking cars at a restaurant in Beverly Hills and happen to strike up a conversation with a producer who invites him to read for a part. The chances of this happening are extremely poor. I'm not necessarily trying to discourage you. I'm suggesting you think about these issues. If you're convinced you want to give acting a shot, you have my support. You could certainly study acting in college and see how it goes. Nothing would give me greater satisfaction than to see you succeed. I believe you'll be successful at whatever you ultimately decide to do. If you become disillusioned, you can always change course. Some-

times we have to drive down a few dead-end streets before we find the entrance to the freeway. At the same time, we have to be careful. We don't want to drive down a dangerous dead-end street and get robbed or shot while we're looking for the freeway.

The parent has expressed his concerns nonjudgmentally and has calmly presented his "take" on the realities of the situation and the potential problems. In so doing, he models his own analytical thinking process. He expresses faith in his son, suggests a reasonable compromise, and leaves the door open for the child to reconsider his decision later. By not frontally assaulting his son with the "flaws" in his decision and by not causing him to become defensive, the parent encourages analytical thinking and creates a win-win context.

When Overt Parental Pressure Is Justified

In some situations, the use of overt parental pressure or coercion as a means of getting a child to modify counterproductive behavior or reverse a flawed decision may be justified. For example, a parent may observe that her son rarely studies and spends most of his time watching TV and socializing with his friends. She legitimately concludes that intervention is imperative. If her attempts to reason with her son prove unsuccessful, and he continues to avoid his school responsibilities, she would certainly be justified in insisting *autocratically* that the TV remain off during certain time periods and that social time be limited. Other incrementally unpleasant consequences may also be necessary if the child refuses to modify his counterproductive behavior.

A wide range of crisis situations may require an autocratic response from parents when logic and reason have failed. For example, a teenager may inform his parents that he wants to drop out of high school and get a job. In this situation, it's urgent that the parents intervene. Ideally, they would make a last-ditch effort to bridge the gap and help their child recognize the consequences of his decision before the situation becomes a showdown. Their intervention strategy would involve several key steps that include:

- attempting to identify the underlying factors that might cause their son to consider dropping out of school.
- attempting to reason with their son about the implications of his decision.
- communicating their position about the value of education.
- resisting lecturing, sermonizing, and threatening seeking professional assistance if they're stymied.

If the parents conclude their son wants to drop out of school because learning problems are causing him to become frustrated and demoralized, they would seek the most competent educational therapist they can find. If they conclude their son is depressed, taking drugs, or being negatively influenced by his friends, they would seek out the most competent psychologist, psychiatrist, or drug counselor they can find. If they conclude their son is confused about the family's rules and values, they would reiterate these rules and values using the best communication skills they possess. If their son resists their attempts to deal with the problem and is clearly on a collision course with society's rules and realities, they may conclude that autocratic intervention is their only recourse. This might translate into insisting that the teenager enter a counseling or drug rehabilitation program.

In crisis scenarios involving grave potential risks, parents must make a judgment call. When noncoercive attempts to help him have proven ineffectual, then autocratic intervention, coercion, forced participation in a mental health or drug rehab program, and/or "tough love" may be what a teenager needs to keep a risky situation from getting out of hand. Parents should rely on their intuition and professional advice in these difficult situations.

Handling Disagreements

- Reason with your child whenever possible.
- Remember that your child is not an extension of your own ego.
- Keep in mind that your child is not responsible for your happiness.
- Remember that your child does not necessarily have the same aptitudes, desires, and interests that you have.
- Remind yourself that your child must learn certain lessons about life on her own.
- Trust your intuition.
- When disagreements arise, create a win-win context whenever possible and appropriate.
- Do not use guilt trips to modify your child's behavior.
- Intervene autocratically in crisis situations when reason, empathy, and efforts to communicate noncoercively have failed.
- Communicate empathy, trust, and respect.
- Clearly reiterate the family rules and values when necessary.
- Seek professional help when you can't handle the problem.

When children believe their parents respect them and have faith in them, despite a difference of opinion, they are far more receptive to a "let's look at this issue and see if we can work it out" approach. Conversely, when children conclude their parents are judgmental, dictatorial, and highly critical, they often become secretive, noncommunicative, and emotionally distant. These children will typically resist or reject their parents' instructions, rules, recommendations, and admonitions. Parents should not be surprised when they're unable to establish a good relationship and good communication with children who perceive them as unreasonable and unfair. Resistance and rebellion are the two most potent weapons children can use when they feel misunderstood, oppressed, or abused.

The following figure represents how your influence decreases as your child matures. The phase of greatest impact is clearly before the age of 8, when peer pressures are less powerful. Although the window of influence begins to close between the ages of 8 and 12, your child will still be quite receptive to you during this time frame. When your child becomes 12, however, peers begin to exert more influence. This will continue until age 17. Then your influence will begin to increase, and peer influence will begin to decrease. Although it's certainly possible for you to affect your child's attitudes and behavior during the teenage years, you must recognize that powerful social forces will make this very challenging. Your only recourse in counteracting negative peer pressures is to develop first-rate parenting, communication, and conflict-resolutions skills.

Figure 5.5. Influencing Your Child*

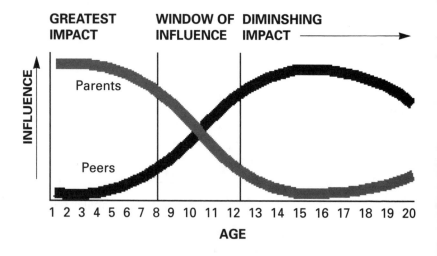

*Adapted with permission from *Family Wellness Workbook* (George T. Doub and Virginia Morgan Scott, San Jose, 1987). The original concept was adapted from an audio tape by H. Stephen Glenn, "Dealing with the Hostile Child/Adolescent." (Humansphere Inc., 1981)

Future Time: Predicting What Might Happen

Many children have a marginal appreciation for future time. Living almost exclusively in the present, they pay little heed to what they must do to prepare for the future. They don't plan ahead, or if they do make an attempt to plan, their efforts are cursory and unrealistic.

Some decisions will be relatively easy for your child to make and will be relatively spontaneous ("I'm going to buy the red shirt. It will match the outfit I bought last week.") In other situations, your child should be able to anticipate with little difficulty the future implications of a particular choice ("If I get into a fight with my brother about who rides in the front seat, Mom will get mad and won't take us to the amusement park this afternoon.") Sometimes, however, the outcome will be in doubt until the situation "plays out" ("If I tell him I like him, he might reject me.")

Choices with future implications may involve few risks, or they may involve grave risks ("We could go swimming in the tide pool where the water is shallow, or we could swim out to the sandbar even though the water seems very choppy.") The risks may be highly unlikely or highly probable ("I might not get an A on this test if I don't review my notes" or "He's really into drugs. If I accept a date with him and go to the party with his friends, we could get arrested.") When making a decision, your child may have a "lock" on the situation ("I just need to complete the report, get a minimum of B, and I'll have an A– in the course), or the decision may be a "crapshoot." In this case, all your child can do is make his best choice, "throw the dice," and hope for the best ("I'm not certain Mr. Tanaka will give me a good recommendation to college because I only got a B- in his class, but I think he likes me because I worked hard. I think he's my best chance.")

Despite the most careful analysis and most meticulous risk assessment, there are no guarantees that things will turn out as planned. The best you can do is show your child how to make "educated" predictions and intelligent, calculated choices that reduce the chances of disappointment, failure, or harm. The steps include:

- Analyzing the situation carefully
- Resisting the temptation to respond impulsively
- Utilizing logic and reason
- Assessing the risks
- Responding to challenges and problems with balanced emotions and critical intelligence
- Identifying the desired outcome
- Identifying a fallback position
- Weighing the pluses and minuses of each option
- Considering past experiences
- Foreseeing possible glitches
- Utilizing intuition
- Planning strategically

Your child must realize that if she's serious about becoming a scientist, she'll need to work hard, plan strategically, and make sacrifices. To attain her goal, she'll also have to make many judicious, future-directed decisions along the way.

Ideally, your child will factor into her decision-making process her previous positive and negative encounters and the wisdom and insights she's derived from these experiences. Of course, the irony is that your child may *not* have any previous experience with the particular issue with which she is wrestling. If her experiential data base is limited, your guidance can be especially vital.

To reduce the risk of flawed decisions, encourage your child to get into the habit of asking a series of key future-oriented questions:

What outcome would I ideally want in this situation?
Is this outcome realistic and attainable?
What are the potential barriers, glitches, and challenges?
What have I learned from past experience in similar situations with similar conditions?

What problems might I face?

How can I neutralize the problems and knock over or detour around the obstacles?

Who can I go to for advice?

How can I avoid repeating mistakes?

How can I increase the odds of getting what I want?

Should this questioning procedure indicate the odds are poor or the risks are high, your child will ideally factor this into her decision-making process. She may choose to proceed or not proceed. When the situation plays out, her choice may ultimately prove to be wrong, but at least her decision was calculated and reasonable. Despite occasional miscues, the chances of her making good decisions are significantly improved if she *steps back and considers the future implications of her choices before acting on impulse.* For example, you would obviously want her to consider the future implications of being disrespectful to her math teacher. You would also want her to recognize that this behavior is likely to alienate him and that he might retaliate by lowering her semester grade. When she begins to work, you would want her to consider that if she lies to her supervisor, she's jeopardizing her job. You would want her to recognize that this lie could create major problems for her. At the same time, you would also want her to consider the issues of honesty, morality, and ethics (see Chapter 4).

Children carry the imprint of their childhood training with them through life. A child may one day become an officer in a bank. He may overextend himself financially and may be tempted to embezzle desperately needed money from the bank. This temptation may be fleeting, or he may actually consider embezzlement as a viable option for extricating himself from his problems. At this critical juncture, it's vital that he step back and consider the temptation carefully and objectively. If he's able to think rationally and has engraved the procedure of asking himself future-oriented questions before acting impetuously, he'll realize that it's virtually certain he'll be caught, prosecuted, convicted, and sent to prison. The bottom line is that he must find another way to extricate himself from his problems.

Despite good planning, there's always the possibility that the unexpected may happen. Someone may act differently than anticipated. Conditions may change quickly. Acts of God may upset the best plans and most carefully thought-out choices. The coach who recruited your daughter to play basketball at a university may be fired. The company your daughter wanted to work for may hire her and then fire her because management has decided to downsize. Even these unanticipated and clearly devastating setbacks can have value and expand your daughter's experiential data base. If she's strategic, she'll analyze and learn from her negative experience. She'll use *in the present* the wisdom and insight she has derived *from the past* to guide her actions and choices *in the future.* Her ability to utilize this time-based learning curve will profoundly affect her success in life.

Trial and Error

Your instinct to protect your child from pain and danger should not be used as a rationale for preventing him from having valuable trial-and-error experiences. Some of your child's most meaningful insights are derived from mistakes: His friend may betray a secret, or he may fall off his bike because he didn't take time to tighten his handlebars. Or he may get an A on a test because he used a highly effective new study technique. From both negative and positive experiences, he'll learn whom to trust, how to keep safe and healthy, and what steps to take to be successful. The information will form the foundation for his evolving wisdom. By urging him to store and refer to his trial-and-error experiences, to figure out what went wrong, and to use the acquired data to guide his future decisions and actions, you're helping him acquire insight. His data base of trial-and-error/cause-and-effect experiences will be an invaluable resource that he can use to avoid calamities down the road.

Points to Remember about Trial and Error

- Trial-and-error experiences produce insight and wisdom, and enhance intuition.
- Carefully analyzed miscalculations provide vital learning-curve data.
- Miscues enhance your child's awareness of cause and effect.
- Wisdom and insight are cumulative and are acquired through reflection about both positive and negative life experiences.

Deciding whether or not to intervene when your child faces a tough call that could have potentially serious repercussions can be traumatic for parents. There are many situations in which trial-and-error experimentation should not be an option for your child. In such situations, your guidance or direct intervention may be vital. Obvious examples include experimenting with drugs, associating with teenagers who manifest antisocial or criminal behavior, making blatantly flawed school-related choices, and taking potentially catastrophic physical or emotional risks. You would also need to intervene if your child's actions indicate he's seriously depressed or potentially suicidal. Your child may resist your guidance or intervention, as teenagers often do. He may argue that his actions are not dangerous, he doesn't care about graduating from high school, the person he's dating is not taking drugs, his friends are "cool," or he's not depressed. If you cannot sort things out together, you'll need to see a well-qualified mental health professional to help you defuse the resistance and find a workable resolution to the problem.

From time to time, you'll need to make difficult judgment calls about whether to encourage or discourage trial-and-error experimentation in a particular situation. Obviously, you must factor safety considerations into your deliberation. Although experiential learning curves can be invaluable, they can also be counterproductive or even deadly. Most parents would agree that it would be very dangerous to allow a sixteen-year-old to hitchhike across the United States with a friend or to allow a sixteen-year-old girl to date a twenty-five-year-old divorced man. Each situation that poses potential risks for a child also poses a potential dilemma for parents. You clearly cannot permit trial and error when the wrong choice could prove catastrophic (for example, going to a party in a gang-infested area of town). As a responsible parent, you have a compelling obligation to establish reasonable boundaries, safety nets, and support systems for your child. You may conclude, however, that other situations would be an appropriate context for trial and error (for example, a child's decision to invite, or not invite, a popular but "stuck up" child to her birthday party). Because the line demarcating appropriate and inappropriate trial-and-error experimentation is not always clear, you must trust your intuition.

The need to experiment with trial and error will vary among children, and their motivation or lack of motivation to experiment is often linked to personality type. Children who are impulsive, oblivious to danger, thrilled by risks, particularly strong-willed, or very self-confident will be more insistent that they be allowed repeated opportunities for trial and error. Although these children may discount or be unaware of the risks, the risks will be very apparent to their parents. Such children tend to climb trees they shouldn't climb and ride their bikes down treacherous trails they shouldn't take. They like challenges and seem to enjoy the adrenaline rush. Usually things turn out okay, but occasionally something goes wrong, and a broken wrist or broken collarbone results. All you can do is vigorously discourage (or forbid) blatantly dangerous behavior and hope that your child derives wisdom from reasonable trial-and-error experiences.

Some children are at the opposite end of the experimentation gamut. These children are extremely cautious about taking risks. Tentative and even fearful about trying anything new, they often look to their parents for guidance and counsel whenever they're faced with difficult decisions that might involve even minimal danger (for example, crossing a slow-moving stream, using rocks as stepping stones). Because they are more tentative, these children rarely act impulsively. Their fears may cause them to miss out on many valuable (and relatively safe) learning experiences.

Children who are emotionally needy and insecure are typically quite dependent on their parents. They don't like to venture outside their comfort zone (that is, their circle of friends, their routines, or their "home turf"). Lacking self-confidence, they are less adventurous and tend to resist experimentation. (Unfortunately, the crime and violence that is rampant in so many communities has contributed greatly to the insecurity and fear many children legitimately feel. These children might be far more adventurous if they weren't afraid for their lives.)

Given the range of personality types and the different levels of emotional independence that children have, you must determine the appropriate trial-and-error guidelines. Certainly, you must factor your child's age and level of emotional and physical development into this decision. You must also recognize that as your child becomes older and more independent, your options to intervene (either diplomatically or autocratically) will be reduced and your control over her daily actions will diminish. Establishing reasonable boundaries and examining these boundaries with your child during the formative years is both strategic and pragmatic.

interactive activity

Age Range: 6–14
Objective: Learning to Differentiate Right from Wrong

ASSOCIATED PRESS

Town Is Angry at Teenager Accused of Killing a Swan

Manlius, N.Y.

The father of a 17-year-old boy accused of sneaking into a park and beheading a swan named Obie says he can't understand what all the fuss is about.

Daniel Doney has received threatening calls and letters since the swan was killed April 30 while defending his nesting mate. Nearly 100 people, the majority angry, showed up for the boy's arraignment Thursday night.

About 30 people peppered the boy and his lawyer with verbal abuse as they left the courthouse.

The boy's father, Floyd Doney, said he also caught a woman trying to put a "swan killer" sign on his front door. Daniel no longer goes to Fayetteville-Manlius High School because it would be "too dangerous" for him, said his lawyer, Mark Blum.

"All this over a . . . duck," Daniel's father said. "I thought we lived in America where you're innocent until proven guilty."

Daniel and a 15-year-old admitted they had been drinking the night the swan was killed.

The swan's head was left at the entrance to the police station in Manlius, near Syracuse in upstate New York. The 15-year-old admitted he tortured and stabbed Obie repeatedly, then broke his legs.

Questions and Issues for Discussion

1. Do you think people had a good reason to be upset with the boys that killed the swan?

2. Why do you think they were upset?
3. The boys killed the swan, but were there specific conditions that made this crime even more horrible? Let's go back into the article and identify these conditions. For example, what was Obie trying to do when he was attacked?
4. How do you feel about the way the boy's father reacted to his son's behavior? Why do you think he tried to justify or rationalize (explain these words) that his son's actions were not all that serious?
5. Do you think the boy's father should have defended his son despite what he did?
6. How do you think I would respond if you had hurt the swan?
7. How would you respond if you were the boy's father?
8. How would you rate the father's parenting skills?

1	2	3	4	5	6	7	8	9	10
Poor				Average					Excellent

9. What could the father have done *before* this happened that might have prevented it from happening?
10. Let's say a friend proposed that you sneak into a park and hurt an animal, what would you say to your friend?
11. What would you do if your good friends dared you to do something you didn't believe was right?
12. If your friends make fun of you because you're "scared," would this cause you to go along with their plan? If you would be tempted, tell me why.
13. What would you do if you discovered that someone you knew was torturing birds or cats?
14. Let's say you refuse to do something you feel is wrong. How willing would you be to lose a friend or become unpopular with other kids in order to follow your conscience and be true to your own personal sense of right and wrong?

1	2	3	4	5	6	7	8	9	10
Unwilling			Somewhat Willing					Very Willing	

15. Would you be willing to turn in a friend who did what the boy in the newspaper article did?

Triggers in Parent-Child Confrontations

Family run-ins are unpleasant for everyone. When parents and children are angry, they often say or do things in the "heat of battle" that hurts the other person. These triggers cause bombs to burst and shrapnel to fly. Statements such as "You're always trying to control my life!" (from children) and "This is just one more example of your irresponsibility and self-centeredness!" (from parents) are all but guaranteed to elicit anger, resentment, and defensiveness. Although there's certainly a downside to these altercations, family disagreements offer an opportunity for parents to model how effective reasoning skills and effective communication skills can defuse potentially explosive encounters.

When parents allow themselves to become "unglued," hostile, argumentative, vindictive, dictatorial, or irrational, they're modeling how *not* to handle family showdowns. Their emotionally charged responses will be imprinted in the child's unconscious mind, and she may replicate these responses whenever she confronts a crisis in her life.

Parents who intentionally avoid emotional triggers, neutralize volatile situations, and model how to argue rationally are demonstrating to their child that interpersonal problems are soluble when everyone remains reasonable. By demonstrating that you're willing to debate and argue fairly, make just compromises, and concede a point when appropriate, you provide your child with a powerful dispute resolution model she'll be able to use throughout her life.

Most families have predictable stimulus-response scripts. The child might say: "I don't have any homework. I did it in school." Then the parent might respond: "Even if you don't have any homework assigned, which I'm not certain is true, you can always begin reviewing for your next test." It's almost certain that a dispute will then ensue in which the child argues he has nothing to review and his parents argue that because he received a C- on his last history test, he has plenty to review. This exchange will probably be repeated in one form or another *ad infinitum*.

One might compare scripted family interactions to a videotape loop on which the same scene from an old sitcom you've seen many times before is continually replayed with the same emotions and the same outcome. The parents and the child enmeshed in a family script are simply pressing the "rewind" and "play" buttons over and over. The drama, albeit boring and predictable, can, nevertheless, become quite addictive.

Although it's easier said than done, you must do everything you can to alter counterproductive scripts that typically produce misunderstandings, hurt feelings, and resentment. If you're strategic, you can restructure and reframe family showdowns so that everyone can derive a positive payoff (a win-win situation). For example, you might say: "I have a proposal. Study fifteen minutes each night this week for your next history test. I'll ask you questions about the unit on Saturday morning. If you know the material, we'll pack a picnic lunch and go fishing at the lake Saturday afternoon."

When you defuse a family run-in and successfully reframe the interaction, you're modeling for your child how to:

Diffuse emotionally charged encounters so that those in disagreement can communicate and reason more effectively.

Identify his own needs and objectives accurately.

See issues from another person's perspective.

Compromise when appropriate.

Capitulate when it's smart and strategic to do so.

Win what he wants or needs without making the other person feel he or she has lost (a win-win resolution—see page 156).

Produce positive results when arguments and disagreements arise.

These skills provide your child with potent conflict-resolution resources. You must be realistic, however. You cannot reasonably expect your child to acquire these skills if *you* don't consistently model them in the "heat of battle."

Angry and unhappy children may unconsciously manipulate discussions so that they inevitably deteriorate into altercations. Although it appears to defy logic, these children may actually be seeking a negative payoff. Their behavior is a red flag that signals emotional turmoil and a need for attention. In many cases, this behavior is a form of aggression. Your reactive anger and punishment recharge the self-sabotaging loop, and the negative payoffs often become integrated into an addictive and highly predictable script.

Children who are unhappy and angry generally act in ways that affirm their poor self-esteem. They might refuse to study and do poorly in school. They might associate with skinheads or join a gang. They might take drugs or become promiscuous.

If you conclude that your child is entangled in a chronically self-sabotaging script, and your attempts to communicate and reason with him have proven unsuccessful, you must seek professional help. A highly skilled psychologist, psychiatrist, social worker, or family therapist can help you and your child sort out the issues. You can then begin to realign the family dynamic and reduce the hostility, stress, and unpleasantness. The alternative is to allow the counterproductive situation to continue. Clearly, the consequences of this "strategy" would be disastrous.

---

interactive **activity**

Age Range: 6–14
Objectives: Difficult Decisions and
                      Reasonable Compromises

The Boy Who Didn't Want to Visit His Aunt

Jeremy was angry. He didn't want to waste an entire day visiting his aunt. He especially didn't want to have dinner there.

Jeremy had known for some time about the visit. He liked his Aunt Flo, and at first he was actually looking forward to going to her house. Aunt Flo was a great cook. But then he learned three days ago that one of his friends was having a party, and the cute girl he liked would be there. Why couldn't his parents go without him? Just because Aunt Flo was his dad's favorite sister didn't mean that he had to spend six hours visiting her and his dumb cousins. Jessie and Ronnie were much younger than he was, and he didn't have one thing in common with them. It was unfair of his parents to make commitments for him!

When Jeremy approached his dad and suggested he stay home, his father got upset. He told Jeremy that the trip had been planned for over a month, and Aunt Flo was very much looking forward to her favorite nephew spending the day. She would be disappointed and hurt if he didn't come.

Jeremy told his dad that he loved his Aunt Flo, but he had made plans to go to a party with his friends. He said that family get-togethers were boring, and he preferred to hang out with his friends.

At this point, Jeremy's father got mad. He told Jeremy he wouldn't allow him to hurt his aunt's feelings. They had made a commitment to visit her, and they would keep the commitment. He told Jeremy he could get together with his friends another time, and there would be other parties. He then informed Jeremy that the discussion was over and they would be leaving in thirty minutes. Jeremy stormed off to his room. It wasn't fair! It was his life, and his parents were always telling him what to do with it!

Questions and Issues for Discussion

1. Do you think Jeremy was justified in feeling angry that he had to visit his aunt?
2. Why do you think he was angry?
3. Were his parents justified in committing Jeremy to accompany them to visit Aunt Flo?
4. Do you agree with Jeremy's dad that Aunt Flo's feelings would be hurt if Jeremy didn't come to visit?

5. If Aunt Flo would be upset, does this justify insisting that Jeremy accompany his parents on the visit?
6. Whose feelings should be the priority in this situation?
7. Do you think Jeremy communicated effectively to his dad about his problem?
8. How might he have handled the problem more effectively?
9. Do you think Jeremy's dad handled the disagreement effectively?
10. How might he have handled the issues more effectively?
11. Have you ever been in a similar situation?
12. If this problem ever arose in our family, how would you suggest we handle it?

Guidelines for Responding to Your Child

1. If your child has difficulty empathizing with the father's dilemma . . .

   Parent: Have you ever made a commitment to do something and realized it would be more convenient to back out? Did you have any qualms about doing so? Have you ever had a friend who at the last minute backed out of a commitment to you? Describe the situation. How did it make you feel?

2. If your child believes Jeremy's father was "out of line" in making a commitment for his son without consulting him . . .

   Parent: Kids obviously have more power over their own lives when they get older and demonstrate they're mature and responsible. How do you think parents should handle the transfer of power? Should they do it all at once, or should they do it gradually? Do you think the parents of a fourteen-year-old have the right to make commitments for him?

3. If your child has difficulty understanding the issue of responsibility . . .

   Parent: Jeremy had known about the visit for some time and had not complained. It was only after he learned about the party that he wanted to back out. Do you think this was fair to his dad or his aunt?

4. If your child has difficulty empathizing with his aunt's feelings . . .

   Parent: Let's say you had a date and this person broke the date at the last minute to go out with someone else. How would you feel? Do you think this person could justify the decision of breaking the date at the last minute? Would you do the same thing to someone else? What would have been the honorable thing to do?

5. If your child has difficulty suggesting alternative ways to handle the argument between Jeremy and his dad . . .

   Parent: Was a compromise possible in this situation? Is there anything Jeremy's dad might have said that could have made his son less upset and resistant?

Without your guidance, feedback, empathy, and support, many of life's most important experiences can be difficult for your child to understand and assimilate. By intentionally expanding your child's awareness of his own attitudes, behaviors, values, and choices, you become a major contributor to his acquired storehouse of wisdom and insight. This wisdom and insight will produce good judgment, and good judgment will, in turn, produce many of life's most coveted rewards.

chapter 6

Dilemmas, Crises, and Run-of-the-Mill Problems

*R*ebecca knew she should be happy, but all she could feel was sadness. Her eleventh birthday party would be in ten days. She had prepared the list of kids she wanted to invite, planned the activities, and selected the cake (chocolate with hazelnut and raspberry filling). Yesterday she had been so excited about the party, she couldn't wait for March 13th to arrive. Today she was dreading the birthday she had been looking forward to for so long.

Rebecca's problem involved her best friends, Kristin and Amy. The three girls had been inseparable. They did everything together. Then something terrible happened. Kristin and Amy had a big fight, and now they weren't talking to each other. Both girls told Rebecca they wouldn't come to the party if the other was invited. The other kids were choosing sides. Those who liked Kristin best told Rebecca they also wouldn't come to the party if Amy was coming. Those who liked Amy best said they wouldn't come if

Kristin was coming. Both girls were urging their friends to boycott the party if they didn't get their way.

It was so unfair! The fight was over something dumb. Amy had accused Kristin of revealing a secret and telling everybody she really liked Martin. Now everything was ruined. Rebecca didn't even want to have her birthday party anymore.

Kids and Their Crises

Like adults, children periodically face crises in their lives. And like their adult counterparts, they sometimes have difficulty differentiating the minor from the major events. Certainly, a serious illness, the divorce of one's parents, an F in a required course for graduation, or trouble with the juvenile authorities would qualify as major calamities. (Some children may not be willing to admit that these are *bona fide* crises. Such denial is common when a problem is highly unpleasant or appears overwhelming and insoluble. To protect herself from feeling inadequate, a child may rationalize: "I don't care if I'm getting F's. I hate school!)

From an adult perspective, many children's dilemmas seem trivial. To the child, however, these upsets are significant traumas, and the emotional fallout can be devastating. Rejection, hurt feelings, and real or perceived humiliation from a seemingly inconsequential event can cause children to suffer intensely.

Your child may not be invited to a slumber party. She may quarrel with her best friend. She may be stood up for date. The pain will be every bit as intense as that of the adult whose boss does not invite her to a party for key employees being targeted for promotion, or who learns that her "good" friend has described her to other people as self-centered and shallow.

From the vantage point of an eleven-year-old, the unraveling of an eagerly awaited birthday party was indeed a legitimate trauma. Rebecca's world had crumbled. The feud between her two best friends shattered her fantasy and produced a chain reaction that enmeshed all of her friends. As is so often the case in a feud, others felt compelled to express their loyalty by taking sides.

Rebecca could see only one solution: cancel the party. She had become a victim in a battle that was not of her making. The scenario has its parallels in the adult world where bruised egos, pettiness, irrational behavior, and vindictiveness are all too common. The friends of a divorcing couple may reluctantly be forced to choose sides. Even those who normally think and act rationally may be reluctantly sucked into the quicksand.

Stepping Back for Perspective

Because children's life skills are limited by their "real world" experiences, they may respond impulsively and irrationally to complex, emotionally charged dilemmas. If they are to handle these difficult problems, children must learn to step back from the situation so they can rationally assess the issues. This emotional distancing permits greater objectivity which, in turn, permits clearer thinking and more effective problem solving.

Rational, dispassionate problem analysis can be challenging in the heat of the moment when there's a strong temptation to "shoot from the hip" and react emotionally. It's precisely at this point that rational thinking is most critical. For example, an impatient driver on a one-lane mountain road may try to pass you despite the oncoming traffic and a double yellow line. He becomes infuriated, honks his horn, and makes an obscene gesture that you see in your rearview mirror. You then become angry and beep your horn. This impulsive, emotional response could have disastrous consequences. The man may be a borderline psychopath recently released from prison. He could go berserk, force your car to the side of the road, and attack you with a tire iron.

It's reasonable to infer from the anecdote that Rebecca had never faced a similar crisis. Responding emotionally, she threw up her hands in despair and decided that the problem was insoluble. Although her parents might have suggested some viable solutions, she may have been too distraught and emotionally enmeshed in the crisis to accept their help.

Other solutions were also possible. Rebecca's parents could have taken "ownership" of the problem, called the parents of the two feuding girls, and set up a meeting to help the children resolve their disagreement. Although this type of direct parental intervention would have addressed the immediate crisis and would have probably put the party back on track, it would have also sent a clear message to Rebecca: "Mom and Dad are here to help you whenever you face a tough problem." This is, of course, a legitimate message to send to a young child in crisis. There is, however, a downside (usually unintended) to this message, namely: "You don't have to solve your own problems. You can *always* depend on us to rescue you." A child has little incentive to develop her own thinking skills, problem-solving resources, and emotional independence when such a tempting symbiotic support system is dangled in front of her.

There was another option. Rebecca's parents could have guided her through a problem-identification/problem-solving procedure that would allow her to figure out what *she* needed to do to resurrect her party. The instruction would have taught her a vital procedure for handling crises and would have provided her with a powerful problem-solving resource she would be able to use throughout her life.

The problem-solving procedure Rebecca's parents might have taught their daughter is called **DIBS***. The procedure, which is described in detail on the following pages, allows children to achieve the requisite emotional distance from a problem so that they can get an objective, rational handle on the issues, think clearly, and develop a viable solution.

***DIBS**, a proprietary problem-solving technique, is an integral component in the strategic thinking/study skills programs that I have written for elementary, high school, and college students.

The first step in solving any problem or crisis is to *define the problem accurately*. This is easier said than done. Because children wrestling with a problem tend to get caught up in the symptoms and emotional fallout from the problem, they often have difficulty identifying the actual problem. For example, your child may complain that her teacher is unfair and mean when, in fact, the teacher is responding to your child's misbehavior in class. If the real problem is your child's behavior, and she doesn't want to admit this, then she's denying her responsibility for eliciting her teacher's "unfair or mean" response. This tendency to deflect blame makes the problem-identification and problem-resolution process even more challenging. It's not pleasant to admit one's role in creating a problem. (Please note: it's conceivable that the teacher is indeed being unfair to your child. This possibility, albeit remote, should certainly be considered if your child can cite concrete examples of the teacher's unfair behavior.)

If your child cannot identify a problem accurately and is preoccupied with the symptoms ("The teacher doesn't like girls. She's always picking on me and accusing me of disrupting the class."), she'll probably have difficulty resolving the problem. As is the case in mastering any new skill, problem-solving must be practiced systematically until the analytical process becomes automatic and the associated logic and reasoning become an integral part of the child's response pattern. Just as a basketball player must spend many hours practicing— until her brain can automatically compute the complex relationship between distance and arc and her muscles can imprint the eye-hand coordination requisite to sinking three-point shots consistently—so, too, must a child practice problem solving until her brain imprints an efficient procedure for breaking problems down into their component parts and for putting the parts back together so that the problem is solved. This "divide and conquer" process is central to all problem solving.

As you examine how DIBS is used to solve Rebecca's crisis, please note that *you must take the time to study the method carefully before guiding your child through the steps*. You'll probably find that the most challenging component in this method is Step 1: defining the problem. Don't be surprised if your child gets entangled in the *symptoms* or the *causes* of Rebecca's problem and struggles to pinpoint the *actual problem*. For example, your child may say the problem is that Rebecca's friends were angry at each other. This is certainly true, and they were indeed angry. It's also true that their feud was a major causative factor in the crisis. The actual problem for Rebecca, however, is more basic: her party is in jeopardy. Learning how to strip away the symptoms and identify the actual problem requires practice, not only for children, but also for adults!

Using the DIBS Problem-Solving Method

The word **DIBS** is an acronym for

> **D**efine the problem
> **I**vestigate the causes
> **B**rainstorm solutions
> **S**elect a solution to try out

Before modeling for your child how to use this method to solve Rebecca's problem, carefully study the technique. You must understand and master the procedure before you can competently teach it. You'll be provided with many opportunities in this chapter to guide your child through the process. By the time you complete the chapter, your child (*not you!*) will know how to analyze the problem, examine the underlying issues, and devise solutions.

Define the Problem:	Rebecca's party may be ruined.
Investigate the Causes:	Kristin and Amy are angry at each other.
	Each refuses to go to party if the other is invited.
	Other children are taking sides and have threatened not to attend.

Brainstorm Solutions:	Talk with Kristin and Amy and try to help them patch up feud.
	Invite either Kristin or Amy, not both.
	Convince Amy and Kristin to come to party even though they are angry at each other.
	Invite Amy and Kristin and persuade other kids to come to the party even if the feuding girls decide not to.
	Ask parents to talk to parents of Amy and Kristin and to parents of other kids.
	Cancel the party.
	Postpone the party.
	Have the party even if some kids don't come.
Select Solution to Try Out:	Talk to Kristin and Amy and try to help them patch up feud.

Examining the Process

The specific **Define**, **Investigate**, **Brainstorm**, and **Select** steps that appear above are models. Your child may come up with different brainstormed ideas or may select another solution to try. Encourage your child *not* to "edit" her ideas (be highly critical) when brainstorming. Brainstorming is the spontaneous, creative part of the method. She may come up with "way out" or even silly ideas that she may subsequently reject, but she should allow her mind to "wander freely" through a range of possible solutions when she brainstorms. It would be a good idea to record these ideas on a form that allocates space for each of the DIBS steps. The format might look like this:

DIBS PROBLEM-SOLVING METHOD

D : _____

I : _____

_____

_____

_____

B : _____

_____

_____

_____

S : _____

You could then make several photocopies of this form to use with other problems described in this chapter and with actual problems your child will encounter in her own life. Emphasize that if the solution she selects doesn't work, she can always select another of her brainstormed ideas to try.

Your child may define Rebecca's problem somewhat differently from the modeled definition. For example, she might say: "Rebecca is upset because her friends may not come to her party." Although there should be some latitude, the thrust of her definition should parallel the model. At the risk of redundancy, it should be reemphasized that defining the problem is the most difficult step. Differentiating the actual problem from the fallout and associated emotions requires objectivity and logical thinking. Your child must discipline herself to step back and make a rational assessment when her natural inclination may be to respond emotionally.

Identifying the causes of a problem can also be very challenging for children. For example, let's say your son is doing poorly in school, and you encourage him to use **DIBS** to examine and handle the problem. Although he may need some guidance, ideally he will define the problem accurately: poor or disappointing grades. Confronting unpleasant problems can be difficult for a child (or an adult!) The temptation to avoid having to face the unpleasantness can be very strong, especially if you are causing the problem. Your child may attempt to protect himself emotionally by denying that he actually has academic difficulties. ("Don't worry, I'm doing okay. You know I can always pull out at least a C-.") He may also attempt to deflect responsibility by blaming someone else, or he may rationalize by citing conditions beyond his control. ("The teacher makes up unfair tests." "The teacher never tells us what his tests will cover." "You and mom made me go to that family picnic on the Sunday before the big test, and I didn't have enough time to study.") You must keep your objective clearly in mind: You want him to gain insight into *his role* in the situation. To avoid triggering defensiveness and resistance, you must guide him to this insight without frontally assaulting him with the "truth." You might say: "Are there risks in leaving things to the last minute and somehow trying to pull it off at the end?" "Why do you think a teacher makes up difficult tests? Is it unfair of him to try to find out how much you know and to want to challenge you intellectually?" "You're right, we did plan a family picnic. But you knew about it two weeks in advance. What could you have done differently? How could you have planned ahead?"

Your goal is *not* to prove your child wrong or make him feel guilty. Rather, your goal is to encourage honest introspection and to stimulate insight. You also want to help your child develop and refine his analytical thinking skills and recognize his role in creating certain problems in his life. Finally, you want your child to accept responsibility for defining and solving his own problems.

During the investigation phase, he might attribute his poor grades (the defined problem) to the teacher being boring. Although this may be true, you want him to realize that he may be using this as an excuse for his lack of effort. Children can become quite adept at rationalizing their behavior and attitudes and quite resistant to breaking the habit of denying responsibility.

If it becomes apparent during the investigation phase that your child is denying or deflecting responsibility for his school performance and is blaming the teacher for his problems, you must be patient and skillful in helping him identify and acknowledge the *actual* causes of the problem. Your attitude will play a pivotal role. If your child perceives you as highly judgmental and critical, he'll resist your attempts to help him achieve insight into his behavior.

Even though you may have serious doubts about some of the causal factors your child identifies during the investigative phase, allow him to list reasons that appear implausible to you. He may be right: his teacher may be mean, and his educational methods may be boring! (Unfortunately, many teachers do put their students' toes to sleep. Because they fail to teach creatively, their students get bored, misbehave, and, in some cases, are erroneously described as having attention deficit disorder. In Orwellian fashion, many of these children are then medicated into compliance.*) If you believe your child is in denial about his behavior, gently help him consider other possible explanations for the problem. Frontally assaulting your child with the "truth" as you perceive it will probably cause him to become defensive and resistant. If he "turns off" to the DIBS method because he feels assaulted, you've clearly defeated your purpose. With sufficient practice, denial of responsibility and distortion of the truth can become an ingrained behavior pattern. Your ability to help your child expand his awareness and understanding of his behavior hinges on your being empathetic, sensitive, and patient.

Discuss your child's explanations with him nonjudgmentally, even if some of these explanations are improbable. *Listen to what he is saying.* During the brainstorming section, explore ways he might handle the teacher's "boring" style more productively. You might say: "Let's assume your teacher is boring. I certainly understand how this can make learning less enjoyable. Although you probably can't change your teacher's style or make him more interesting, I wonder if you could somehow

---

*See my book *1001 Ways to Improve Your Child's Schoolwork* for more information.

make the material more exciting so that you can get more involved in studying and get a better grade on the next test. You're studying about lasers. Perhaps we could go to the library and look at some reference books and find out some of the new uses for lasers. I read in the newspaper that lasers are being used in plastic surgery. Doctors actually use them to remove scars and even tattoos. I'd certainly like to know more about that."

You want your child to realize that *he* has a responsibility to solve *his* problem (that is, poor grades). You also want him to realize that he must figure out how to deal with a less-than-perfect situation (that is, a boring teacher). His success in school, and subsequently in life, will depend on his being able to deal with reality, handle problems, and neutralize obstacles.

During the **S**election step of DIBS, encourage your child to select a solution that appears most likely to produce a successful resolution to the present problem. If this solution doesn't work, tell him not get discouraged. He can analyze what went wrong and then select another solution from the brainstormed list to try. Explain that this trial-and-error process (see page 166) will provide him with important data that he can put into his "mental computer" for future reference. You want him to understand that a "learning curve" is comprised of both positive and negative experiences. By analyzing setbacks objectively and learning from mistakes, he will acquire information and insight that will permit him to solve similar problems more effectively. Although it's certainly preferable to avoid making serious mistakes whenever possible, everyone occasionally makes a mistake or miscalculation. It's the price we pay for being human and imperfect. However, the smart person learns from his miscues, and, in so doing, turns negatives into positives. The key is to recognize when it is appropriate to experiment with trial and error and when it's inappropriate. He doesn't need to try crack cocaine to find out it's a poison that could kill him.

With sufficient practice, your child will go into a DIBS "mode" automatically when faced with a problem or crisis. At some point, he'll be able to run through the steps in his mind without having to write down the actual problem definition, causal factors, brainstormed ideas, and selected solution. This mental process will require practice. It will also require that you provide copious amounts of encouragement, empathy, and affirmation.

Practicing DIBS

The short scenarios below will offer you and your child an opportunity to practice DIBS. You don't need to do all the practice exercises, although you certainly can if you're both enjoying the activity. You may want to select scenarios that are most relevant to your child's age and life experiences. Another option is for you and your child to make up your own scenarios and work together to solve these problems. A third option is to examine *real-life problems* your child is currently experiencing or has experienced. **A word of caution**: if your child is initially reluctant to focus on personal problems, respect her desire for privacy. She may first have to be convinced that DIBS works and that she can trust you with intimate information before she would be willing to analyze personal problems with you. Trust hinges on your child feeling you're empathetic, nonjudgmental, and noncontrolling. Trust is vital in the case of teenagers who are highly protective of their privacy and who are often beset with identity crises and social dilemmas. During this difficult and confusing developmental stage, teenagers want more independence and control over their own lives and may perceive their parents as the "enemy." To interact successfully with a teenager, you must use finesse and be respectful and sensitive. If you're intrusive or heavy-handed, you can count on eliciting resentment and resistance.

As you work with your child, maintain a positive, supportive attitude by saying, for example, "This is an opportunity for both of us to learn how to use this technique."

Remember that our goal is to help your child develop the ability to think analytically and solve problems.

Common Sense Guidelines for Making DIBS Work

- Recognize that a *perfect* solution (or the one *you* would choose) is not required for your child to benefit from DIBS and to improve her problem-solving skills, especially when she is first learning the method.
- Remind yourself that your child's skills will improve with practice.
- Be affirming.
- Be patient.
- Be sensitive to your child's feelings, especially when examining real (as opposed to hypothetical) problems.
- Allow your child to have a different perspective on issues.
- Guide your child gently to an expanded awareness of causal factors and possible solutions.
- Acknowledge your child's efforts and expanding skills in problem solving.
- Gear your expectations to your child's level of development and maturity.
- Encourage creative solutions.
- Have fun.

Practice Scenarios for DIBS

D = **DEFINE** the problem (say exactly what the problem is).

I = **INVESTIGATE** what is causing the problem.

B = **BRAINSTORM** as many solutions to the problem as you can.

S = **SELECT** an idea to try out as a possible solution.

Complete the following practice scenarios on separate pieces of paper.

1. Your friend wants to borrow your bicycle. The last time he borrowed it, he scratched it and broke your gear shift.

D*: _____

I : _____

_____

_____

_____

B : _____

_____

_____

_____

S : _____

2. Your friends want to go to the amusement park on Saturday, but you've told your parents that you will do some chores at home that you've been putting off for several weeks.
3. Your teacher has been lowering your grade because your math homework has "silly" mistakes.
4. You've missed a week of school because you had the flu, and you've fallen behind in all of your classes.
5. Your sister has been telling your parents that you've been teasing her, and you've been punished twice.
6. Your parents say you're not spending enough time doing your homework, and they've told you that you can't watch television on school nights.

---

*The accurate **D**efinition of this problem is: "I don't want to lend my bicycle to my friend, but I also don't want him to be mad at me." The **I**nvestigative step (causes) might be: "My friend is irresponsible." "I had to spend money to repair my bike." The **B**rainstormed ideas might be: "I'll charge a deposit." "I'll refuse to lend my bike." "I'll ask for collateral." "I'll lie and say my bike is broken" (a not-very-ideal solution).

7. Someone is spreading a false rumor about you in school, saying that you cheated on a test.

8. You made plans to go with your friends to a movie, and your parents want you to baby-sit for your younger brother so they can go to a party.

9. You suspect a friend may have stolen something from your house. Your parents have noticed that several of their videotapes and CDs are missing.

Using DIBS to Neutralize Family Disagreements

DIBS can be a powerful resource, not only in your child's life, but in your own life. You can use the method to get to the heart of virtually any problem or misunderstanding. It can be especially effective when you become entangled in predictable, counterproductive, emotionally charged arguments that strain family relationships and interfere with effective communication. By helping your child accurately identify the problem (for example, "I feel that you're not giving me enough freedom."), dispassionately investigating the causal factors ("I feel that you don't trust me."), and creatively brainstorming solutions ("To convince you I deserve more freedom, I'll prove during the next two weeks that I can be responsible in school and make wise choices."), these conflicts can usually be resolved. DIBS can help you avoid the emotional "triggers" that make children defensive and resentful, parents frustrated and angry, and everyone unhappy.

For practice, ask your child to identify and describe a predictable, repetitive family conflict. (If she's reticent or finds this emotionally threatening, you may help her by suggesting a scenario that is *not* emotionally charged. For example, you might select the issue of taking responsibility for cleaning *her* cat's litter box.) Then ask her to use DIBS to find a solution to the problem. Have her sit at her desk or the kitchen table and do all four steps on her own. Ideally, she'll be able to do so after having completed the practice section that appears above. If she cannot yet use DIBS on her own, have her work with your spouse or a cooperative older sibling who knows how to use the method. While she's doing this, use the format independently to work out your own solution to the same problem. Don't compare notes until you've both completed the process on separate pieces of paper. Once you've both finished, examine together each of your DIBS solutions. Be open-minded. Try to learn from each other. Be empathetic to the fact that your child may perceive certain issues differently. See if you can cooperatively produce a DIBS solution that incorporates the best features of both your plans. The alternative is to try each of your plans for solving the problem and see which one works best. Be objective. If your child's plan is better, acknowledge this. In some respects, the process is akin to playing chess with a child who has just learned how to play. You want to challenge her, but you may deliberately make some mistakes so she doesn't get discouraged. Your goal is not to prove that you have better problem-solving skills. Rather, your goal is help your child improve her own skills and develop self-confidence.

At all costs, make this interaction with DIBS fun! Your goal is *not* to use the time you're spending together for recriminations about a pet peeve. Rather, your goal is to teach your child a problem-solving method that she will ideally be able to use throughout her life.

Your child will undoubtedly want her plan to work best, and she'll want to show you how good she is at solving problems. This is precisely what you want to happen! It goes without saying that you should acknowledge and sincerely affirm her. Let her know how proud you are of her problem-solving skills.

Most difficulties can be resolved in several different ways. Some solutions may be better than others, but there may not be a consensus about this. Evaluating the efficacy of a particular solution can be quite subjective. For example, Republicans and Democrats may propose very different solutions to the problem of homelessness. If both plans are tried experimentally, each political party would be biased in assessing the effectiveness of their respective strategies, unless, of course, there's indisputable evidence that one program is unequivocally better than the other.

If your child's plan doesn't work, be sensitive when pointing this out. You don't want to demoralize her. You might say: "That was a good try. Sometimes, even the best strategies don't work. You discover that you've run into an unexpected glitch, and you have to make changes. A football coach may have an excellent game plan, but the other team may react differently than he anticipated. On the sidelines, he and the team will have to make adjustments. When your plan doesn't work out, you go back to the drawing board, try another brainstormed solution, or take a fresh look at the problem and brainstorm some new ideas. This is what it means to learn from mistakes. We all make them, but smart people learn from them."

Using Goal-Setting to Solve Problems

Although DIBS is a powerful resource for solving problems and dilemmas, *goal setting* is another highly accessible and effective problem-solving option. Your child may not realize it, but she's probably already using this method to handle many of the difficult situations she encounters. Let's say she's not doing as well as she would like in her history class. She might say to herself: "If I want a B in this course, I'll have to study at least forty minutes each night for the next five days so that I can get at least an A- on the next exam." Without necessarily being conscious of her problem-solving procedures, she has defined:

The Problem:	her current grade in history
The Challenge:	improve her grade
The Long-Term Goal:	a B in the course
The Short-Term Goal:	an A- on the next exam

By establishing a specific long-term goal and by creating specific short-term (or interim) goals (such as study longer, study with a friend, etc.), she addresses the challenge and resolves the problem. *If she achieves her specific goal, she has, in effect, produced a solution to her problem.*

Despite the fact that your child may not be aware that she is using goal-setting as a problem-solving resource, her unconscious mind has, nevertheless, set in play a sequential series of steps intended to resolve the problem. Let's look at how this plan might appear if it were represented on paper as a conscious, systematic strategy. You will note that the short-term goals have been expanded and amplified and very specific data have been included.

Problem:	My grades in history are not as good as I would like.
Challenge:	Get a minimum of B as my course grade in history.
Long-Term Goal:	Get at least a B in history.
Short-Term Goals:	Get an A- on next exam.
	Study at least 40 minutes for 5 nights.
	Study a minimum of 2 hours over weekend.
	Reread assigned unit in textbook.
	Recopy class and textbook notes.
	Study with Kelly over weekend.
	Make up practice test questions.
	Answer practice questions.
	Review all previous quizzes.

The short-term or interim goals are the steps your child would need to take to attain the long-term goal, meet the challenge, and resolve the problem. These steps in the Goal-Setting Method are similar to the brainstorming section in DIBS. The critical difference, however, is that in the Goal-Setting Method, your child implements *all* the ideas as opposed to selecting one idea to try out.

Whereas DIBS can be especially effective in helping your child define and resolve a thorny or perplexing problem in which there may be complex, underlying issues, the Goal-Setting Method can be especially effective in helping your child develop a strategy for solving a more obvious problem in which there may not be complex or perplexing significant underlying issues. For example, let's say your daughter uses the Goal-Setting Method to improve her history grade, and she develops the plan described above to address the challenge. She subsequently realizes, however, that she's procrastinating. At this point, she could use DIBS to **D**efine this new problem with precision ("I'm procrastinating"). She could use the **I**nvestigate step of DIBS to identify the causal factors ("I'm having trouble concentrating," "I'm having difficulty prioritizing my schoolwork over my social life," etc.). She could then **B**rainstorm ("I could make up a study schedule." "I could limit my social life this week and go out with my boyfriend on Saturday night.") Finally, she could **S**elect a reasonable solution to try out ("I'll set up a study schedule and discipline myself to keep to it.") This procedure demonstrates how the two analytical thinking strategies *overlap* and can be used in tandem or sequentially to solve problems.

Although many children unconsciously use goal-setting as a problem-solving resource in certain contexts, they may not realize its application in other contexts. For example, your fifteen-year-old son may realize his batting average is low because he's swinging the bat a split-second too late. He decides that he wants to improve his hitting (the challenge and problem), and he asks his high school coach to help him improve his timing (the long-term goal). He may decide to stay after practice for fifteen minutes of private coaching and spend several hours practicing in the batting cage during the weekend (short-term goals). If he attains his short-term and long-term goals, he has met the challenge, and he will have ideally resolved the problem.

Another teenager may be upset and angry at his parents because they've taken away his driving privileges. They've explained that they've done so because he's not spending enough time studying. He could use the Goal-Setting Method to regain their confidence in his work ethic and to solve the problem.*

Problem:	My parents have taken away my driving privileges.
Challenge:	Convince my parents that I'm spending sufficient time studying.
Long-Term Goal:	Get back my driving privileges.
Short-Term Goals:	Spend a minimum of two hours studying on school nights during the next two weeks.
	Get good grades on tests and papers and show these to my parents.
	Demonstrate to my parents that I'm serious about my studies.

The child who learns to use goal-setting to solve problems has acquired a powerful resource for meeting life's challenges. One of the major advantages of the Goal-Setting Method is that it can often circumvent the need to analyze the underlying issues. It is practical, expedient, and fast, and it requires far less introspection. This can be very appealing to the child who wants to deal quickly with an irksome issue and get on with his life. The child simply needs to say: "This is the problem. This is the challenge. These are the steps I must take to solve the problem."

Many bright children do not intuitively recognize all the possible pragmatic applications of goal-setting as a problem-solving resource. Other children, who unconsciously use the technique in certain contexts, fail to recognize its potential use in other contexts. On the playing field, a child might say to

---

*He could also use DIBS as an alternative problem-solving method. Some children will prefer one method, and others will use DIBS in certain situations and Goal-Setting in other situations.

himself: "On ground balls, I've got to keep my eye on the ball and field it *before* looking at the runners and deciding where to throw the ball." The child has intuitively defined the problem: too many fielding errors. Although these are probably *not* the actual words the child would use in his mind to describe his goal-directed solution to his problem, he intuitively recognizes the challenge and prioritizes proper fielding of the ball before deciding where to throw it. He also intuitively realizes that he can solve the problem by establishing and attaining a specific defined goal: to improve his self-discipline when fielding ground balls. The child's actual analytical mental process will be quick and spontaneous. The words used above describe the child's nonverbal evaluative process and translate how his mind intuitively defines the problem and establishes a specific goal to address and resolve it.

Your goal is to make your child more aware that he can *consciously* choose to use the Goal-Setting Method when he is faced with virtually any problem that can be resolved through clearly defined goals, focused intention, strategic thinking, systematic effort, and perseverance. By practicing together how to apply the Goal-Setting Method with a wide range of problems or challenges, you can help your child make this powerful resource more accessible, "user friendly," and, ultimately, more automatic.

Practicing the Goal-Setting Method

The following scenarios provide opportunities for you and your child to practice the Goal-Setting Method. Your child doesn't need to do all the exercises. She may, of course, want to do them all if you're both enjoying the activities and she's feeling a sense of accomplishment. You may decide that it would be most productive to select only those scenarios that are especially relevant to your child's interests and level of maturity or that best reflect the types of problems she's likely to encounter.

The same words of caution applied in DIBS (see page 190) apply in teaching the Goal-Setting Method to your child. It's critical that you maintain a positive and supportive attitude ("This is an opportunity for both of us to learn and practice this technique").

Practice Scenarios Using the Goal-Setting Method

Sample problem: *Let's say you want to persuade me to allow you to have a party. I've said no. I'm upset with you because you haven't been doing your chores around the house.*

Problem:	I can't have a party because I haven't completed my chores.
Challenge:	To get Mom to change her mind and say "yes."
Long-Term Goal:	To convince Mom I am responsible about doing chores.
Short-Term Goals:	Write down all assigned chores
	Voluntarily add some non-assigned chores to list of chores.
	Each day check off the chores I've completed.
	Ask you to inspect the job I've done.
	Give you the completed checklist at the end of the week.
	Write up a signed "contract" agreeing to continue completing chores in the future.
	Ask you to reconsider your decision.

Choose at least three of the following problems to solve using the Goal-Setting Method (or substitute other real-world problems that your child is currently facing). Write down the steps and fill in the ideas your child develops. Your child may be able to do the problems without necessarily writing down the format, although this procedure would certainly reinforce mastery of the method.

1. You received a low grade on your last book report.
2. Your soccer coach benched you.
3. You need at least $15.00 to be able to go with your friends to the amusement park.
4. Your teacher told us that you're misbehaving in class (or not completing your assignments).
5. You want to get a good recommendation from a teacher so that you can get a particular summer job.
6. We are upset because we feel you're acting immaturely, and we won't allow you to get your driver's permit.
7. You want us to help you pay for a new bicycle.
8. You want to persuade us to allow you to stay up thirty minutes later on school nights.
9. You want to persuade us that you no longer need a baby-sitter on the weekends when we go out.

Figuring Out Who Owns the Problem

One of the most difficult challenges parents and children face is figuring out who owns a particular problem and who is responsible for solving it. Parents sometimes unwittingly take ownership of problems that rightfully belong to a child, or they may assign ownership of a problem to a child when it rightfully belongs to them. For example, let's say you're upset because your child is not keeping her room neat. Your child, however, seems perfectly content with the situation. As a parent, you may define the problem: "My child is a slob, and her room is a mess. I'm sick and tired of arguing with her about cleaning it up!" The condition of the room, however, may not be the problem from your child's vantage point. She may define the problem as: "My parents are always on my case about my room being a mess. I like my room the way it is. I don't mind if it's messy. Why don't they just leave me alone!"

Before you can solve this dispute, you must figure out who owns the problem. Inasmuch as *you* are concerned about the mess in your child's room, and she is not concerned about it, then *you,* the parent, own the problem. If you respond by punishing her and taking away her television or telephone privileges, then your child now owns a problem, but it's not the same problem you own.

The tendency to fall into the common, recurring scripted admonishment "Clean your room!" with the associated pre-dictable resistance and resentment is quite common. The script is dysfunctional, of course, but it's accessible and habit-forming. DIBS and the Goal-Setting Method are more effective alterna-tives. (A model for how to use these methods in the "clean your messy room" drama is given on pages 205 and 208.)

Let's now assume your child's English grades are being low-ered because there are too many spelling and grammatical mis-takes on her essays. You're upset, and you talk about the problem with a good friend. You tell her: "We're not doing well in English because there are too many grammar and spelling mis-takes on our essays." In this case, the use of the plural pronoun "we" and the possessive adjective "our" are red flags. You may not be consciously aware that you're using this pronoun or pos-sessive adjective, but the words signals that, on an unconscious level, you've taken ownership of a problem that rightfully be-longs to your child. Your child, however, may not consider low-ered grades on English essays to be a major concern. Your first challenge in dealing with this legitimately important issue is to guide her to the realization that *she does indeed have a problem* (lowered grades because of mistakes). Your next challenge is to help her develop a strategy for solving the problem. To meet both challenges, you'll need to use your best communication and teaching skills. (A model for how to handle the "improve your English grade" drama is also examined on pages 206 and 209.)

Figuring out problem ownership must *precede* any attempt to define and solve the problem (using DIBS) or to establish a goal to resolve the problem (using the Goal-Setting Method). For highly protective parents, relinquishing ownership of problems that rightfully belong to their children can be challenging. These parents may have an unconscious psychological need to play the role of savior or to be in control. One unfortunate repercussion of highly protective parental behavior is that the child may become dependent or helpless. This learned helplessness ("Mom will always be there to rescue me whenever I have a problem.") could become an engrained, albeit unconscious, personality trait that may undermine the child's self-esteem, self-confidence, and self-reliance throughout her life. Her unconscious mindset may become: "Why take chances, why work hard, why strive for personal goals? I could never do it on my own."*

Other parents have a very different reaction when faced with the challenge of figuring out appropriate problem ownership: they resist taking responsibility for resolving a family problem that rightfully belongs to them. For example, a high school student may complain that he can't study and concentrate at night because his younger sisters insist on cranking up the stereo and playing rock music. Although he clearly owns a problem, his parents also own a problem. They must figure out how to reduce the noise and create an environment at home that is conducive to studying and academic achievement. It's their responsibility to define, own, and solve this problem. If they don't, they have no right to complain about their son's grades. The onus rests on their shoulders.

In extreme cases, a child can become the scapegoat (the "identified patient") and be unjustifiably held responsible for causing a family disharmony that the parents created through their own choices and behavior. Denial-oriented parents might say or think: "If only Susan would behave and be nicer to her sister, our family would be much happier." At issue is whether the parents have overtly or covertly, wittingly or unwittingly, consciously or unconsciously communicated to Susan that they love her sister more and believe she is brighter, prettier, more charming, or more talented. If they have, they must be willing

---

*See my book *1001 Ways to Improve Your Child's Schoolwork* for a more comprehensive examination of the phenomenon of "learned helplessness" in school.

to take responsibility for their own behavior and they must be willing to work on "fixing" the family dynamic. This will probably require professional assistance. If, on the other hand, Susan has *inaccurately* perceived that she is less loved, this, too, will need to be addressed with counseling. Although Susan may own the problem, the entire family is clearly enmeshed in the problem, and the parents must assume a major role in finding a solution. To make Susan *exclusively* responsible for the family unhappiness is ineffectual and unfair.

Let's assume that Susan's parents are willing to accept partial or complete responsibility for Susan's perceptions. Before they can solve the problem, they must accurately define it. DIBS certainly lends itself to this.

Define: Susan feels unloved even though this is not true.

If after honest and objective introspection, the parents conclude that Susan's misbehavior is *not* attributable to mistakes they've made and that the problem exclusively belongs to their daughter (*this is highly unlikely!*), they would define the problem very differently. In this situation, the following would be more appropriate.

Define: We must find ways to help Susan examine her behavior and make appropriate changes and, at the same time, clearly communicate that we love her.

Another reasonable definition might be:

Define: We must help Susan take responsibility for her behavior.

Once appropriate ownership of the problem is determined and the problem is accurately defined, the **Investigate**, **Brainstorm**, and **Select** steps can proceed systematically and logically. Clearly, the content of these stages hinges on who owns the problem. Parents who accept ownership will identify different causative factors and produce different brainstormed solutions than parents who believe the problem belongs to their child. In this case, the goal is to help the child accept ownership of the problem and find solutions to *her* problem.

> ### *Modeling How to Use DIBS in the Real World:*
> ### *Defining the Problem, Assigning Ownership,*
> ### *and Solving the Problem*

The Messy Room Scenario

(Remember: the child does not believe there's a problem.)

<u>D</u>efine:
- *I* have a problem, and I'm going to use DIBS to solve my problem. Although I believe your room belongs to you, it's still part of the home in which our entire family lives. There are times when I must go into your room to put washed clothes away or change the sheets. I get upset by the lack of hygiene and the messiness. There's partially eaten food on your bed and on your dresser. Empty soft drink cans are on the floor. I'm afraid this will draw insects. We must find a compromise with which we can all live.

<u>I</u>nvestigate:
- You've told me that you feel your room is your own private domain to do with as you wish.
- You do not place the same value on order, hygiene, and neatness as I do.
- You don't want me to interfere.
- I want our home to be reasonably present-able if my friends or your friends should visit.
- I have to enter your room occasionally, and it distresses me greatly.
- I feel I have parental rights, which are within reasonable limits and apply to all rooms in the house.

<u>B</u>rainstorm:
- I could never again enter your room.
- I could leave the washed clothes outside your door, but you will have to agree to a minimum standard of neatness and cleanli-ness.
- You will be responsible for changing your sheets, but you will have to agree to a mini-mum standard of neatness and cleanliness.

> - You could pay for the exterminator if we get insects.
> - You could make a reasonable list of clean-up tasks that you would agree to perform each week, and I'll get off your case if you do these tasks.
> - I could autocratically require that you clean your room every day and impose a punishment if it is messy or dirty.
>
> **S̲elect:** - We can arrive at a compromise if you agree to do a reasonable list of clean-up tasks as agreed. (Assuming both the parent and the child are satisfied with the solution, it is a **win-win resolution**.)

If your child refuses to compromise, you'll either need to drop the issue or impose an autocratic solution. This will require a judgment call on your part. You must be prepared to create a positive context for reaching a mutually acceptable compromise to resolve the problem. To do so, you may need to explain that when compromising, everyone has to give up something. Compromising successfully is not the equivalent of feeling compromised. You give up something and you gain something. In a sense, you will either see the glass as being half-full or half-empty. If you value having something, then a compromise is a win-win resolution.

Modeling How to Use DIBS in the Real World:
Defining the Problem, Assigning Ownership,
and Solving the Problem

The Poor Grade Scenario:

Your child agrees she's doing poorly in her English class. You would need to guide your child through this application of

DIBS. Her insights may not necessarily parallel exactly those modeled below.

Define:
- I'm getting bad grades on my English assignments.

Investigate:
- I'm making too many grammar and spelling mistakes.
- I'm not carefully proofreading my assignments.
- I'm not budgeting enough time to complete the assignments.
- My effort and conscientiousness could be improved.
- My teacher is unreasonable.*
- I don't care about book reports and analyzing poems.
- My teacher is unfairly lowering my grades because of silly mistakes.

Brainstorm:
- *You* should proofread my work and find the mistakes.*
- I should do my assignments on a computer or a typewriter with a spell-check.
- I should allow sufficient time to proofread my assignments carefully.
- I should review the mistakes on my assignments and look for the ones I make over and over. If I can't figure out why they're mistakes, I'll ask my teacher.

Select:
- I'll write my papers on a computer with spell-check, and I'll budget enough time to proofread my assignments carefully.

---

* You want your child to consider all possibilities, even those that appear improbable on the surface. This also applies to the brainstorming section. You don't want your child to "edit" her ideas, as this will inhibit her creativity. She can always reject or discount implausible ideas during the **S**elect phase when she carefully evaluates her options and chooses the best.

To use DIBS as modeled above, you'll need the cooperation of your child. If she's resistant or denies there's a problem, the process will not run as smoothly as described. You must assure her that DIBS is not her enemy, but, rather, is a practical problem-solving tool she'll be able to use to solve many different types of problems in her life. If her ideas are not as insightful as those modeled, be patient, supportive, and affirming. Resist any temptation to say: "That doesn't make any sense." or "You can certainly come up with a better idea than that." If you're distressed by your child's insights, you might expand her range of ideas by saying "What do you think about this as a possibility . . . ?"

Modeling How to Use the Goal-Setting Method in the Real World: Defining Who Owns the Problem and Establishing a Goal to Solve It

The Messy Room Scenario

Problem:* ■ *I* have a problem. I believe your room belongs to you, but it's still part of the home in which the entire family lives. There are times when I must go into your room to put washed clothes away or change the sheets. I'm upset by the lack of hygiene and the messiness. There's partially-eaten food on your bed and on your dresser. Empty soft drink cans are on the floor. I'm afraid this will draw insects.

Challenge: ■ To reach a mutually acceptable compromise about your room.

---

*Defining the problem is the same in both DIBS and the Goal-Setting Method. In this case, the parent acknowledges *she* owns the problem, and she uses the method to define specific short-term and long-term goals, produce a compromise, and solve the problem.

Long-Term Goal:	■ Keeping your room sufficiently neat and clean so there's peace in the family and I can get off your case.
Short-Term Goals:	■ Remove all food before going to bed.
	■ Put dirty clothes in hamper.
	■ Hang up or put away any clothes that have been laying around for more than 24 hours.

Obviously, most parents would want their child to make her bed and put her possessions away. This may be asking too much, however, of some children, especially those who consider their rooms to be their private sanctuaries. You must be prepared to make reasonable compromises. In fact, even short-term goal #3 may be too optimistic. Deciding whether to press for hanging up clothes will require a judgment call. Using the Goal-Setting Method with a child is akin to negotiating a contract. You have to read the situation, define what objectives are realistic, decide how much leverage you have (it may *not* be very much with a resistant teenager!), and negotiate specific short-term and long-term goals with which everyone can live.

Modeling How to Use the Goal-Setting Method in the Real World: Defining Who Owns the Problem and Establishing a Goal to Solve It

The Poor Grade Scenario

Problem:	■ My poor grade in English.*
Challenge:	■ Reduce the spelling and grammar mistakes on my assignments and improve my grade.

*This assumes your child admits he has a problem. If he claims he doesn't care about his grade, the problem then belongs to you and would have to be defined differently. In this case, you might define the problem as: "I'm distressed by your poor English grade. I feel you're capable of doing better, and I have a responsibility to insist you make the effort to work up to your true ability. I'd like to help you develop a plan for improving your grade." Defining specific long- and short-term goals would require negotiation.

Long-Term Goal:
- Get at least a B in English this semester.

Short-Term Goals:
- Budget enough time each evening to check my work over carefully.
- Proofread each written assignment at least twice each evening.
- Look up the spelling of any word I'm not sure of (or use spell-check).
- Ask a friend to proofread my assignments in exchange for me proofreading his or hers.
- Speak to my teacher about any repeated errors I'm making so that I understand the mistakes and can be on the alert for them.

Practice Assigning Ownership of Problems

Read the following short scenarios with your child and decide who owns which problems. Have your child give his or her reasons for the decision.

1. We helped you study for a test, but you got a bad grade.
2. You lost your wallet and it contained the money you were going to use for Dad's birthday present.
3. We're upset because you and your brother (sister) are continually teasing each other, and it's driving us crazy.
4. You're doing so poorly in a class that you might fail the course and be required to take it again in summer school.
5. You got a ticket from a police officer for riding your bike at night without a light. You have to pay a fine.
6. You disobeyed our instructions and invited friends to the house on Saturday night while we were out.
7. We've grounded you because you haven't been doing your chores.

8. We're upset with you because the teacher says you haven't been handing in your assignments on time.
9. Your sister (brother) is borrowing your things without asking permission.

After assigning ownership of all the problems, select two (or more if you and your child are enjoying yourselves) and practice solving one using **DIBS** and the other using the **Goal-Setting Method**. If you wish, substitute a real-life problem from your own life that you could use as a vehicle for practicing problem solving. You and your child should discuss whether DIBS or the Goal-Setting Method would be more effective in solving either the following problems or any problem you might choose to substitute.

In the final interactive activity in this chapter, be prepared to share a personal problem with your child and ask her to help solve the problem. This procedure sends a clear message: you have confidence in your child's ability to think effectively and apply the problem-solving techniques you've practiced in the chapter. By examining a personal problem, you also model that sharing is a form of intimacy, which reflects trust and respect. Ideally, this will stimulate her to share her own feelings and problems with you.

Examining the Issues with Your Child

As you discuss the anecdote on the following page with your child, explain that this is a practice activity. Ask her to pretend that you're asking for help, even though you may not actually be an employer who would be faced with the described situation. Don't ask all the modeled questions. Encourage your child to ask *you* some of the questions. If you decide to use the anecdote as opposed to a real problem from your own life, you'll have to make up plausible answers to the questions your child asks. For example, she might ask, "How many people are you considering for the job?" You might reply, "three." Both of you will need to "play act" in this hypothetical scenario, which should be fun!

The questions which follow are intended to help your child get a better handle on the issues. You need not cover all the questions before you and your child decide on a method (**DIBS** or **Goal-Setting**) to define and solve the problem.

---

interactive activity

Age Range: 9–14
Objective: Evaluating Options and
Solving Difficult Problems*

Deciding Who to Promote

I have a problem, and I thought you might help me solve it. One of the people at the office is retiring. She was a wonderful employee, who worked for me for more than twelve years. I'll be very sorry to see her leave.

My problem is that I have to replace this person. I don't know whether I should give the job and the promotion to one of her assistants or whether I should try to hire someone from outside the company.

I have some good people on staff, but they don't have the skills or the training to do the job as well as I would like. The advantage is that they know my business better than someone from the outside. On the other hand, if I hire someone who has had more experience working for another company, this outside person would have certain skills my in-house staff lacks. There are two other important considerations. If I select a person within my company to promote, the people who are not promoted might be jealous and resentful. If I hire someone outside the company, my staff might become resentful, and this could hurt morale. I sort of feel like I'm between "a rock and a hard place." What would you do?

*Explain that this is a "pretend" problem. Feel free to substitute a real personal problem that you've experienced at work.

Questions and Issues for Discussion

1. Let's define the problem I've described as accurately as possible.
2. What would be the pluses and minuses of hiring someone from within the company? (Include those listed in the anecdote and any others you can think of.)
3. What would be the pluses and minuses of hiring someone from outside the company? (Include those listed in the anecdote and any others you can think of.)
4. Which method do you think would be most effective for solving the problem?
5. Choose one method (or, even better, practice using *both* methods) and develop a reasonable and practical solution to the problem. (Your child may enjoy the process and actually want to continue practicing. This would, of course, be ideal. If your child masters both procedures, she'll be far more predisposed to using them to solve real day-in and day-out problems.)
6. If you want to experiment with both methods, discuss the relative merits of each method in handling this problem.
7. Let's say one of my employees really wants the job. Pretend you're this person on my staff, and *you* want the job. (We'll have to pretend for this activity that you're not my child.) Let's use either DIBS or the Goal-Setting Method to define and solve the problem and produce a possible solution. You choose the method. If you want, we can try both methods. (By urging your child to look at a problem from someone else's vantage point, you're helping her become more empathic and sensitive to another person's perspective. This is a key prerequisite to solving disagreements.)

If after completing this activity, your child wants to continue working, ask her to describe a thorny problem in her own life, and then work together using both methods to solve it. Examine the pros and cons of each method in dealing with the particular problem. You might even select a problem described in the media (gang violence, drugs, AIDS) and use one or both methods to produce a solution. If, however, you see that your child is fatigued or losing interest, stop. You can always set time aside to practice the techniques later.

chapter 7

Deciding What Counts Most

*K*risten had a tough decision to make. She desperately wanted to work at the animal hospital during the summer, but she also desperately wanted to go to basketball camp.

When she had first asked the veterinarian if she could work for her, Kristen was both surprised and delighted when she said "yes." Her job would be to bathe and exercise the dogs who were staying in the hospital. She would be paid $25.00 a day for working six hours. It was a perfect summer job for a fourteen-year-old.

Kristen had decided in fifth grade that she wanted to be either a veterinarian or a physician. Working at the animal hospital would provide wonderful experience. The vet told her she could even watch some surgery at the clinic. Kristen realized the job would be a great opportunity to find out what was involved in being a real veterinarian.

Now, everything had become very complicated. Her parents had offered to send her to basketball camp for the month of July. She had been wanting to go for two years, but her parents couldn't afford it. Her father had recently gotten a better paying job, and her parents wanted to send her to camp as a special birthday present.

Kristen was an excellent athlete. She knew that going to basketball camp would improve her chances of making the junior varsity squad when she started high school in the fall. There was something else that made the idea even more appealing: her best friend Katie would be going to the same camp. Kristen knew they would have a great time together.

Kristen didn't like having to choose between the two appealing options. She wanted to do both things, but this seemed impossible. The vet told her she would have to hire someone else if Kristen couldn't work during the entire month of July.

As delighted as she had been about the working at the animal hospital during the summer, Kristen was equally excited about going to camp. She had to make a tough choice: Stay home and have a great summer job or go away to camp, have fun, and improve her basketball game. Her parents said they wouldn't try to influence her decision, but they did offer to help her look at the pros and cons of her options. What a dilemma!

Indecision

Choosing between two very appealing options can pose a major crisis for any child, especially when good arguments can be made for each option. Kristen's dilemma underscores how heart-wrenching it can be for children to make a difficult decision and feel confident they made the *right* choice.

As she struggled with her dilemma, Kristen must have felt like she was swinging on a pendulum. She would be decisive one moment and indecisive the next. She'd add up the plus and minus columns for each option and come up with a score. Then, she'd do the math again and come up with a different total.

There are no simple answers or guidelines for making tough choices. Despite a meticulous calculation of the pros and cons and the potential consequences, the decision often comes down to intuition. The person simply concludes: "This choice *feels* right." (See "Intuition," page 54.)

Intuition can certainly be a valid criterion for making a difficult choice, but in some situations, a more deliberate, systematic analysis can make the decision-making process less stressful. If Kristen were to analyze the issues strategically, she would ask herself a series of key questions that include

- What is the likely payoff for each option?
- What are my short-term goals?
- What are my long-term goals?
- How well does each option fit with my goals?
- What are my priorities?
- Is there any way I can "finesse" this situation so that I can get as much as possible from it?
- Can I "live" with my choice and not look back and try to second-guess the decision?
- If my first choice doesn't work out, do I want to leave the other option open?
- What's the worst that could possibly happen if I make the wrong choice?
- Can I adjust the timetable so that I can somehow do both things?

These practical questions clearly emphasize not only "future time" considerations and implications but also tactical planning. The questions may not necessarily resolve the dilemma, but they can reduce the anxiety and uncertainty associated with the deliberation process. In tandem with intuition, a careful analysis of the issues can often produce a viable, rational strategy for handling tough choices that involve more than one appealing option.

Examining the Issues with Your Child

Read the introductory anecdote with your child. It can be used with children from ages 8 to 14. You may also decide to use the anecdote with an older child. If you analyze it with a child under the age of ten, adjust your expectations so they are congruent with your child's level of maturity.

---

interactive activity

Age Range: 8–14

Objectives: Evaluating Pros and Cons and
                Making Difficult Choices

Questions and Issues for Discussion (anecdote found on page 215. For Parent-Response Guidelines, refer to pages 31–36)

1. If you were faced with the same situation, would you find this decision difficult?
2. What makes the decision difficult?
3. What issues do you think Kristen should consider as she wrestles with her decision?
4. Do you see any way out of the problem other than choosing either to work for the vet or to go to basketball camp?
5. What are the pluses of going to basketball camp?
6. What are the minuses of going to basketball camp?
7. What are the pluses of working for the vet?
8. What are the minuses of working for the vet?
9. If you tried to look into the future, would one option have better long-range benefits for Kristen than the other option? Why?
10. If Kristen decides to work for the vet and not go to basketball camp, how would you rate this decision?

1	2	3	4	5	6	7	8	9	10
Not Smart				Fairly Smart					Very Smart

11. If Kristen decides to go to camp, how would you rate this decision?

1	2	3	4	5	6	7	8	9	10
Not Smart				Fairly Smart					Very Smart

12. In the story, Kristen's parents offered to help her with her choice. If she asks for help, how would you rate this decision?

1	2	3	4	5	6	7	8	9	10
Not Smart				Fairly Smart					Very Smart

13. What would you do if you were Kristen?

As you and your child examine this anecdote and the related issues, it would be beneficial to explore alternative solutions that might help Kristen resolve her dilemma. For instance, she could offer to serve as a volunteer at the animal hospital during those weeks when she's not at camp. She might make arrangements to work at the animal hospital the following summer, or she might put off going to basketball camp until the following summer. Kristen could also offer to work for the vet on Saturday mornings during the school year. Explain to your child that these alternative solutions might not work. If this happens, Kristen would have to "go back to the drawing board" and brainstorm something else. At some point, she may "simply" have to make a choice and accept the fact that she can't get everything she wants.

Using Priorities to Make Choices

To attain her short-term and long-term goals, your child must be able to rank her responsibilities in order of descending or ascending importance. She must also learn how to rank options in order of appeal and viability. This process of establishing a hierarchy based upon specific criteria can simplify the decision-making process and make it less painful.

Many children intuitively prioritize when confronted with a decision, challenge, problem, or project that requires careful planning. For example, your daughter may be invited by her friends to go the mall on Saturday. Another friend may invite her to go with her family to a water slide. Realizing that she can go to the mall some other time and that an opportunity to go to the water slide doesn't present itself often, she would probably prioritize going to the water slide. (If she had already made a commitment to going to the mall with her friends, she might want to honor this commitment and sacrifice the water slide opportunity.)

Although many children do intuitively prioritize, others do not. These children do not realize that this procedure can help them get a handle on "tough calls" and seemingly overwhelming dilemmas. Your objective is to help your child realize that by stepping back from a problem and taking the time to establish her priorities, she can often simplify her deliberations and reduce wheel-spinning and counterproductive anxiety. This can be a very valuable insight. Once the procedure becomes a habit, choosing from among appealing options is usually less traumatic.

Establishing priorities is a relatively straightforward process. For example, Kristen could list all the pluses of working at the veterinary clinic. Then she could list all the pluses of going to basketball camp. To avoid inhibiting her thinking, she should initially create her list without considering the importance of each plus. Finally, the last step would be to rearrange the list in order of how important each issue is to her. Her final ordered list might look as follows: (Please note: this might not be the way *you* would prioritize the list. Ranking what's important involves logic, values, esthetics, *and* subjectivity. It requires personal decisions as to what counts most.)

Pluses of Working at Veterinary Clinic

I could get important experience working with animals.

I would have a much better sense of what it's really like to be a vet.

I would have an opportunity to see surgery and examinations.

I would make money.

If I do a good job, I could probably get a job at the clinic next summer as well. Perhaps I would be given more responsibilities so I could learn more.

I would get to spend time having fun with animals and helping those that are frightened and homesick.

I would learn how to groom and bathe animals.

If I do a good job, I could ask the vet for a letter of recommendation to college and, later, to veterinary school.

My experience at the clinic would probably impress the admissions committee when I apply to college.

Even if I decide not to become a physician or a veterinarian, my experience working with animals would be interesting.

Pluses of Going to Basketball Camp

I would learn a lot from the coaches, and my game would improve.

I would have a much better chance of being a starter on the junior varsity team next year when I start high school.

I'll have lots of fun.

I'll get to make new friends.

I'm a kid, and I should have fun during my summer vacation. There will be plenty of time to work later in my life.

Although the plus list for working at the veterinary clinic is clearly longer, this does not necessarily mean that these reasons outweigh those for going to camp. Kristen might decide that at fourteen, the most important thing is to have fun during her summer vacation. This would certainly be a legitimate conclusion. On the other hand, she might decide that the experience of working with a vet is more important than having fun, especially if she's serious about becoming a vet or a physician. Her choice could be easier if she can decide what her most important priority is— fun and sports or practical work experience that will help her confirm (or abandon) her current career orientation.

By acting as a sounding board and helping their daughter expand and rank her plus list, Kristen's parents could provide invaluable guidance. By suggesting issues she might consider, they can help her develop and refine her analytical decision-making skills. By showing Kristen how to prioritize and link her short- and long-term goals with her priorities, they can help her develop her planning skills. By allowing her to struggle with her choice (rather than telling her what she should do), they can affirm their faith in her judgment. Her parents are, in effect, saying: "Sometimes we have tough choices to make. The best we can do is consider the issues, figure out what we want most, look at what might happen in the future, make our decision, and accept the consequences. Occasionally, we'll make the wrong choice. If we do, we don't beat up on ourselves. We did the best we could, and sometimes things don't work out. That's part of life."

If your child chooses to respond spontaneously when faced with an important decision, you must make a judgment call about whether your intervention or guidance is appropriate. For example, she may say she's decided to take French in high school rather than Spanish. If you believe that her decision is too spontaneous and she hasn't considered key issues that should be factored into her decision, you may want to encourage a more conscious, systematic analysis of the issues.

DIBS and the Goal-Setting Method can be useful resources if, during the discussion of a particular issue, your child identifies specific problems that are influencing her decision or affecting her behavior. For example, she may realize that she gets distracted when she has to study something she's not interested in or that she experiences stress when she has to talk in front of the class.

Problem-solving and decision-making techniques often go hand-in-hand. In some cases, utilizing these techniques either concurrently or sequentially may the most effective strategy for handling a difficult issue (for example, first figure out what's most important, then establish specific goals). Your goal is to provide your child with a range of thinking, planning, and problem-solving resources. In a sense, these resources are analogous to having a well-equipped and well-organized shop in the garage or basement. When you need to do a repair job around the house, you have the tools to handle it.

Examining the Issues with Your Child

Read the anecdote below with your child and have him respond to the questions and issues that follow. This exercise can be used with children from ages 8 to 14. As you explore how establishing priorities can help you handle challenges, realize that younger children may not fully understand the realities of physical survival in a jungle. You may need to explain to your child why a particular item would be more vital to survival than another item. You may also need to help him patiently with his math. Be careful not to criticize your child for flawed judgment. He may put the rifle at the top of his list because he is frightened of jungle animals, whereas you might place water first. Certainly, a rational argument could be made for putting either item at the top (you might explore your respective rationales nonjudgmentally). Your goal is to expand your child's awareness and insight and to help him acquire facility in using priorities to solve problems. If you unwittingly criticize him, you'll probably make him defensive, and he will resist doing the activity with you.

---

interactive **activity**

Age Range: 8–14
Objectives: Establishing Priorities;
Planning; Anticipating
Potential Problems;
Thinking Strategically;
and Making Choices

How Can I Make It Work?

Paul was fascinated by the survival exercise he was assigned in science class. His teacher told the eighth graders he wanted them to apply what they had learned about human physiology and biology to a real-life situation. He wanted them to pretend they were bush pilots working for a U.N. relief agency. Their job was to drop off emergency medical supplies in a remote village in an African jungle. The village was over 700 miles from the nearest town. During the day, the temperature on the ground would be above 110 degrees Fahrenheit and the humidity would be 95 percent. The plane they would be flying had two engines and could seat two people. The rear compartment could hold 500 pounds of supplies.

The assignment was to design a contingency plan for an emergency landing. The teacher told them that they might be stranded in the jungle for two weeks so they had to be certain they had the necessary supplies to survive until a ground party could find them.

Each student was told to make up a list of survival gear to pack in the plane. Because of the weight of fuel and medical supplies the plane was carrying, the survival gear could not exceed 50 pounds. If it weighed more, they would not be able to carry enough fuel to make it to the village and back.

Figuring out what to pack was challenging. Paul had images of fighting off wild animals and surviving the terrible heat. After careful thought, he made up a list of items he felt were essential and the estimated weight of each item. Below is his list.

Item	Weight (in pounds)
2 Flashlights	$1/2$
Flares	1
Sleeping bags	2
Freeze-dried food	6
Charcoal	8
Tent	7
Fishing gear	3
Radio and transmitter	7
Rifle and ammunition	5
Flare gun	1
First aid kit and emergency medicines	2
Brightly colored signaling cloth	1

Chocolate and other candy for energy	2
Hatchet	1
Ten gallons of water	10
Knife	$1/4$
Cooking utensils	2
Matches and kindling	2
2 Canteens	$1/2$
Waterproof tarp	2
Maps	$1/4$
Toiletries (soap, sun block, toothbrushes)	1
Reading materials and games to pass time	2
Compass	$1/8$
Insect repellent	$1/2$

Paul was convinced he had included all the supplies and emergency survival gear he would need. When he added the weight of the items, however, he discovered the supplies exceeded the weight limit by almost 17 pounds! It was clear he would have to eliminate some items and reduce the weight of others.

Realizing he'd have to revise his list, Paul began the difficult process of deciding which supplies were not absolutely essential. He could certainly reduce the weight by replacing the charcoal with some other emergency cooking fuel. In fact, he only needed a supply of waterproof matches, as he would undoubtedly be able to find wood or leaves to burn in the jungle. By eliminating the charcoal, he'd save over 7 pounds. He decided he would only need one flashlight, and he could survive without a waterproof tarp. This would save 2 pounds. On the other hand, he could keep the tarp and use it as a tent at night. By eliminating the tent, he could save seven pounds. Each time he decided to eliminate an item, Paul could think of reasons not to eliminate it. For example, if he took only one flashlight, and it was damaged during the emergency landing, they'd be in trouble. Paul realized he would have to make a judgment call about the flashlight once he eliminated everything else.

The teacher advised the students to place each item on their list in order of priority. This meant placing the most important item or gear at the top of the page and listing the less essential items below it in descending order of importance. To help students understand the process of establishing priorities, the teacher wrote on the chalkboard three steps for prioritizing a list.

Steps for Establishing Priorities

1. Write down items essential to survival.
2. Number the list in order of importance (the most essential items should be at the top).
3. If necessary, eliminate items at the bottom of the list that are least essential.

Paul realized he couldn't survive for long without water. Not knowing whether they would be able to find water on the ground that they could boil and drink, he decided to make water the #1 item on his list. Although having reading materials and games to pass time would be nice if they made an emergency landing, these items weren't essential to survival and had a low priority. After listing all the gear in order of priority for survival, Paul could then do the final step—decide what to eliminate. As he struggled to reduce the weight of the supplies, he found that the tough decisions were easier because he had prioritized the list.

After some very difficult decisions, Paul produced a survival gear package that met the weight limit. His science teacher told him he had done a great job and gave him an A on the project.

Questions and Issues for Discussion

1. What conditions in the jungle would be the most threatening to the crew's survival?
2. If you made up a list of items in order of importance to survival in the jungle, what would you put at the top?
3. Would you add anything to Paul's list (such as money to pay the natives to guide him out of the jungle)?

4. Look at Paul's list. Add any items you think are important and create a list of priorities beginning with the
   most vital and descending to the least vital.
5. When you complete the list, add up the weight.
6. Now eliminate the less vital items or reduce the weight.
7. Add your list up again. If you don't make the weight
   limit, you'll need to make more adjustments or find alternatives that weigh less.
8. Tell me your reasons for eliminating specific items from
   the list.
9. Let's take this exercise and apply it to a situation that is
   more likely to happen to you. Describe a problem
   (such as packing a suitcase for a vacation or loading a
   car with gear for a camping trip) in which you might
   need to prioritize. Let's make up a list of the gear and
   prioritize it. Remember, if you're packing a car, you'll
   want to put in *last* the gear you'll need *first*. You want
   to be able to get to it without having to unpack the entire trunk.

Using Priorities as a Planning Tool

Your child's academic and vocational success hinges on her
being able to figure out what needs to be done, ranking what's
most important, and sequencing her efforts and responsibilities. Your child must realize that studying for a math test is
more important than watching her favorite sitcom on TV or
going to the beach with her friends. She must realize that she
must do her library research, take notes, record her sources,
and develop an outline before she can expect to write a good
science term paper.

Children who can plan sequentially and establish a logical hierarchy of importance or urgency are more organized
than those who work in a haphazard, disjointed way. Children
who can prioritize have a much easier time dealing with

irksome challenges, handling complex projects involving many variables, developing effective strategies, and attaining their targeted goals. They also experience less stress. Unlike the child who becomes overwhelmed, spins his wheels, and fishtails from side to side like a car on ice, the child who establishes priorities can progress sequentially from point A to point B to point C. If she wants to get a good grade on her biology final, she realizes she must review the textbook, review her class notes, review her textbook notes, identify important information, memorize key facts, review previous tests to get a sense of what the teacher is likely to ask, make up and answer practice questions, and perhaps study with a friend. She also realizes that she has to budget enough time *in advance* to do these things. This might translate into studying for the history final thirty-five minutes every evening for eight days (See "Time Management," below). The same child also realizes that to get a summer job, she needs to begin canvassing and networking in April.

For strategic children, the process of prioritizing is standard operating procedure. Children who are not as "naturally" strategic must be taught the principles and provided with repeated opportunities to apply these principles in real-life situations. Most children achieve mastery of a particular skill when the concept underlying the skill is made concrete and relevant through application and practice.

Establishing priorities and goals are intrinsically linked procedures that usually overlap. Children who can do both are on a track that leads to success in school and in life.

Time Management

The ability to manage time effectively is critical to planning efficiently, thinking strategically, establishing goals, and setting priorities. Children who don't know how to budget their time will struggle to meet their academic and family obligations. Unless they acquire time management skills, they will also struggle to meet their vocational obligations down the road. A chronic pattern of "fighting the clock" invariably triggers stress and anxiety. It also triggers resentment in those who are continually kept waiting.

Because time awareness is a left-brain activity (functions involving logic occur in the left hemisphere), some would argue or rationalize that the person who is predominately right-brained (functions involving creativity and artistry occur in the right hemisphere) would have great difficulty managing time efficiently. Certainly, people do have *natural* talents in specific areas that reflect their aptitude and inherited neurological "style" (they are predominately right-brained or left-brained). Nevertheless, as previously stated, no one is *exclusively* right- or left-brained, and human beings must learn to utilize both cerebral hemispheres. The creative, artistic person who primarily relies on the right hemisphere must be able to plan projects, and the systematic, linear-thinking, highly organized scientist who relies primarily on the left hemisphere must be able to think creatively when she conceptualizes a research project or encounters a problem or challenge.

If your child is to manage time effectively, he must be able to create a reasonable, practical schedule for completing projects. The amount of time he budgets will reflect his perceptions about the complexity and difficulty of the project and the amount of time realistically available to complete the job. Quality and quantity are critical in the equation. If your child wants to do a first-rate job on a term paper, he'll have to allocate more time than if he's willing to do a mediocre job. If doing the assignment requires extensive library research, then he must factor this into his time frame. If he realizes he has a tendency to make spelling and grammatical errors, he must plan ahead and allocate extra time for proofreading.

Some children appear to have a "natural" appreciation for time constraints. Their "inner clock" helps them intuitively order their obligations efficiently. This natural talent notwithstanding, good time management skills can be taught to all children, and the sooner the teaching process begins, the better (see "Setting Up a Schedule," page 234). The child who acquires these skills during the formative years possesses a resource he'll be able to use throughout his life. ("This project should take approximately eight hours to complete, and I have five days to do it. This means I must spend an average of one and one-half hours a day beginning tonight.")

Examining the Issues

Read the following anecdote about time management with your child. Although the suggested age range is 6 to 14, with children younger than eight, you must have realistic expectations. You cannot reasonably expect young children to be as time-conscious as fourteen-year-olds. Your goal is to make your child aware that when she has a deadline, planning her time is vital if she wants to get everything done.

---

interactive activity

Age Range: 6–14
Objectives: Managing Time, Planning Ahead,
          and Prioritizing

Oops, I Ran Out of Time . . .

There was no way Michelle could possibly get everything done. She felt desperate. Although she and her sister and brother were leaving on an eagerly awaited vacation in five days, she hadn't even thought about what she was going to take with her. She needed to buy some new clothes, but finding the time to get to the shopping mall was going to be a major problem. Her scholarship application for college was due in one week, and she hadn't even started it. She estimated it would take at least ten hours to complete the form and write a first-rate essay. Her car also needed to be serviced before they left, and she needed at least two new tires.

Michelle made a mental list of all the other things she had to do before she, Rebecca, and William could leave for Yosemite. She had to wash her clothes, assemble the camping gear they would need, and pack the car. She had to go to the bank to get travelers checks, buy a map, and make arrangements for a kid in the neighborhood to feed her cat. Since her parents would be away on a trip to Canada, she couldn't count on them to take care of Whiskers.

Then there was the matter of finding time to say good-bye to her boyfriend, who was upset because she was leaving for two weeks. Her parents wanted an itinerary, and she would have to look in the touring book, call ahead for reservations, and tell her parents what motels they would be staying in on the way to and from Yosemite. She also wanted to buy some books to read on the trip, and she needed to pick up her hiking boots at the shoe repair shop. Of course, she also needed to buy food, soft drinks, and snacks for the trip. How could she possibly find the time to get it all done?

Questions and Issues for Discussion

1. Michelle was in a bind. What caused her to get into this bind?
2. What could she do to solve the problem?
3. Let's examine the story and underline and number all of the projects Michelle must complete before she leaves on vacation. We'll make a list and rank the list in order of priority, importance, and urgency (see below). After making up this list, what would be the next step? (Remember that Michelle has a limited amount of time before she leaves. She has to figure out how much time each task requires and when to do each task.)
4. Figuring out how much time each task requires and having a schedule certainly makes sense. The challenge is for Michelle to make a schedule in which each task she needs to do before leaving on vacation is carefully planned. For practice, pretend *you* are Michelle. (Boys

could pretend to be Michael and could substitute saying good-bye to a good friend or a girlfriend.) The first step is to write the list of tasks, and then to prioritize the list. (Emphasize that completing the scholarship application and getting the car serviced are vital!) Now make up a schedule of each day remaining before the trip (see opposite page). Use your estimate of how much time each task would take. Write down each task on the schedule and indicate the estimated completion time. Let's assume today is Monday, and you're leaving on vacation at 7:00 A.M. on Saturday. That leaves five days to complete everything. Start with Monday. Which tasks do you want to do today? Plug the tasks into the schedule below (using a pencil in case you need to make modifications) and indicate the time when you propose to do it and how long you estimate it will take.

List of Tasks, Target Date for Completion, and Time Required

Order	Task	Day	Time
———	—————————	———	———
———	—————————	———	———
———	—————————	———	———
———	—————————	———	———
———	—————————	———	———
———	—————————	———	———
———	—————————	———	———
———	—————————	———	———
———	—————————	———	———
———	—————————	———	———
———	—————————	———	———
———	—————————	———	———

5. You can move things around and play with the schedule until it works, that is, until you complete everything before leaving on vacation. This is called fine-tuning your schedule.

Schedule

	Mon.	Tues.	Wed.	Thurs.	Fri.	Sat.	Sun.
8–9 A.M.							
9–10							
10–11							
11–12							
12–1 P.M.							
1–2							
2–3							
3–4							
4–5							
5–6							
6–7							
7–8							
8–9							
9–10							
10–11							

6. Now let's pretend the problem of preparing for the trip belongs once again to Michelle. If she concludes she can't possibly do everything on the list, are there any tasks she might eliminate? What would they be? Could she ask her sister, brother, or parents to help her? Perhaps someone could take the car to the service station for her. Is there anything on the list she might put off until later or not do at all before leaving? For example, if she needs new jeans for the trip, and she doesn't have time to buy them before she leaves, could she

stop at a store along the way? Can you think of any other adjustments she could make if she finds it impossible to do everything? Could she leave Saturday afternoon if she can't finish everything she has to do? Could she leave one day later and use Saturday to complete her preparation for the trip?

7. Hindsight (looking back on what happened later) often tells us what we *should* have done. Unfortunately, we don't have hindsight until we've already made the mistake. All we can do with hindsight is learn from it so we don't make the same miscalculation again. Let's assume Michelle becomes stressed out. She has an argument with her sister, brother, or parents. She realizes she cannot get everything done by Saturday, and she's forced to leave on Sunday, thus losing one day of vacation. If she uses her hindsight to analyze what went wrong so that she can avoid the same problem in the future, what specific things might she have done differently the next time she plans a trip?

Setting Up a Schedule

At one time or another, everyone becomes convinced there's too little time in the day to complete everything that needs to be done. Time pressure can be a major source of stress and anxiety. Your tax return may be due, and you may not have finished organizing and tabulating the figures. Your daughter may have five final exams and a term paper due within a three-day period. An assistant may be sick, and you may face an important deadline with no one to help you.

People with "natural" time awareness may be able to keep track mentally of their responsibilities, obligations, pending projects, and deadlines. Most people, however, must make a list of what they need to do, and they must carefully budget the necessary time to fulfill these obligations.

By teaching your child how to create a practical schedule, you provide her with an invaluable planning resource that can significantly reduce the stress in her life. For example, if her book report is due in two weeks, she must allow enough time to read the book, write her first draft, edit, rewrite, and proof-read. If she doesn't budget adequate time, she'll find herself in a crisis. She may not submit the report on time, or she may do a shoddy job.

There are many possible formats for schedules. The one on page 237 is similar to the schedule in the "Questions and Issues for Discussion" section on page 233. Designed to be practical and simple, it divides the week and the day into segments and encourages your child to make judgments about *when* she wants to do her work and *how* much time she estimates she'll need to complete this work.

interactive	activity

Age Range: 8–14
Objectives: Learning to Budget
Time and Plan Ahead

Ask your child to list all the tasks he wants or needs to do during the next week (finish his Boy Scout project, adjust the gears on his bicycle, etc.) and all of the obligations he has been assigned by you or his teachers (mow the lawn, complete his math homework, etc.). Have him decide when he wants to do these projects and have him estimate how much time it will take to complete the work. Finally, ask him to plug the task into his weekly schedule. For example, he may need to spend approximately two hours fixing his bike and may decide to do this on Saturday morning from 9:00–11:00 A.M. He may conclude that he must spend one hour each evening during the six days reading a book for his book report. He may choose to do this from 7:00 to 8:00 P.M. beginning on Monday evening. If he doesn't want to do homework on Saturday, he may decide to read on Sunday night.

Your child should indicate on his schedule how he proposes to use a particular time segment. He may want to create a color code. Blue might signify study time. Yellow might signify sleep. Red might indicate mealtime. For practice, have your child fill in every activity during a typical day. He should include time in school, after-school sports, homework, study breaks, R & R (rest and relaxation), etc. This procedure of meticulously indicating the time frame of every activity during the day may seem overdone, but the procedure is intended to make your child more time-conscious and help him become better organized.

Because of space limitations in this book, the schedule may be too small for your child to use. You may want to redraw the schedule to make it larger. It would be a good idea to punch holes in the schedule so that your child can put it in his binder.

You will note that the schedule divides the day into one-hour blocks of time until three o'clock, the traditional end of the school day. After-school time is divided into half-hour segments so that your child can indicate with precision how much time he wants to spend studying and relaxing. If you prefer, you can redraw the schedule and divide the entire day into half-hour segments.

Make several copies of the schedule. After your child completes this week's projects and obligations, have him schedule next week's likely projects and obligations. As an experiment, ask him to keep to his schedule as best he can. Explain that although schedules are not chiseled in stone, they are far more effective when someone makes a concerted and sustained effort to keep to them. If the schedule doesn't work or if conditions change and your child wants to make adjustments, this is, of course, both acceptable and advisable. For example, the football season may end, and your child may no longer be participating in an after-school sports program. Since he would have more time available after school, it would make sense to modify the schedule.

Your child may be able to do this activity with little help or guidance from you, or he may require a great deal of assistance, especially if he's younger than twelve. You might model how to create a schedule by completing one for yourself and asking your child to help you create your schedule. You could then reverse roles, and you could help him.

Weekly Schedule

Time	Mon.	Tues.	Wed.	Thurs.	Fri.	Sat.	Sun.
A.M.							
7:00–7:30							
7:30–8:00							
8:00–9:00							
9:00–10:00							
10:00–11:00							
11:00–12:00							
P.M.							
12:00–1:00							
1:00–2:00							
2:00–3:00							
3:00–3:30							
3:30–4:00							
4:00–4:30							
4:30–5:00							
5:00–5:30							
5:30–6:00							
6:00–6:30							
6:30–7:00							
7:00–7:30							
7:30–8:00							
8:00–8:30							
8:30–9:00							
9:00–9:30							
9:30–10:00							
10:00–10:30							
10:30–11:00							

Organization

Some children appear to have an inborn need for order and organization. Although they are not necessarily obsessive about organization, they realize that they function best when they know where their possessions are and when their environment is neat and functional.

Children who have a compelling need to create order in their lives may neatly organize their closets and their drawers, group their socks and clothes according to color, and arrange their pencils according to size. (Psychologists would probably say that this extreme behavior has obsessive overtones indicating rigidity and, perhaps, repressed emotional turmoil. It also strongly suggests an obsessive need for control.)

Other children could care less about order, neatness, and organization. They surround themselves with chaos and seem perfectly content with never being sure where anything is located. Their rooms are typically disaster areas with their clothes, schoolbooks, and papers strewn everywhere. Partially eaten food can usually be found on their dressers and their beds. Resigned to spending hours looking for their possessions, these children cope with, and in some cases seem to thrive on, the stress and frustration associated with continually losing, and occasionally finding, their possessions.

Certain children are organized in specific areas of their lives and disorganized in other areas. They might throw their school papers on their desks and their football gear on the floor, but they may, paradoxically, have an elaborate system for keeping track of their CDs or videos.

Although a child's need for order and neatness is strongly influenced by environmental factors, there are many exceptions. Messy, disorganized children can often be found in families where parents highly value organization and cleanliness. The behavior of these children suggests that they may be reacting negatively to their parents' compelling, and perhaps obsessive, need for order. These children actually seem to delight in being disorganized and slovenly. Their reaction may indicate resentment and an "I don't want to do it your way" attitude. Certainly this behavior, whether a conscious or unconscious expression of anger or assertion of independence, is guaranteed to press "hot buttons" in the parents.

If your child's disorganization is creating family stress, reducing efficiency, and causing school performance to suffer, then *you* have a problem. You clearly do not want your family immersed in stress, and you clearly do not want your child to flounder in school. Your child, however, may be unwilling to acknowledge that *he* has a problem, and, in fact, may be quite resistant to discussing the matter or exploring alternatives to his counterproductive behavior.

At this point, you will probably decide to intervene. The efficacy of this intervention hinges on how you handle the issues. Remember, if your child doesn't feel he has a problem, then *you own the problem, and you must figure out how to solve it,* ideally with your child's cooperation and active participation. DIBS could be a very useful tool at this juncture. The first step is to define the problem accurately and assign proper ownership. Let's look at how this might be done in a non-emotionally-charged context.

Define:	I have a problem that is causing me a great deal of stress. When you're disorganized and can't find your books and your assignments, I get upset. For my own mental health, I need to solve this problem.
	I'd like you to work with me as I use DIBS to figure out a mutually acceptable solution to my problem.
Investigate:	You own your room.
	It's not fair for me to try to control all areas of your life.
	We share this house.
	Our lives overlap.
	Your possessions and my possessions take up mutually shared space in the house.

We have areas in the house that we primarily
"own"—your room and my room.

We affect each other when we're stressed out.

We have to make compromises if we're
going to live together harmoniously.

I have trouble handling a lot of disorder in
the areas of the house we share.

I get irritated and uptight when you get
upset because you can't find something
you need.

It would reduce my anxiety if you were willing to make some compromises and help
keep the house and your room more orderly.

Brainstorm: All personal possessions that are not being
used but are left in shared areas of the
house will be put back in our own rooms.

I will build more shelves in your closet for
your possessions.

I will put shelves on the wall above your desk.

I will buy you a file cabinet and help you set
up a filing system for your school papers
if you want my help.

I will buy you an assignment organizer for
your binder.

I will put a closet in the garage for your
larger possessions.

Select: I'll put a closet in the garage for your possessions and buy you a file cabinet for your
school papers.

Most of the ideas developed in the brainstorming section
could reduce the child's disorganization, and it might seem reasonable to implement *all* of the ideas, assuming this is financially feasible. Rather than risk "overkill," it would be more
strategic to select one brainstormed idea to implement at first.
Other ideas might be implemented later.

The key component in this modeled DIBS solution to a disorganization problem is that the parent avoids recriminations and triggers that would probably cause a child to become defensive. It's possible, of course, that the child will become defensive irrespective of the parent's methodology, especially if the issue of disorganization has previously been handled in a confrontational or punitive fashion. Defensiveness often becomes a conditioned response when a child feels that he's continually on the receiving end of a great deal of overt or covert criticism. The context, spirit, tone, and mechanics of your communication can profoundly affect your child's willingness to work on the problem and arrive at reasonable, mutually acceptable compromises.

Examining the Issues with Your Child

An alternative to DIBS is modeled below. The questions are designed to help you and your child examine the anecdote in a non-emotionally charged context. In most cases, examining the behavior of another child is less threatening to a child and usually avoids "knee-jerk" resistance. The parallels between the behavior of the child described in the anecdote and your child must be handled with subtlety and diplomacy. If you say "Lauren sounds just like you!" you are going to trigger defensiveness, resentment, and resistance.

interactive **activity**

Age Range: 6–14
Objective: Learning to Value Organization

It's Gotta Be Somewhere!

Lauren raced into her room and began searching desperately for her roller blades. She began pulling out her dirty clothes from the floor in her closet, hoping to find her skates underneath. When she couldn't find them, she searched under the pile of CDs and videos near her boombox. The roller blades weren't there either. She pushed aside the books and shoes under her bed, but to no avail. Where could they be? Julie and Lisa were waiting for her downstairs. The boys would be in the park by now, and the girls were anxious to join them.

In exasperation, Lauren screamed to her mother "Have you seen my roller blades and my helmet? I can't even find my knee and elbow pads. Please help me find them. I'm late!" There was a tone of panic and exasperation in her voice.

Lauren's mother shook her head. She had heard this lament many times. "Did you look in the garage near the dryer?" she called up to her daughter.

"Could you look for me, Mom?" Lauren pleaded. She began to rip off her school clothes, which she dropped on the floor. From a pile of clothes by the foot of her bed, she extracted her shorts and her favorite tee-shirt.

"I found them!" Lauren's mother yelled.

Lauren smiled and bounded down the stairs. She grabbed the skates, the helmet, and the pads from her mother's outstretched arms and raced out the door. As she ran by, she muttered "Thanks, Mom. I forgot that I left them out in the garage yesterday."

Questions and Issues for Discussion

1. Why do you think Lauren was upset about not being able to find her roller blades?
2. Do you have the impression that she often loses things?
3. How would you rate her organization?

1	2	3	4	5	6	7	8	9	10
Poor				Fair					Excellent

4. What are your reasons for evaluating her this way?
5. Do you think she's disorganized when doing homework?
6. What effect do you think Lauren's behavior is having on her family?

7. Do you feel her mother has a legitimate right to be upset?
8. Form a picture in your mind about her room and describe what you see.
9. What specific things could Lauren do to make her life more organized? Let's see how many ideas we can come up with.

If your child likes the suggestions and ideas you developed to improve Lauren's organization (shelves in her closet, a filing system for school papers, etc.), ask her if she would be interested in using some of these ideas herself. As you can see, this questioning procedure achieves the same objectives (that is, ideas for becoming organized) as the DIBS method described on page 239.

---

interactive activity

Age Range: 6–14
Objectives: Organizing a Major Project
and Establishing Priorities

Getting the Job Done

"There's a major home-improvement project I want to do, and I'd really like you to help me with it. As you know, the deck and deck furniture are in bad shape. I'd like to sand, stain, and weather-coat the deck. (You can substitute wallpapering the living room, painting the garage, organizing an annual block party, etc.) It would be neat to plan this project with you. We would need to figure out what specifically has to be done, the steps for getting it done, the material we need to buy, the deadline for finishing the project, and a schedule for completing each step. If you want, you can help me plan the project. Let's plug the data into the format below."

*Project:*_____

Target Date for Beginning Project: _____

Target Date for Completing Project: _____

| *Specific Steps for Doing Project:* | *Target Date:* | |
| | *Start* | *Complete* |

1. _____ _____ _____

   Person(s) Responsible for This Step: _____

2. _____ _____ _____

   Person(s) Responsible for This Step: _____

3. _____ _____ _____

   Person(s) Responsible for This Step: _____

4. _____ _____ _____

   Person(s) Responsible for This Step: _____

5. _____ _____ _____

   Person(s) Responsible for This Step: _____

6. _____ _____ _____

   Person(s) Responsible for This Step: _____

7. _____ _____ _____

   Person(s) Responsible for This Step: _____

8. _____ _____ _____

   Person(s) Responsible for This Step: _____

9. _____ _____ _____

   Person(s) Responsible for This Step: _____

10. _____ _____ _____

   Person(s) Responsible for This Step: _____

11. _____ _____ _____

   Person(s) Responsible for This Step: _____

12. _____ _____ _____

   Person(s) Responsible for This Step: _____

Materials Needed: *Target Dates for*
                                                      Procurement:

1. _____   _____

   Person(s) Responsible for Procurement: _____

2. _____   _____

   Person(s) Responsible for Procurement: _____

3. _____   _____

   Person(s) Responsible for Procurement: _____

4. _____   _____

   Person(s) Responsible for Procurement: _____

5. _____   _____

   Person(s) Responsible for Procurement: _____

6. _____   _____

   Person(s) Responsible for Procurement: _____

7. _____   _____

   Person(s) Responsible for Procurement: _____

8. _____   _____

   Person(s) Responsible for Procurement: _____

9. _____   _____

   Person(s) Responsible for Procurement: _____

10. _____   _____

   Person(s) Responsible for Procurement: _____

Using a schedule, let's create a master plan with specific dates for doing work and procuring the materials (see page 237).

If effective strategic thinking skills comprise the foundation for achievement and success in our society, then effective organizational and time-management skills are the nuts and bolts that hold the superstructure together. By teaching your child how to line up the holes properly, how to insert the correct bolts, and how to tighten the nuts with washers, you are helping him build a superstructure that will hold together in both good and inclement weather.

chapter 8

The Thinking Child

Brian was upset and scared. He couldn't figure out how or why it all had happened. For some reason, one of the school gangs had targeted him, and they were out to get him.

A serious student who wanted to go to college, Brian had scrupulously avoided the gangs on campus. The sixteen-year-old socialized with his own select group of academically oriented friends. They had their own private parties, which they were careful not to publicize at school so they wouldn't be crashed. When he went on a date, it was always with a girl who was college-bound and serious about doing well in school.

As Brian struggled to understand how he had gotten entangled in this nightmare, the only explanation he could come up with for the threats and harassment was a seemingly insignificant incident that had occurred the previous week at a convenience store near school. Brian had unintentionally walked in front of a kid wearing a gang bandana who was waiting to pay for something. When Brian realized what he had done, he apologized, but this didn't satisfy the other teenager. He became upset and muttered a curse. Brian ignored his "remarks." He apologized again, smiled in a friendly way, paid for his candy bar, and left the store. He couldn't believe his life was now being threatened for something so minor. But that morning three boys who were gang members had approached him in the hallway and told him he was "dead meat."

Brian was terrified. Knowing that some gang members came to school with guns and knives had made him afraid to walk down the hall between classes. The sixteen-year-old now continually looked over his shoulder and was convinced he was being followed. "If only I hadn't gone to that store to buy that stupid candy bar, none of this would be happening!" he thought with sadness and disgust. "One dumb thing has totally screwed up my entire life."

At first, Brian hoped the problem would go away if he was careful to avoid the places at school where the gang members congregated. From the looks on their faces when he had to pass them on the way to class, he knew they wouldn't forget. They stared at him, hatred mirrored in their eyes. As he was headed to the gym for PE, one gang member ran his index finger across his neck, mimicking how he would slit Brian's throat. Another pointed an imaginary gun at Brian and pretended to fire it. Brian felt terror surge through his body. His pounding heart seemed to sink into the pit of his stomach, and he could barely breathe.

Brian was tempted to tell his parents, but he feared his mom would become hysterical and tell the school authorities or the police. If she did, things would be worse. He was certain the school couldn't protect him. Brian became distraught when he realized his family might have to move from the neighborhood, or they might have to use the money his parents were saving for college to send him to a private school. What a nightmare his life had become!

Brian knew his dad kept a small handgun in a locked box under his bed. He also knew where his father kept the key, and that afternoon after school he began toying with the idea of taking the gun to school in his backpack. At least he'd be able to protect himself, and if the rumor spread that he was "packing," maybe the gang would leave him alone.

When his parents went to the shopping mall that evening, Brian went to their bedroom and used the key to open the steel box. He took out the gun, loaded the clip with seven shells, pulled back the receiver, chambered a shell, and pushed in the safety button. He had gone target shooting with his dad a few times, and he knew how to handle the gun. As he stared at the weapon in his hand, Brian began to tremble. He couldn't believe he was actually considering taking a gun to school. Two days ago his biggest concern was the next calculus test. Now his biggest concern was staying alive.

The Moment of Truth

As your child matures and becomes increasingly independent and self-reliant, it may be disconcerting to accept the fact that you won't always be present to offer wise counsel, guidance, and advice at each major decision point in his life. At these crossroads, your child may have to make choices on his own that could profoundly affect the future course of his life. If he makes a good choice, he may not even realize the significance of his decision. He may simply proceed to the next event in his life, oblivious to the fact that, had he made the wrong choice, his life might have changed forever.

It's precisely because your child will make many momentous decisions on his own that the process of teaching him to think clearly and rationally is so essential. This teaching process is vital to preparing him to meet life's challenges, handle life's problems, and avail himself of life's opportunities.

Some of your child's choices will be innocuous. Discovering that he's invited a "boring" person to the prom may cause temporary discomfort, but the choice will not alter the course of his life or have an impact on his future.

Certainly, your child is entitled to make an *occasional* bad choice. Unfortunately, one flawed choice involving a serious or life-threatening issue could be disastrous. Accepting a ride home from a party with a friend who's drunk *just once,* trying crack cocaine *just once,* or taking a weapon to school *just once* are clear and blatant examples of flawed monumental choices that could have life-destroying implications.

In reality, of course, your child is never truly "alone" when he faces a major decision point in his life. You are with him in spirit, or ideally, you are with him. Your values, attitudes, modeling, admonitions, rules, teaching, parenting methods, and imparted wisdom will be part of a complex mix of considerations your child will consciously or unconsciously factor into his decision-making process. Although he may not be aware of your influence as he struggles to sort out the issues, your imprint, in one form or another, will be stamped on his ultimate choice.

If the engraving process has been positive, and your parenting and training have been effective, your child will factor what you have taught and modeled into his decision-making. As he responds at an important juncture in his life, he may not necessarily act as you would prefer, but he will nevertheless use the decision-making template you've provided to assess critically and strategically the situation he's confronting. If he has learned how to think effectively, he'll add the pluses and the minuses of each option, consider his goals and priorities, draw upon his past experiences, predict the potential consequences, and make what he believes to be the best choice. This analytical procedure will help him determine whether he should or should not "borrow" your car without your permission, study for an important exam, dive from a boulder into a mountain pool, or have unprotected sex with a girl he meets at a party.

Your child's computing of the pros and cons will not only reflect your distinctive parenting benchmark, it will also reflect a gamut of other crucial factors that include self-esteem, self-confidence, social pressure, stress, hormones, societal values, and fear. Because you may not be with him physically at the moment of decision, it's vital for your *own* mental health that you know you've done everything in your power to provide him with the values and analytical thinking resources he needs to assess problems rationally, sort out his options, and identify choices that are in his best interests.

If your training has not been effective, or if your child, for complex psychological reasons, is consciously or unconsciously compelled to reject the values and thinking skills you've taught him, he may respond impulsively and mindlessly when faced with a critical decision. The result of this behavior is usually a pattern of chronically flawed choices that frequently produce terrible consequences. Your child might accept any dare that offers the possibility of a quick thrill. He may sabotage himself in school by not completing his assignments or studying for tests. He may cut corners, break the rules, or break the law. When faced with the option of making a good or a bad choice, he will typically make the wrong choice. Wandering through life in a mental haze, he'll repeatedly suffer the effects of his own flawed decision-making process. Unfortunately, he may not realize, or he may deny despite convincing evidence, that his own decisions are responsible for his negative experiences and failures in life. Refusing to accept that he is his own worst enemy, he may curse his fate, blame others, or rationalize that he's simply unlucky.

When Everything You've Taught Hangs in the Balance

Brian, the teenager described in the introductory anecdote, is clearly at one of the most critical junctures he will face in his life. His ultimate decision about how to handle his terrifying dilemma could shape the course of his future. That a sixteen-year-old would have to make such a momentous life-and-death decision underscores the sad state of affairs in our violent society. As if in a time warp, our children seem to be back in the wild west where anyone who feels offended or threatened can resolve his dispute by shooting it out in the street. These shoot-outs are not some computerized fantasy game in a video arcade. The bullets are real, and the dead teenagers are real.

Some might question whether the situation described in the anecdote is realistic. The following newspaper article should lay to rest any reservations about realism as well as underscore the mindless violence that can so quickly and so easily envelop our children.

ASSOCIATED PRESS

'Hard Looks' Lead to 2 Deaths at Birthday Party
Sacramento

Sheriff's deputies are seeking four young men who shot and killed two birthday partygoers because of "hard looks."

Manuel Hernandez, 22, and Jason Hatch, 16, were killed outside a Rancho Cordova home Saturday night.

"From all indications, it appears to be gang related," sheriff's spokesman Jim Cooper said. He said the gunman was angered by "hard looks" from partygoers.

Raquel Fischer, mother of two sisters who gave the party at their home, said the affair was a nonalcoholic birthday bash for a 15-year-old girl.

The gunman was among the 40 guests but left during the party with three other youths to pick up a girl. The four returned later, apparently intoxicated, with several carloads of people, witnesses said.

"Nobody here was drunk," said the older sister of the party hosts. "Everything was cool until somebody showed up drunk."

Terrible things happen to children today. Kids will actually *kill* other kids because of a facial expression or a perceived "slight." Our children, through no fault of their own, can easily become entangled in this epidemic of madness. Tragically, parents are often powerless to protect their children from the mindless violence.

In the anecdote that opens this chapter, Brian's life is threatened for an unwitting, seemingly inconsequential act. Three paths stretch before him. All three are fraught with danger and frightening consequences. If he does nothing and "goes about his business," his life is at risk. He might be attacked on the way to school, in the hallway, or on the way home. He may leave a party and become the victim of a drive-by shooting.

If Brian decides to take his father's gun to school for protection, his life is still in jeopardy. He might be expelled, or he might use the weapon and end up in jail. He might also end up in a gunfight and be killed.

If Brian tells his parents, and they inform the authorities, his family might be forced to make radical changes in their lives. They might have to move to another community, or Brian might be forced for his own protection to attend a private school and, in so doing, use the money that had been saved for his college education. Even if he does change schools, Brian realizes that his life would be in peril whenever he walked down the street or went to a movie or a party. Gang vengeance is brainless and unforgiving.

Faced with three awful options, Brian must make a gut-wrenching choice. Should he try to protect himself as best he can? Should he ask for help? Should he try to "blend into the woodwork" and hope everything will "blow over"? As he adds up the pluses and minuses of each option, he'll find far more minuses than pluses. No wonder the situation seems hopeless.

Brian's decision would clearly be an ultimate litmus test of his strategic thinking skills, critical thinking skills, and judgment. As he wrestles with the nightmare, his fear and despair could easily cloud his judgment, prevent him from going through a systematic and meticulous assessment of his predicament, and cause him to act irrationally. This systematic and meticulous assessment of the dangers and his potential responses could save his life. To extricate himself, Brian must be able to think clearly and rationally. Despite his justifiable fear, he must force his mind to process what he knows about gangs, codes of "honor," revenge, and self-preservation. He must force his mind to compute carefully the pros and cons and the potential consequences of each available option. He must force his mind to search for better options. If he is incapable of this mental discipline, he may indeed be "dead meat." Surrounded by a jungle and stalked by predators, Brian must either somehow escape the jungle, or he must learn to survive in it. The perils are real, and Brian *must* make himself smarter than the tigers stalking him.

The parallels between the urban jungle and the actual jungle are striking. In remote areas of India, where attacks by man-eating tigers are relatively common, the predators typically attack from behind. Some villagers wear masks that look like human faces on the *backs* of their heads to trick the tigers and avoid attack. This behavior illustrates how the thinking mind can compensate for physical inferiority to offset danger. Survival in the face of peril and terror can hinge on being able to analyze their situation, learn from experience, acquire insight, utilize imparted wisdom, and think strategically.

As Brian consciously and unconsciously sorts out what he has to do to survive, he must adjust strategically to the stark realities of a violent teenage world. At some point in his deliberation, he would ideally ask himself a key question: "What would my parents do in this situation, and what would they expect me to do?" This one question could save him. It would force him to take a step back from his terror so that he can carefully examine his options before he acts impetuously.

Although Brian will perceive and assess his plight through his own lenses and filters, the tint and shape of these lenses and filters, and his judgment, will be colored by his upbringing and by his parents' values and beliefs, and the analytical and strategic thinking skills they taught him. His ultimate choice about how to extricate himself from his horrible dilemma will hinge on whether he's learned how to think effectively in a crisis.

To survive, Brian must be able to:

- **Make realistic predictions about consequences.** ("If I take the gun, I might get caught or I might get shot.")

- **Appreciate cause and effect and link his actions with logical repercussions.** ("Taking the gun to school is a no-winner. I might get expelled, arrested, or shot. None of these options are good. I've got to come up with something else.")
- **Realize how his behavior might affect others.** ("My parents would be devastated if I brought a gun to school and got expelled or shot.")
- **Deal with frustration.** ("I'm scared. I need to protect myself, but carrying a gun isn't the way to do it. I just need to take the time to figure out a better solution.")
- **Avoid mistakes by considering rather than denying the reality of the situation.** ("I have a major life-threatening problem, and I've got to think smart.")
- **Consider moral and ethical issues.** ("I don't want steal my dad's gun. I don't want to break the law.")
- **Link values with specific choices and actions.** ("I can't take a gun to school and shoot someone. I'm not a killer. There has to be a better way to protect myself.")
- **Draw reasonable conclusions from available data.** ("I can't continually look over my shoulder, and even if I do, this won't protect me. There must be people who have figured out a way to get out of this type of jam. I'm probably going to need help in dealing with this problem.")
- **Factor "future time" into decisions.** ("If I make the wrong choice, I won't be able to go to college, and I won't have a future.")
- **Appreciate risks.** ("I can't have a gunfight with an entire gang. Even I shoot someone, they're still going to get me. There are too many of them, and they'll want revenge even more. I have to come up with a strategy that really protects me even if I don't like some aspects of the plan.")
- **Control impulses.** ("Even though packing a gun may seem like protection, I know it would be a dumb thing to do.")

- **Suspend immediate gratification.** ("I may not be able to solve this crisis immediately. While I search for a solution, I may need to make up an excuse for not going to school today.")
- **Think for himself even when under pressure.** ("I'm brighter than these idiots. I can use my head to save myself.")*

Some might argue that a terrified sixteen-year-old would be incapable of demonstrating these characteristics in a life-and-death situation. They would contend that Brian would be so frightened and his thinking would be so clouded by fear that he would be incapable of rational thinking. Perhaps this is true. But it's also true that those who cannot think clearly and rationally in a life-and-death crisis often end up in the emergency room or the morgue. Certainly there are sixteen-year-olds who do think clearly in a crisis. These are the kids who have been trained to be analytical, who can figure out how to extract themselves from a jam—even a deadly jam—and who can think critically and strategically. These are the kids who, when the chips are down and things look bleak, function like the well-trained football tailback who is about to be tackled. Seeing imminent danger, he quickly scans the field, instinctively evades the tacklers by "going against the grain," finds a lane, shifts into high gear, and streaks down the field. He prevails because he's been physically and mentally conditioned to make the smart moves that allow him to win.

Every parent dreads that his or her child mght act brainlessly and impulsively in a crisis. The antidote to mindlessness is for parents to teach their children to remain calm, assess the situation rationally, and make the right choice.

Examining the Issues

Read the anecdote that begins this chapter with your child. You can use it with children ages 6 to 16 with the proviso that you

---

*If the clear-thinking traits look familiar, they are. They have been borrowed, with minor modifications, from Chapter 1.

recognize and accept that the life experiences, reasoning skills, and communication skills of younger children are obviously less advanced. You will need to patiently guide them through the examination of the issues. While the anecdote may be scary for younger children, it unfortunately encapsulates what your child may face in middle school and high school. The better prepared he is, the less likely he'll become a tragic statistic. This interactive exercise also provides a final opportunity for you to reinforce the analytical thinking skills and decision-making skills you and your child have practiced together.

interactive **activity**

Age Range: 8–14
Objectives: Assessing and Devising Strategies for
Getting Out of Dangerous Situations

Questions and Issues for Discussion (anecdote found on page 247. For Parent Response Guidelines, see pages 31–36.)

1. Do you think that the situation described in the story could actually happen? Could it happen at your school? Has something similar happened to you or to a friend? Are gangs a problem at your school?
2. What's going through Brian's mind as he struggles with his decision? What are the specific issues he's considering?
3. Do you think his fear is justified? Do you think his life is truly in danger?
4. The story indicates that Brian is considering three options. What are they?
5. What are the pluses and the minuses of doing nothing and hoping the situation will settle down?
6. If Brian does nothing, how would your rate this decision?

1	2	3	4	5	6	7	8	9	10
Not				Fairly					Very
Smart				Smart					Smart

7. What are your reasons for making this evaluation?

8. What are the pluses and minuses of telling his parents or the school authorities?

9. If Brian does tell his parents or the authorities, how would you rate this decision?

1	2	3	4	5	6	7	8	9	10
Not Smart				Fairly Smart					Very Smart

10. What are your reasons for making this evaluation?

11. What are the pluses and minuses of taking his dad's gun to school?

12. If Brian does take the gun to school, how would you rate his decision?

1	2	3	4	5	6	7	8	9	10
Not Smart				Fairly Smart					Very Smart

13. What are your reasons for making this evaluation?

14. Brian apparently sees only the three options for solving the problem. Can you think of anything else he might do to solve his crisis? For example, could he try to talk to the gang member he offended and apologize again?

15. If Brian's life is truly in danger, would this justify moving to another community or changing schools?

16. If you were going to describe Brian, what adjectives would you use?

17. Let's assume Brian decides to take the gun to school and he gets caught by the school authorities. What excuse would he use to justify his actions? Would they "buy" the excuse? What do you think the consequences would be?

18. How do you think I would respond if I were Brian's dad, and Brian tells me his life is in danger? Would I be mad at him? Would I be upset that we might have to make changes in our lives to protect him? Would I want him to tell me what had happened?

19. Let's say I am Brian's dad, and I own a gun that I keep in a locked steel case under my bed. If I discover that Brian has taken it to school, how do you think I would respond?

20. If you faced the same dilemma Brian faced, what would you do?
21. Let's pretend *you* are Brian's parent. What would you want his decision to be about how to handle his crisis?
22. Let's try an experiment. Let's use DIBS to examine the crisis and see what we come up with. Perhaps this might suggest some possible solutions that Brian hasn't considered.

Define _____

_____

Investigate _____

_____

_____

_____

_____

_____

_____

Brainstorm _____

_____

_____

_____

_____

Select _____

_____

At this point, it would be a good idea to summarize what can be learned from Brian's terrible experience. A model can be found below. Certainly, it makes sense to put the ideas in your own words. If you can, avoid sounding "preachy." You want to communicate to your child that you, too, have learned something from examining the crisis.

Parent: We both know that Brian's problem is very real and very serious. If we find ourselves in a serious jam or in danger, we would need to think carefully before we respond impulsively. An exception, of course, would be if someone were trying to hurt you or kidnap you, and you had to scream and run way immediately to save yourself. Sometimes the solution to a problem such as the one Brian faced is not the one we first consider. As frightened as we might be by the danger confronting us, we would still need to keep a clear head. We would need to take a step back from the problem and get some emotional distance so that we could think calmly and find the best solution. We would need to control the impulse to act without thinking carefully. We may also need to ask for help from someone who has had more experience. Requesting assistance is not a sign of weakness. It's a sign of smartness and intelligence. I think you would agree that Brian needs help from someone. If he tries to protect his parents from his terrible dilemma, it wouldn't be fair to him or to them. If he's going to survive, he has to be smart and strategic. His problem is a *family* problem, and the family needs to help him find a solution. If they decide they have to move or send Brian to another school, this would be a small price to pay for saving their son's life. Sometimes, we have to make tough choices that involve sacrifices. Doesn't it really comes down to priorities? Do you move or spend your savings to save your child's life, or do you risk your child's life. What do you think is more important?

Taking Another Look at the Checklist

You have now completed a systematic program for training your child to think rationally and to make good choices in a highly competitive and often dangerous world. In reality, you haven't actually completed the program. Interactive family problem-solving activities and effective family communication should continue for as long your child lives under the same roof with you. Ideally, this interplay will continue, in one form or another, for many years after that. Certainly, as your child matures, the tone and thrust of your interaction will change. Although your child will justifiably want to make more and more independent decisions, you will, to some extent, still be her mentor and guide. She may not always agree with you or do as you might wish, but if you've "played your cards right," she'll honor you, respect your opinion, and continue to use the thinking tools you've provided throughout her life.

Although you will now put this book aside, the instructional process is not over. Your child will need to practice the methods, and she'll undoubtedly need your guidance and support from time to time. She'll inevitably have to make momentous decisions at some point in her life, and her choices at these crossroads could have significant repercussions. You want her to be prepared when she arrives at these decision-making junctures. You want her to assess the situation rationally. You want her to make a good choice about how to handle the challenge, temptation, obstacle, setback, or problem effectively. You also want her to make good choices about how to respond appropriately to the opportunities that will present themselves.

To gauge the effectiveness of the instructional process you have just completed with your child, it would be a good idea to complete again the checklist introduced in Chapter 1. This reassessment procedure will allow you to identify issues that may still need to be reviewed.

As has been repeatedly emphasized in this book, the abilities to think analytically, logically, rationally, strategically, and critically are skills. All skills, even those that have seemingly been mastered, must be practiced and used, or they will diminish. Seasoned professional athletes will confirm that if they don't practice, they lose their competitive edge. They'll also confirm that even highly competent, well-trained professionals continue to require good coaching.

You are your child's primary coach, mentor, and guide. You are also your child's biggest fan. If you do your coaching job well, you can significantly increase the likelihood that your child will not only make good decisions in her life, but that she'll become your biggest fan as well. What more could you desire from your child?

Statements particularly relevant to older children are placed at the bottom of the checklist and are preceded by an asterisk.

Checklist: Does My Child Have Effective Reasoning Skills?

0=Never   1=Rarely   2=Sometimes   3=Often   4=Always

My child has difficulty making realistic predictions. *(Even though I won't study for the test, I'll do okay.)*   _____

My child has difficulty appreciating cause and effect and linking her actions with logical repercussions. *(Even though I haven't done my chores, Mom will let me go to the movies on Saturday.)*   _____

My child has difficulty realizing how his behavior affects others. *(Big deal. All kids lie to their parents.)*   _____

My child has difficulty analyzing mistakes and setbacks and learning from these experiences. *(Just because my teacher lowered my grade because my book report was late, she may not lower it next time if it's late.)*   _____

My child cannot deal with frustration. *(I didn't get the part in the play. I can't act. I'll never try out again.)*   _____

My child has difficulty suspending immediate gratification. *(I can't afford it, but I'm going to buy it anyway.)*   _____

My child refuses to admit when he's wrong. *(I didn't break the window because we were playing too close to the house. The ball went foul.)*   _____

My child will persist on a particular course even though it's clear the strategy isn't working. *(I don't care if the teacher says these problems are incorrect! This is how I'm going to do them!)*   _____

My child makes flawed judgments because he doesn't look at key issues or denies the reality of the situation in which he finds himself. *(I don't care if John has lied to me many times before. He's my friend and I believe him!)*

My child has difficulty linking values and principles with specific choices and actions. *(If I miss practice this week, my coach won't care. I'll make the varsity team anyway.)*   _____

My child often fails to consider ethics and morals when making a decision. *(When the teacher turns her back, I'll ask my friend for the answer to this test question.)*   _____

My child disregards danger. *(Jumping off this bridge looks like fun.)*   _____

My child is having difficulty with impulse control. *(I'll put this candy in my pocket when the clerk's back is turned.)*   _____

* My child has difficulty developing a strategy that will allow him to attain his goal. *(I don't want to take the advanced placement science course, even though I heard you need them for pre-med.)*   _____

* My child has difficulty perceiving the progression and sequence of events and ideas. *(I don't need to take the introductory course to get an A in the advanced class.)*   _____

* My child has difficulty drawing reasonable conclusions and inferences from available data. *(Everybody is taking coats to the stadium, but I don't think I'll need one.)*   _____

* My child uses non sequiturs (conclusions that don't follow from the premise or evidence) when expressing ideas. *(The book says communication skills are linked to intelligence. Dolphins have a very complex communication system, but I don't really think they're very intelligent.)*   _____

*My child has difficulty planning ahead and factoring "future time" into her decisions. *(I'll probably have enough time to read the book and do the report even if I start next week.)*   _____

As the author of this book, it is my sincere desire that your child's thinking skills have improved. If your child is still having difficulty in specific areas, refer to the chapters that address the particular skill that needs review and reinforcement. You may want to repeat a particular exercise, or you may want to change the content, using different information but focusing on the same issues. You may also decide to substitute a personal experience as a catalyst for discussion. The key is to stimulate your child's interest and direct involvement in the activity.

Encourage your child to use the problem-solving and analytical thinking methods described in this book to address and resolve family, school, and personal issues that arise in her life. Continue to examine with her not only those newspaper and magazine articles that underscore mindlessness and irrational thinking, but also those articles that underscore good choices, rational thinking, and ethical behavior. Discuss hypothetical situations and urge your child to share with you how she might respond. However, a word of caution is in order: *Don't overdo it!* You don't want your child to grimace every time you open a newspaper and get your feathers ruffled by something you read. Be selective. Use your discretion. Overkill will defeat your objectives.

By keeping your child's cerebral engine stoked, you can significantly improve the likelihood that she'll make good, rational choices in this dangerous world of ours. Keep shoveling coal into the furnace. There's room for more, and there's plenty of track ahead!

Index

A

Activities. *See* Interactive activities

ADD (Attention Deficit Disorder), 26, 127

ADHD (Attention Deficit Hyperactivity Disorder), 26

Age
and decision-making skills, 2–3
and insights, 38–39
and judgment, 49–50
and length of sessions, 35–36
range this book addresses, 8, 10
and reasoning skills, 29–30, 47–49

Alcohol, 65–68

Analysis, 74–75

Applied intelligence, 73–74, 76–77. *See also* Critical thinking; Strategic thinking
chart of forms of intelligence, 98
interactive activities, 80–83, 104–107
smartness, 78–80

Attention Deficit Disorder (ADD), 26, 127

Attention Deficit Hyperactivity Disorder (ADHD), 26

Autocratic responses, justified, 159–162

Awareness, 102

B

Betrayal (informing on others), 109–115, 139–140

Bike anecdotes, 36–37, 71–72

Birthday party crisis, 179–181

Boundaries, setting for children, 115–120

Brain power, 71–107
chart of forms of intelligence, 98
critical thinking, 83–95, 101–107
intelligence, 76–78
interactive activities, 74–75, 80–83, 91–95, 99–101, 104–107
smartness, 78–80
strategic thinking, 96–107

Brainstorming solutions. *See* DIBS problem-solving method

C

Career guidance
coercion vs., 145, 146–147, 149–150
interactive activity, 151–152

Cause and effect. *See also* Logic; Reasoning skills; Strategic thinking
checklist for skills, 27–29, 262–263
child's perception of, 26

Helping Your Hyperactive/Attention Deficit Child, Revised 2nd Ed.

John F. Taylor, Ph.D.

Written to help parents and professionals learn about the many effective ways to deal with and even overcome hyperactivity/attention deficit disorder, this book is a leader in the field. Instead of prescribing only one approach, Dr. Taylor offers a comprehensive point of view, detailing the strengths and weaknesses of the various methods, including nutritional, psychological, and medical. An exclusive feature of this book is the author's own Taylor Hyperactivity/Attention Deficit Screening Checklist to help parents determine if their child is truly hyperactive.

Positive Discipline for Teenagers

Jane Nelsen, Ed.D., and Lynn Lott

There is no such thing as perfect parents or perfect children. This book shows parents how to turn off the cycle of guilt and blame and begin working toward greater understanding and communication with their adolescents. Parents can learn how to:

- win cooperation without having to threaten
- see the world through the child's eyes
- tell if a teen's rebellion is normal or excessive

With the strategies found in *Positive Discipline for Teenagers*, you can begin now to strengthen and build your relationship with your teens.